AF252001

BETWEEN FAITH AND THOUGHT

STUDIES IN RELIGION AND CULTURE

Frank Burch Brown, Gary L. Ebersole,
and Edith Wyschogrod, *Editors*

BETWEEN FAITH AND THOUGHT

AN ESSAY ON THE ONTOTHEOLOGICAL CONDITION

JEFFREY W. ROBBINS

UNIVERSITY OF VIRGINIA PRESS
CHARLOTTESVILLE AND LONDON

Library of Congress Cataloging-in-Publication Data
Robbins, Jeffrey W., 1972–
    Between faith and thought : an essay on the onotheological condition
/ Jeffrey W. Robbins.
        p.   cm. — (Studies in religion and culture)
    Includes bibliographical references and index.
    ISBN 0-8139-2163-5 (alk. paper)
    1. Philosophical theology. 2. Faith and reason—Christianity. I.
Title. II. Series: Studies in religion and culture (Charlottesville, Va.)

    BT50 .R63 2003
    230' .01—dc21

                                                                                    2002154226

For Noëlle,
and
in memory of Charlie (1944–2002)

Why should philosophy accept a division which in all probability will not correspond to the articulation of the real? This division, however, it does usually accept. It accepts the problem as it is posited by language. It is therefore condemned in advance to receive a ready-made solution or, at best, simply to choose between the two or three only possible solutions, which are co-eternal to the positing of the problem. . . . One might just as well assign to the philosopher the role and the attitude of the schoolboy, who seeks the solution persuaded that if he had the boldness to risk a glance at the master's book, he would find it there, set down opposite the question. But the truth is that in philosophy and even elsewhere it is a question of finding the problem and consequently of positing it, even more than of solving it. For a speculative problem is solved as soon as it is properly stated.

—Henri Bergson, The Creative Mind

CONTENTS

PREFACE

It is difficult to know precisely where and when this study began. The occasional biblical references that are interspersed throughout point to its prebeginning, which I suppose, borrowing language from the study itself, I might designate as the formal conditions of this work's possibility. As such, this study owes its spirit to what I consider to be the rich, awe-inspiring, and all-too-often overlooked ambiguities of the biblical tradition. As scholars of Judaism and Christianity are pleased to point out, the Bible is not *a* book as much as it is a book of books, or a collection of texts with unknown authors engaging in a prolonged dialogue reflecting their best guesses at the meaning of God's care for human existence. My own concerns with the problem of philosophical theology are meant to reflect this same generous and cooperative spirit. I believe it will have succeeded only to the extent in which it invites further reflection and future dialogue.

Beyond this broad background of prehistory, however, there are three moments that, when looking back over the development of my own thought, stand as watersheds. The first was my introduction to theology through the work of Martin Luther. I happened upon Luther's biography and theological writings as a history major in the senior year of my undergraduate studies. While coming relatively late in my career as a student, I still consider my first exposure to Luther's work as the true beginning of my education, for it was only then that my studies spilled over outside the classroom and into the very recesses of my mind. It was only then that I discovered myself in the pages of a text, but the self I discovered was a self put in question, because my words—perhaps for the first time—were found in the words of another. And these words, which I had thought were my own, when set in the context of another time, another place, and another voice, suddenly took on a wholly new meaning. In other words, reading Luther raised certain fundamental questions that up to that point in my life I had somehow managed to avoid. But even while discovering myself suddenly exposed, it should come as no surprise that I was also thrilled by the encounter. An unknown, mysterious vista opened up before my eyes. I was made thirsty for knowledge, while at the same time, I felt free from the compulsion to know. My ignorance was my ticket to a whole lifetime of discovery. Most importantly, what I learned from Luther was the fundamentally affirmative nature of theological thinking, God's "Yes!" to me as an existing and thinking subject.

The second key moment occurred during the course of my subsequent theological studies as I began to reflect on the impact of multiculturalism on the contemporary theological understanding. Certain religious trends such as the growing commitment to the ecumenical movement and interreligious dialogue, along with the development and spread of various liberation theologies, struck me as being the obvious and absolutely necessary responses to some of the issues raised by the realities of cultural pluralism. But what interested me most about these movements was not their shared emphasis on praxis over theory, but rather how such a practical emphasis fundamentally transformed both theory and practice, even to the point that one might say the dichotomy itself between theory and practice is no longer a hypothesis that might be sustained. It was with this in mind that I first encountered the field of postmodern theology. By its incorporation of deconstruction and psychoanalytic theory into a traditionally theological discourse, postmodern theology effects its own transformation, much like the death of God theology, which was its predecessor. By so doing, it extends the critique of the dualism that manifests itself in the dichotomy between theory and practice, explicitly questioning the nature and ground of truth itself. Its suggestion that theology has always had more to do with desire than with truth opens wide at least a two-thousand-year-old history of theological thought such that its presumed grounding in the truth of God's revelation is made indeterminate by the ambivalence of desire.

The third moment develops out of the second, as the conviction that the theological shift from truth to desire characteristic of postmodern theology carries with it an added ethical urgency. As Charles Winquist writes, "Epistemic undecidability does not prevent or even inhibit ethical decidability. It simply shifts the responsibility for ethical and political decision making into an experimental and pragmatic frame of conscious freedom. It is a work of becoming, becoming self and becoming community."[1] Or in the words of John D. Caputo, "Undecidability does not detract from the urgency of decision; it simply underlines the difficulty."[2] It is in this sense that my work draws on the thinking of Emmanuel Levinas and the priority that he gives to ethics in contemporary philosophical and religious thought. His is a metaphysical desire that is supplemented and made complete by responsibility—a responsibility for desire and a desire for responsibility, never fulfilled but only deepened, never satiated but rather nourished by its hunger.

From affirmation to desire and responsibility, philosophical theology is no longer required to speak in dogmatic or foundational terms. It answers for itself not by its conformity to a doctrinal rule of faith, but rather by its enfranchisement of the thinker, its articulation of the unsayable, and its assumption of an impossible obligation that is beyond its own power to meet. As with the moments of my beginnings as a thinker, these also remain as the points of my continued striving.

ACKNOWLEDGMENTS

For this work, I am thankful to many. To my colleagues in the Department of Religion and Philosophy at Lebanon Valley College, thank you for your support of my work, and a special thanks to Brad Fuhrman for compiling the index. To the editorial staff at the University of Virginia Press, most especially Cathie Brettschneider and Ellen Satrom, thank you for your enthusiasm from the start and your professionalism throughout. To my family, without your encouragement, and without the constancy of your convictions, this self-involved and at times self-indulgent labor of love would have been unrealized. To my teachers, most especially Jim Wiggins and the recently departed Charles Winquist, thank you for your confidence in me, for your model of intellectual integrity, and for your friendship. To my friends from the Department of Religion at Syracuse University, for Andrew, Chad, Heath, and Oz, thank you not only for the encouragement that you have given to me along the way, but even more, for the making of a genuine community where learning and laughter go hand in hand. Most of all, to my wife, Noëlle, whose understanding surpasses words, and whose words give beauty and meaning to my life, thank you.

BETWEEN FAITH AND THOUGHT

INTRODUCTION
THE ONTOTHEOLOGICAL CONDITION

The world of illusions—the world of religions—brings to light or embodies the prohibition that has us speak. Thus, it gives legitimacy to hatred if it does not invert it into love. Embodying, legitimizing—today we are too aware of their techniques to yield to them. The worlds of illusions, now dead and buried, have given way to our dreams and deliriums if not to politics or science—the religions of modern times. Lacking illusions, lacking shelter, today's universe is divided between *boredom* . . . or . . . *abjection* and *piercing laughter.*

—Julia Kristeva, Powers of Horror

Weary therefore of dogmatism, which teaches us nothing, and of scepticism, which does not even promise us anything, not even to rest in permitted ignorance; disquieted by the importance of knowledge so much needed; and lastly, rendered suspicious by long experience of all knowledge which we believe we possess or which offers itself under the title of pure reason—we have left but one critical question upon whose answer depends our future conduct, vis., *is metaphysics at all possible?*

—Immanuel Kant, Prolegomena to Any Future Metaphysics

IMAGINE AN entire tradition of thought based upon a fundamental misapprehension. It would be like a doctor who had wrongly diagnosed a patient—no matter the proposed remedy, it would be destined to fail. This is to say nothing of the remedy itself. Indeed, it might be the most innovative, potent, and thorough available, but if misapplied or wrongly prescribed, its usefulness would be that of a placebo at best, and at worst, it might be entirely counterproductive—not only failing to cure, but adding illness to illness. Take this same patient once the misdiagnosis and the futility of the remedy have been realized, would he then be justified in rejecting the entire medical profession for the misdiagnosis of a single practitioner? If so, would he then be any closer to a cure?

What if the problem of philosophical theology was the result of a similar misapprehension? The symptoms are real, the problem is grave, but the diagnosis is off the mark. And what if the prescribed course of thought among contemporary theologians and philosophers alike was similarly a wholesale rejection of the values inherent to philosophical theology? The result would be a remedy that perpetuates, if not extends, the problem. Again, this says nothing of the remedies themselves, or even of those who first proposed them, for oftentimes the only way to test and discover the adequacy of a diagnosis is through the implementation of a specific regimen of relief. But there eventually comes a time when a new course of action might be required, when it becomes apparent that one's original evaluation of the problem might have been faulty. If this is the case when it comes to the problem of philosophical theology, then this would require a complete redefinition of the meaning of ontotheology, and correlatively, a reevaluation of the relation between theology and philosophy. For when both theologians and philosophers are asked to describe their task, their diagnosis invariably begins with the ontotheological problem, and the remedy that is more often than not prescribed is the task of overcoming, by which either theology or philosophy is purified of the other.

My position is that this diagnosis is fundamentally misguided, that it ultimately betrays a misunderstanding of the ontotheological condition of being and thought, and that the consequence is that much of contemporary theology and philosophy is inconsequential, if not entirely counterproductive. What this means is that ontotheology must be redefined. The problem is not, as some insist, that God has somehow entered into philosophical discourse, as if the theologians had crafted a carefully orchestrated coup d'état. Nor is the problem the fact that theologians have borrowed a philosophical language in their talk of God, as if theology ever spoke a divine tongue unscathed by human finitude. The ontotheological condition is more than the intermixing of theology and philosophy, for it precedes both theological and philosophical thinking alike. In this regard neither the theologian nor the philosopher is to blame; indeed, ontotheology is no more a blameworthy condition than language is falsifying. Yet, while there is the continuing effort to overcome ontotheology, language is considered both an inevitability and a necessity and, as such, is allowed its own possibility of regeneration and renewal. What I propose, therefore, in the place of the attempt to overcome ontotheology, is the basic recognition that ontotheology is also an inevitability, if not a necessity, of thought. Thus, it is not a question of whether or not one thinks ontotheologically, but rather, how and toward what ends?

Similarly, when thinking through the problem of philosophical theology, it is foolhardy to align oneself with the philosopher or the theologian—as if the two could be so easily disentangled, as if any identity were so simply constituted. Instead, the better approach is with an eye toward how the one informs the other, and vice versa. For modern philosophy and theology illuminate one another, and together they reveal a common nature that both seek to overcome, namely, ontotheology—the constitutive origin and legacy of Western thought. However—and this will be the primary argument of this text—overcoming is a problem where ontotheology is concerned. Indeed, it could be said that the problem of ontotheology is entirely this desire for its overcoming. Therefore, to the extent that the strategy of overcoming is presented as the prescribed path of thought that will lead beyond the problem of ontotheology, then it is itself the problem that must be overcome—but overcome otherwise than by simply overcoming. For the endeavor at overcoming remains trapped within ontotheology, and what is worse, it confuses this trap as the problem when in fact it is the very clue needed for thinking otherwise.

In short, ontotheology is the condition of the problem of philosophical theology. It is more fundamental, more basic, yet also less evident. Thus, in this attempt to redefine ontotheology, the approach will be through an examination of the divided history of contemporary philosophical theology. What this history will show is that no matter the path of thought, whether primarily philosophical or theological in orientation, the root problem remains the same. Philosophical theology, in other words, inevitably manifests the ontotheological condition of thought. This being the case, the issue will be whether this condition might be thought of as a resource for creative and responsible engagement with the world.

The Objectives

This understanding of ontotheology as a condition of thought as opposed to a problem that needs to be overcome signals the first of the three primary objectives of this study; namely, to demonstrate that the problem of philosophical theology is a false problem that exposes a fundamental misunderstanding of the nature of being and the conditions of thought. This misunderstanding belies an uneasiness or a discomfort with the divisions and differences that exist simply by virtue of being. Consequently, it seeks to overcome these divisions and differences through the recovery of either a pure philosophical or pure theological discourse. In contrast to this misunderstanding, this work proposes that many of the differences that do exist—whether these differences are thought of in terms of the existing divisions between philosophy and theology, between the self and the other, between the sexes, between the races, between the nations —are merely symptomatic of a graver problem or of a more fundamental condition. Therefore, they are not the outcome of faulty logic; nor are they the result of a lack of resolution, persistence, or fortitude; nor certainly are they explained simply by malicious intent or narrow-mindedness. Some differences are simply irreconcilable, and the purpose of reflection is to expose them as such. Moreover, some differences might be key to better understanding the way beyond the problems and limitations of modern thought. These are the differences that are unavoidable, inevitable, and even necessary to the human condition. These are fearful, awe-inspiring differences that might inspire some to prefer the securities of identity as opposed to the unknown ambiguities that emerge from such an encounter. Thus, the first objective will be a complex one—namely, (1) to examine the current understanding of philosophical theology, both from the philosophical and the theological perspective; (2) to understand why it is a false problem; and (3) to show how this misunderstanding, which leads to this desire for overcoming, in fact exposes an even graver problem or more fundamental condition that is yet to be addressed.

The second objective is related to the first, as it reconsiders the philosophical and theological strategies of thought that have based themselves on this false problem. That is to say, as both philosophy and theology have sought to overcome the "problem" of philosophical theology, their self-prescribed paths of thought have been at best misguided. Because insofar as philosophical theology is a false problem, the desire for its overcoming is not only quixotic, but even more, it does violence to the understanding, as it leads to further distraction from the genuine issue at hand. Thus, the second objective of the work will be to demonstrate the shortsightedness, contradiction, and even violence of the strategy of overcoming, and thereby suggest the urgency for a new, alternative strategy of thought.

The third and final objective is to map out possibilities for this new, alternative strategy and to make a compelling case for why this alternative is both more appropriate and more fruitful when considering the prospects for philosophical theology. For the most part, this third objective will not be addressed until the final chapter, wherein the Levinasian argument for ethics as first philosophy and the Levinasian strategy for giving articulation to that which is "otherwise than being" will serve as a model for the renewal of philosophical and theological thought.

The Urgency

Before turning directly to these objectives, more must be said concerning the dilemma with which we are faced, of which the problem of philosophical theology is but a symptom. For upon first glance, one might not consider the problem of philosophical theology as being a necessarily urgent one. However, if the argument of this text is correct, then not only is this problem urgent in the sense that it demands immediate attention and that it bears certain consequences, but even more, it is fundamental in the sense that it speaks to the very nature of being and thought. That being said, I appeal to Julia Kristeva's *Powers of Horror* as a way of introducing both the urgency and necessity of this present study.

In *Powers of Horror*, Kristeva writes an ontology of the abject and a phenomenology of abjection. Of the abject, she writes that it is, "Not me. Not that. But not nothing, either. A 'something' that I do not recognize as a thing. A weight of meaninglessness, about which there is nothing insignificant, and which crushes me." Of abjection, she writes, "There looms, within abjection, one of those violent, dark revolts of being, directed against a threat that seems to emanate from an exorbitant outside or inside, ejected beyond the scope of the possible, the tolerable, the thinkable. It lies there, quite close, but it cannot be assimilated. It beseeches, worries, and fascinates desire, which, nevertheless, does not let itself be reduced."[1]

For our purposes, Kristeva's distinctive phenomenological ontology demonstrates the futility and the misguided nature of modern efforts at overcoming. Abjection is the subject's disavowal of itself—the subject's effort to rid itself of that which is unclean, disordered, or horrific. Such disavowal, however, is destined to fail. And it is this failure, Kristeva suggests, that then becomes the very condition of the identity of the subject. As Elizabeth Gross explains, "The ability to take up a symbolic position as a social and speaking subject entail the disavowal of its modes of corporeality, especially those representing what is considered unacceptable, unclean or anti-social. The subject must disavow part of itself in order to gain a stable self, and this form of refusal marks whatever identity it acquires as provisional, and open to breakdown and instability."[2] Never fully assimilated, nor completely purged, it is not so much that the abject returns (e.g., Freud's "return of the repressed"), as that the abject is the necessary undercurrent beneath the waves of an ever fluid identity. Again, in Gross's words, the abject is "a necessary accompaniment" to all activities, whether we are speaking of identity formation, art and literary productions, even philosophical theology. Such being the case, we might say that it is only a threat to the extent to which the process of abjection is foreclosed or cut short. Or, mixing metaphors even further, it is no more the poison than it is the cure—the abject as *pharmakon.*

Put differently, if our very nature as a subject is in accordance with the abject, and if our very experience ultimately manifests the process of abjection that drives both our actions and our thoughts, then there can be no escaping or overcoming. The dilemma is without resolution. And if the abject is indeed the irreducible condition of existence, then no matter what path of thought one chooses, one remains nevertheless circumscribed within abjection. This circumscribed condition includes not only philosophy, but religion and theology as well. For, as Kristeva writes, the abject "does not respect borders, positions, rules. The in-between, the ambiguous, the composite. The traitor, the liar, the criminal with a good conscience, the shameless rapist, the killer who claims to be a savior. . . . Any crime, because it draws attention to the fragility of the law is abject, but premeditated crime, cunning murder, hypocritical revenge are even more so because they heighten the display of such fragility."[3] There is no escape, no resolution, no overcoming. The farther one travels, the more one is driven to return to an innocence that never was or a purity forever passed, and the deeper one moves into the violence of the aboriginal and the blindness of the civilized.

Regarding religion, Kristeva writes that its history tells "the various means of *purifying* the abject,"[4] which is the attempt at sublimating the abject through consecration. But the symbolic constructs of religion are never more than secondary acts, negotiations covering over their fundamental essence. Religion exposes itself by its essence. Religion is destined to fail so long as it is understood as a panacea, because, ontologically speaking, religion is still new to the scene. The abject is the secret history behind the history of religion, the very condition that elicits the *homo religiosus.*

To put it bluntly, religion is a deceit—perhaps a necessary one, as it blunts the inevitable powers of horror. But still, never pure, never innocent. It is like the caution Jesus gave to his disciples: *One must be wise like serpents to make one's way in the world* (Matt. 10:16–18). The truth of Jesus' gospel, in other words, does not translate into the false notion of a recovered innocence, but instead issues forth as a command to follow. And where such discipleship leads is toward the cross, wherein the inevitability, if not the necessity, of violence is once and for all exposed. From Kristeva's perspective, therefore, the function of religion is not that it purifies the sinner or that it assures the faithful; on the contrary, this is the great deceit of religion, as it fools the faithful into thinking that they have somehow overcome abjection.

This critique of religion is certainly not original to Kristeva. Indeed, from Feuerbach, to Marx, Nietzsche, and Freud, this critique is the defining feature of the contemporary study of religion. The field has passed through what Paul Ricoeur terms "first naïveté" to a critical posture that is more reflexive but equally troubled by the assurances that religion may or may not provide. A common feature of this latter critical posture toward religious studies, for instance, has been the suspicion of the theological underpinnings or the crypto-theological tendencies of the academic study of religion. Arguments have been made that a more appropriate stance for the scholar of religion, in distinction from the religious practitioner, would be that of a dispassionate observer.[5] In this way, the more theological questions, such as the meaning of religious phenomena, would be left unasked and unanswered, and the legitimacy of Religious Studies as an academic discipline would require its eventual emancipation from this theological residue.

Therefore, like religion, theology is faced with a fundamental problem. Not only have its shortcomings and inconsistencies been well chronicled; even more significantly, the very nature of its intentions has been questioned. With good reason and ample justification, many detect in theological thinking nothing but covert politics and the implementation of religious ideology. Accordingly, philosophical theology must be fundamentally rethought. On the one side stands God, with whom we have grown to have enough sense to question. On the other side stands creation, which we have learned from phenomenology does not need God in order to speak of transcendence and infinity. The once towering heights of human longing have been dispersed along a plane of immanence. The Tower of Babel has been decimated; in its place comes the realization of a divided humanity, an infinitely giving source of human richness that all too often turns against itself in the violence of fear, ignorance, and indifference.

Strategies of Thought

Put otherwise, this circumscribed condition is what is meant by the term ontotheology. And much of contemporary thought has been consumed with "overcoming" variations on this problem.[6] As already stated, this will also be the consuming interest of this particular work in the sense that we must somehow overcome this effort at overcoming if we are to arrive at the requisite new understanding of ontotheology I am urging. As a point of illustration, consider the dual edge of Martin Heidegger's assessment of the continuing legacy of Nietzsche, namely, that Nietzsche is "the last metaphysician." On the one hand, this means that with Nietzsche the age of metaphysics has come to its completion and thereby might effect its own overcoming. On the other, according to Heidegger's assessment, Nietzsche remains trapped between one age and the other, much like Moses leading the Israelites out of bondage to the border of the promised land, which he himself is never allowed to enter. That is because while Nietzsche might have successfully inverted Platonism, he nevertheless failed to overcome the dualism that was at its base. Thus, according to Heidegger, in spite of his praise for Nietzsche's thought, in the final analysis it remains essentially an expression of ontotheology:

> As an *ontology,* even Nietzsche's metaphysics is *at the same time* theology, although it seems far removed from scholastic metaphysics. The ontology of beings as such thinks *essentia* as will to power. Such ontology thinks the *existenia* of beings as such and as a whole theologically as the eternal recurrence of the same. Such metaphysical theology is of course a negative theology of a peculiar kind. Its negativity is revealed in the expression "God is dead." That is an expression not of atheism but of ontotheology, in that metaphysics in which nihilism proper is fulfilled.[7]

Nietzsche remains trapped within the problem of ontotheology as he gives expression to its necessary negative counterpoint. In contrast to Nietzsche's, Heidegger's strategy was to bring the ontological difference to light, to differentiate without falling back into either a metaphysical or theological dualism.[8] And as Heidegger knows well, this effort requires a constant vigilance, for it demands that one skate along the brink, with little comfort and no rest.

The question this work will ask, therefore, of both the philosophical and theological traditions, is whether they accomplish this necessary vigilance, and if not, whether this is to their fault or credit. If the answer to this latter question is neither, then perhaps the failure of both philosophy and theology to overcome ontotheology does not necessarily lead to the conclusion that they must redouble their efforts; instead, perhaps it means that their very efforts are misguided. If such is the case, then what is needed is not yet another strategy of overcoming but another strategy altogether, one that is *otherwise than overcoming* by its recognition of the ontotheological condition of thought.

Hence, to begin, I offer three contemporary views of the relation between philosophy and theology, each of which emerges as a response to the problem of ontotheology. The first two of these views will be explored in an intertwined fashion in the first four chapters. The third view, which is the chief proposal of this text as a whole, will be reserved for chapter 5:

(1) *Theology overcomes ontotheology by escaping the problem.* This view is best articulated by Brian Ingraffia in *Postmodern Theory and Biblical Theology.* According to Ingraffia, biblical theology must be disentangled from Greek philosophy and modern metaphysics; indeed, in Ingraffia's view, this separation has always been at the heart of a theological understanding. From this perspective, the modern and postmodern critiques of religion and theology are entirely misplaced, because they are not dealing with what is genuinely theological; namely, human experience as interpreted on the basis of scripture— but rather with modern philosophy's presumptive appropriation of religion; namely, revelation as judged and criticized on the basis of human experience. As Ingraffia writes, "It is my contention that the god of ontotheology, no matter how descriptions of this god may differ, is always the product of human reason, is always the result of humanity's attempt to formulate an understanding of god rather than the result of God's revelation towards us."[9] From Ingraffia's perspective, this clarification of the modern and postmodern critique liberates theology once again to voice its insights both authoritatively and determinatively, without fear of the predetermined lens of intelligibility as set by philosophy.

This position is echoed by Jean-Luc Marion when he writes concerning the "death of God" that it does not spell the death of the God as articulated by Christian theology, but rather the death of a certain conception of God—in his words, "God according to Being."[10] Like Ingraffia, Marion believes that this realization of the true target of suspicion liberates theology from the self-consuming concerns of modern and postmodern philosophies. In fact, according to Marion's analysis, the theologian is now free to pursue the unique pleasure of writing theology as it transgresses the bounds of reason and faith.

A final representative of this view is Merold Westphal, who, in his essay "Overcoming Onto-theology," contrasts ontotheology with the religious practices of prayer, praise, and sacrifice. From this respect, the problem of ontotheology amounts not so much to the concept of God as it does to the manner in which one thinks and speaks of God. The mistake of ontotheology is the fact that it gives primacy to the theoretical. As Westphal writes, "As a project of rendering the whole of being intelligible in accordance with the principle of reason, onto-theology presupposes and practices the primacy of theoretical reason."[11] Theology, by contrast, "must deny theory, or, to be more precise, the primacy of insight . . . This love, this trust, this relationship— these are the practice for the sake of which it was necessary to deny theory. This is not to abolish theology. It is to see that theology's task is to serve this life of faith, not the ideals of knowledge as defined by the philosophical traditions Heidegger variously calls calculative-representational thinking, metaphysics, and onto-theology."[12]

(2) *Philosophy overcomes ontotheology by passing through and beyond the problem.* This view is represented by and will be explored through the work of Martin Heidegger, Edmund Husserl, and Paul Ricoeur. It is Heidegger's view that through the philosophical question of being, the delimitation of thought as structured by knowledge is overcome by that which is the very ground and presupposition of philosophical inquiry. This ontological revolution in, and transformation of, philosophy sets contemporary thought on a path that is factually unknown and structurally unknowable. This passes through and beyond the problem of ontotheology because this realization of the open-ended nature of thought liberates philosophy from the need to fill the gaps in knowledge. Instead, philosophy's task is to bring such gaps to light, to differentiate. And unlike theology, this task of differentiation offers no assurances. It will be argued that Husserl extends this distinctively Heideggerian project by allowing phenomenology to effect its own transformation and undoing, as Husserl moves from the ideal of phenomenology as a rigorous science to the phenomenological discovery of the life-world.

Finally, it is Ricoeur who articulates this position most explicitly when he writes of his "conscious and resolute bracketing" of biblical faith in his philosophical studies. He also writes that his philosophical hermeneutics is safe from the threat of ontotheology, by which he means that his philosophy is not to be confused with theology. The former proceeds by "arguments alone," while the latter is invested in faith and structured by its conviction of truth. The implication of such a claim is that by virtue of the differentiation of philosophy from theology, ontotheology becomes the sort of problem that might be safely resolved, or at least its threat might be reduced or effectively overcome. This, then, allows the philosopher the confidence to traverse a path once assumed to be too dangerous to tread.[13]

(3) *Ontotheology is not overcome, and this causes both theology and philosophy to be read in light of the Other.* This position disagrees with those who think that the problem of ontotheology is but a problem of a wayward history, a thinking in error, a tradition misunderstood, or a temptation to be resisted.[14] That is because a serious analysis of the problem exposes something much more complicating, something that is endemic to thought; namely, that ontotheology is not a problem to be avoided, for the simple fact that it is not the kind of problem that can be avoided, or corrected, or resolved, or done away with, or thought or willed to extinction. *Ontotheology is not a mistake.* On the contrary, it is the condition of thought in general and the symptom of any and all thinking in particular. This view accepts neither the assurance offered through a dogmatic faith nor the overconfidence in the human subject's capacity for thought. In its place it substitutes the parallel movements of both philosophy and theology, as both forms of discourse are equally conditioned by ontotheology. This in turn forces a reevaluation of the problem of ontotheology: no longer a hurdle to cross along the path toward a purity of discourse, but rather the constitutive destiny that is not to be overcome at all, but instead embraced as the fact of life.

Two recent works that when taken together might serve as an example of this third view are Louis Dupré's *Passage to Modernity* and Jonathan Glover's *Humanity: A Moral History of the Twentieth Century.* Dupré's understanding of ontotheology provides an alternative to that which predominates in contemporary philosophical and theological thought by his understanding of ontotheology as the constitutive synthesis at the origins of Western civilization. In this respect, the problems and shortcomings of modernity are not thought synonymous with the ontotheological problem; on the contrary, from Dupré's perspective, modernity begins with the breakup or disintegration of the ontotheological synthesis.[15] In other words, the failure of modernity is due to its denial of the ontotheological condition. The result of this denial is the fragmentation of meaning into separate spheres of mind/matter, sacred/profane, and theology/philosophy. For Dupré, locating this problem within modernity does not translate into a return to premodern premises. As he writes, "Its [modernity's] problems cannot be treated as errors to be corrected by a simple return to an earlier truth." Dupré understands well that the cultural changes accomplished by modernity have had a "definitive and irreversible impact that transforms the very essence of reality." Instead of nostalgia, what is needed is a "new synthesis" that is based on "newly established principles."[16] Shifting registers, in Glover's terms, this "new synthesis" would be a moral history that brings together ethics with the history of its failures; or as he explains in the preface, "This book is an attempt to give ethics an empirical dimension. It uses ethics to pose questions to history and it uses history to give a picture of the parts of human potentiality which are relevant to ethics."[17]

GLOVER'S ATTEMPT will also be the challenge accepted by this present work, and it is the reason why the work of Emmanuel Levinas is given a place of such prominence in the final concluding chapter. As stated there, the importance of Levinas is his engendering of a kind of questioning that moves beyond the self-consuming problems of modern thought, to its very conditions, which he then emphasizes as the ethical relation. From this respect, it might be said that ethics is the site where philosophy and theology meet. As such, the relation between philosophy and theology is given priority over the secondary question regarding their respective natures. Accordingly, philosophical theology cannot carry on just as before. Neither purely theological nor purely philosophical, its essence is intermingled with the other. Beyond the problem of philosophical theology, therefore, lies the ontotheological condition, which tells of the mixed origins of thought and of the need for thinking otherwise.

1

THE PROBLEM OF PHILOSOPHICAL THEOLOGY

> What serves and helps the Church is not to soften or weaken the heresy which has infiltrated into it, but to know it, to fight it and to isolate it.
>
> —Karl Barth, *Church Dogmatics*

> We understand each other better when each speaks in his own language.
>
> —Martin Heidegger, *The Piety of Thinking*

PHILOSOPHICAL THEOLOGY is at a crossroads. The legacy of the radical theologies of the sixties and seventies that were both continuations and responses to the neo-orthodox theology of the previous generation leaves the question regarding the possibility of theology as the chief aim of theological thinking.[1] This assessment is shared by those on both sides of the traditional theological divide, both liberal and conservative, radical and orthodox, secular and religious.[2] At stake is the status of the relation between theology and philosophy, or more generally, *between faith and thought.* At issue are the bounds of human possibility, the nature of truth, and the conditions and resources for thought. In this way the crossroads is as old as theology itself (e.g., "What does Athens have to do with Jerusalem?"). What is new is the reserve that accompanies the intellectual and cultural realization of diversity. This reserve is a much stronger and more positive force than the reactionary posturing of political correctness.

It springs from the genuine sorrow of a historical awakening to the abject in history, and the resolve to face the totalizing course of history in order to hold the present to account. It is a celebration of the richness of a diversity of resources. What also is new is the interrogative quality of thought reflective of what is loosely termed as postmodernism. Thinking has become a questioning from all sides such that the proclaimed autonomy or superiority of any single vantage point is rightly held under suspicion. There can be no resolution to the problems of representation. This has become as much an ontological and epistemological realization as it is ethical and political. It is within this milieu that the contemporary exchange between contesting theological voices concerning the possibility of theology is set.

It shall be the argument of this work that contemporary theological thought takes its shape from two directions that converged in a shared suspicion of philosophical theology. From the one side there is the Swiss Protestant theologian Karl Barth, often regarded as the most significant theological voice of the twentieth century.[3] From the other side there is the German philosopher Martin Heidegger, not a theologian himself, but whose work set a new agenda for theology in a secular culture.[4] While much separates these two thinkers—not the least of which, the fact that the one proclaims himself to be a theologian and the other a philosopher—more significant is their mutual concern with the dangers of the contamination of thought. For Barth, this concern resulted in a self-critical theology attempting to preserve for the Church the integrity of the Word of God. For Heidegger, it was from the side of philosophy that the purity of thinking was sought, even as he pursued the task of thinking after the end of philosophy and the overcoming of metaphysics. For both, philosophical theology was regarded as both a danger and a capitulation.

The mutual insistence on the dangers of philosophical theology, symptomatic of the work of both Barth and Heidegger, has had a far-reaching effect on twentieth-century thought. It has set a path that the successors to Barth and Heidegger have unwittingly followed, even when these successors are more easily recognized by their differences than their similarities. For this reason, this text considers their very understanding of the problem of philosophical theology to be problematic. That is because by cutting off the possibility of a true dialogue between philosophy and theology, they do not allow a genuine exchange of ideas, perspectives, and methodologies. Even further, by the view that philosophical theology is a problem that needs to be overcome, their efforts are misguided, as they have confused the symptom for the cause and have failed to understand that this cause is the very precondition of thought itself.

This need not be the case. Philosophical theology need not be thought of as a problem to be avoided or as yet another symptom of the degeneration of thought. Instead, perhaps philosophical theology as a mixed discourse stands well suited to voice what is most common, though no less significant, about the postmodern sensibility. Perhaps it is by the wandering and duplicitous path of philosophical theology that the ontotheological condition of thought might be more fully revealed. But this latter claim is reserved for the end of the work, only after there is sufficient clarity concerning the nature of the supposed problem, and after the various ways that the paths set by both Barth and Heidegger have gone untested and perpetuated.

Of course, it should be noted that the desire for purity and the fear of contamination does not begin with Barth and Heidegger. It dates back at least to the biblical injunction of Holiness, a code of purity that, as Kristeva explains, develops from a desire for order, to the desire for the preservation of the symbolic oneness of God, to its fullest articulation in abomination and/or prohibition. This history tells of the development of religion from a religion of sacrifice to a religion of Law. As Kristeva writes: *"Prohibiting instead of killing—such is the lesson of the proliferation of biblical abominations."* In other words, the Law replaces by overlaying sacrifice; it is that which *"restrains the desire to kill"*—the Law as a muted, mediated, and covert violence.[5] In its way this injunction of Holiness accomplishes its task well by providing an apparent foundation for human cooperation and civility. But also, as Kristeva suggests, its utility only goes so far. It does not provide an authentic, thoroughgoing reconciliation with the divide of being that would represent the genuine "overcoming" of violence to which it attests.

A similar dynamic reasserts itself in the twentieth century, if it were ever absent at all, as both Barth and Heidegger articulate their respective critiques of philosophical theology. What this will mean for Heidegger is that disorder will be reined in within the horizon of thought, that the phenomenological reduction stops short of prohibition by its *step back* from abomination to the sacred.[6] And for Barth, he will see the shortcomings of philosophy in its reluctance to complete the transition from sacrifice to Law, or its incapacity to *step out* from impurity through the clarification of a theological language. Theology is distinguished from philosophy because it witnesses to abomination. In the discussion that follows on Barth and Heidegger,

I do not mean to gloss over these significant differences. Instead I mean to suggest that these differences are still propelled by the same driving force, namely, the desire for purity[7]—a desire that very well might stem from a righteous despair; nevertheless, still exposing a misguided hope, a hidden violence, and an incipient force.

Barth's Theological Critique of Philosophy

Karl Barth was schooled in the liberal Protestant theological tradition. It was a time when the historical-critical method had reached its heights and shown its limitations in works such as Albert Schweitzer's *The Quest of the Historical Jesus* and Adolf von Harnack's *What is Christianity?* This early period of the twentieth century was also the time when Western Imperial Rule was at its zenith, a time when the promise of progress appeared unlimited and the reign of reason seemed assured. That was until the outbreak of World War I, when Western civilization discovered itself divided against itself, and the violence of this divide unleashed its destructive power. Theology was slow to read the signs of the times. It continued on in the comforts of its hard-won historical objectivity, fearing the contamination and compromise that would result from self-involvement and political activism. As a result of this psychology of self-preservation, the hidden politics of such a careful theology was exposed.

This was the sounding bell for Karl Barth. Thus, when his once-revered teachers voiced their support for German Nationalistic policies, it was made apparent to Barth and his friend Edward Thurneysen that what was needed was a new way of doing theology, a theology that would be responsive to the times, a theology in a new key. Because modern theology had shown itself to be morally bankrupt, it must rediscover the Word of God.[8] What was needed, pure and simple, was a theology purified from its contamination by culture. This would be a theology free from history, free to speak against the course of history, and free to reclaim God's purposes for history. It would be a theology unbound by the self-imposed limitations of philosophy, unafraid of voicing a word on faith without knowledge, and unfazed by the learned masters' demand to give full and universal account. This, then, was the historical and political context and urgency for Barth's theological renewal. Its first fruits would be the theological commentary on Saint Paul's *Epistle to the Romans*. And it is in this text that Barth first articulates his theological critique of philosophy and first explains why a "Christian Philosophy," or a philosophical theology, should be avoided.

DEFINING THE CRITICAL TASK OF THEOLOGY

In Karl Barth's *The Epistle to the Romans*, first published in 1918, and then significantly reworked and revised for its second publication in 1921, Barth defines theology by its contrast with history, ethics, religion, and most importantly for our present purposes, philosophy. Theological thinking, Barth explains, begins in the crisis that results from opposing ways of thinking, a crisis that, in his words, is "primarily concerned with the permanent *krisis* of the relation between time and eternity."[9] This crisis extends from theology in general to the particular case of exegetical theology, which is Barth's specific interest in his commentary on the Apostle Paul's *Epistle*. Exegetical theology, Barth explains, is devoted solely to the task of interpretation, which he defines on the first page of his commentary as "an endeavor to see through and beyond history into the spirit of the Bible, which is the Eternal Spirit."[10] A theological interpretation is not content simply in deciphering the literal meaning of a text. Its concerns are more complex as it moves "through and beyond history into the spirit."[11] Not only in a state of "permanent *krisis*," the theological exegete is also confronted with a fundamental enigma. As Barth writes: "Intelligent comment means that I am driven on till I stand with nothing before me but the enigma of the matter; till the document seems hardly to exist as a document; till I have almost forgotten that I am not its author; till I know the author so well that I allow him to speak in my name and am even able to speak in his name myself."[12]

Therefore, what must first be stressed about the critical task of theology is the importance of its realization of this permanent state of crisis. Even in the particular case of scriptural interpretation, there is the movement "through and beyond" the document itself to the Word of God, which Barth distinguishes from the given words of Scripture. What warrants this claim, from Barth's perspective, is the theologian's insistence on the event of revelation. That is to say, what makes a particular interpretation distinctively theological is the revelatory event wherein, as Barth states in the first volume of his *Church Dogmatics*, "the biblical word becomes God's Word."[13] A critical theology, therefore, is in a constant state of becoming, following the pattern as manifested in exegesis wherein scripture continually becomes the Word of God by virtue of revelation, and as discerned in and through the act of theological interpretation.

The relation of theological thinking to history, ethics, religion, and philosophy is no different. Theology reestablishes the relation that was purportedly lost, forgotten, or obscured, but in so doing, the objective sciences are eclipsed. Of course, this imbalanced relation should come as no surprise given the prevailing motif of Barth's commentary; namely, the "infinite qualitative distinction" between time and eternity that Barth learns from Kierkegaard and then reclaims in Paul.[14] It should be noted, however, that Barth's theological dialectics disallows a simple Hegelian sublimation so that the spirit of the world is not completely swallowed up in the Spirit of Christ, nor do human words come to an end when God speaks. Barth is much more Kantian than that.[15] For with Barth, at least in this early stage of his theology, theology is always and only *prolegomena*. In other words, what distinguishes theology from the objective sciences is that theology knows its limitations and sets in relief theology as a strictly critical task. Theology is forever and only a beginning; it remains a pointing, never a possession. In this relation between the sciences and theology, which is apparently one of extreme imbalance, theology stands apart in one way as a corrective by pointing toward the infinite if only for the purpose of pointing out what the finite is not. Thus, theologian's primary identity is that of the iconoclast.[16]

This iconoclastic mandate fittingly begins with Barth's critique and reevaluation of theology itself. From beginning to end, Barth was a nonfoundationalist theologian, which is a great irony considering he spent the entire latter half of his career on the colossal, fourteen-volume, never-to-be-completed *Church Dogmatics*. But early in this work, Barth explains his task: "In dogmatics . . . there are no comprehensive views, no final conclusions, no permanent results. There is only the investigation and teaching which takes place in the very act of dogmatic work and which . . . at every point must begin again at the beginning."[17] Moreover, "all conclusions must be intended, accepted, and understood as fluid material for further work. None of the results of dogmatics—really none at all—can be important."[18] And finally, in a later work in which he compares theology to the wonder and mystery in the artistry of Mozart, he writes that theology is "a glorious upsetting of the balance."[19]

Attending to this critical or iconoclastic dimension of Barth's theology is the main objective of William Stacy Johnson's recent study of Barth in which he argues that Barth was a precursor to postmodernity by laying a nonfoundational foundation for theological thinking.[20] In Johnson's words, "Theology cannot be *the*ology without also being a critique of the*ology*."[21] And again:

> To put it plainly, in order to "center" on God one must effect a "decenter-ing" of theology. This is the insight that lies at the heart of Karl Barth's

theological quest. To "center" upon God is to converge upon the untamed and the uncoercible. It is to focus upon that which calls us fundamentally into question, upon that which brings about a shaking of the foundations, of all that was previously considered stable and secure. The mystery of God, far from safeguarding theology, precipitates an act of endangerment, like removing the safety from a loaded gun.[22]

Theology, in other words, has more at stake in questioning itself as a possibility than in preserving itself in its security; it is neither objective nor subjective, but rather a radical interrogation that effects a reversal, an overturning, and most importantly, an opening to a "wholly other" that resists categorization and defies definition.[23] *Theology decenters.*[24] Again, in Johnson's words, "Rather than proclaiming the absence of a 'center,' therefore, Barthian theology insists that it is the divine center itself that infuses the postmodern intellectual task with all its instability and risk."[25] To return to Barth's commentary on Paul's *Epistle to the Romans*, theology, as the response to and striving after the Word of God, is the "question mark" or the "hinge" upon which all else turns.[26]

Unfortunately, often lost in these imperfect analogies is the question of ethics that drives Barth's theological concerns.[27] The fact that Barth views theology as engendering a kind of questioning opens theology to the question of its own justification. And the priority that Barth gives to the Word of God as the decisive key in addressing such questions forces the theologian beyond a rationale that is merely self-justifying. With such a perspective, therefore, it is not a question of whether or not one believes, but what one believes, why, and toward what ends. In addition, it is not a question of whether one thinks, but how and by which standards. The nature of these questions is that they are never completely resolved, which is befitting the permanent crisis that exists by virtue of the relation between God and humanity. In addition, these questions never cease to exert the impossible demand that God's Word be spoken and that God's will be done. This, then, is the ethical demand that emerges from Barth's critical theology. And this demand is distinct from the study of ethics, which insists on either the false notion of human autonomy or the straightforward imposition of divine commands.[28]

Not only ethics, but also history and religion—at least how they are understood and appropriated by scholars—fall short of this demand. Each is reductive as it sets boundaries on the radical transcendence of God, and therefore, each is ripe for a theological rendering. This means that history will then be made relative by the standard of eternity; that the historical method will be useful only insofar as it points beyond itself. As Barth writes in *Romans*: "When history points beyond itself and discovers in itself its own inadequacy, when there emerges in history a horror at history, then its high places are made known."[29] In other words, from a theological perspective, history is best understood when it realizes its fundamental inadequacy. One implication of this is that nostalgia can never be justified theologically. Theology disallows the notion of a "golden age"; this includes the time of Christ, the age of the Church fathers, or the Reformers, and even Barth's own age, which celebrated itself as a time of theological crisis and renewal. As Barth makes the point, "There is no fragment or epoch of history which can be pronounced divine. . . . Everything human swims with the stream either with vehement protest or with easy accommodation, even when it appears to hover above it or to engage in conflict with it. Christ is not one of the righteous."[30] History is nothing more than a tale of loss and forgetfulness, and the undying allegiance to the historical-critical method by scholars of religion is nothing more than a sign of theology's spiritual and moral poverty.

Nevertheless, in spite of the inadequacy of history, and in spite of the continued allegiance by historians to the historical-critical method, history remains a resource of hidden possibilities. In support of this claim, Barth evidences Plato, Luther, and Dostoevsky, all of whom stood within a history while standing apart.[31] As a result, each belongs to history because they set it on a different path. History was not allowed to be lord and master, overwhelming by the power of inertia, but instead, for each of these individuals it was a condition of possibility, a resource for thought, and a motivation for urgent and meaningful action. In this way, history is transformed by theology in serving as a resource for theological renewal. Lost is the objectivity of the dispassionate scholar. Lost is the periodization of history that lends general comprehension to what is otherwise an endless stream of facts and figures. But also lost is the sense of inevitability or the crippling necessity to existence. In its place theology insists on "crisis" as the ontological, and thus perennial, state of affairs, which means that each present is an opportunity for the existential awakening of faith. More directly still, historical crisis means theological demand; and the demand of theology is the moral challenge that Barth issues as the call to heed the Word of God.

Religion suffers the same fate. Barth views religion, like history, as a limited human possibility. Unlike history, religion is the highest human possibility and, consequently, the most dangerous. In Barth's words, "the religious man above all others is not what he is intended to be." The religious life "is nothing more than romantic unbelief."[32] Its danger is its propensity toward self-deception. Barth's theological rendering of religion is the rendering of religious truth as a lie by exposing its knowledge to the unfathomable truth of the Word of God. Barth's bluntness, then, should come as no surprise when he writes: "Religion must die. In God we are rid of it."[33] And elsewhere: "Jesus simply has nothing to do with religion. The meaning of his life is the actuality of that which is not actually present in my religion—the actuality of the unapproachable, the unreachable, the incomprehensible, the realization of the possibility, which is not a matter of speculation: 'Behold I make all things new!'"[34]

FROM CRITIQUE TO "COOPERATION"

Barth's theological critique of science, history, and religion serves as a backdrop to the primary concern of this present work, which is Barth's theological critique of philosophy and the reasons he gives for why a "Christian Philosophy" should be avoided. First, it must be stated that Barth's problem with philosophy is not that philosophy is somehow wrong, nor even that philosophy is misguided. In a 1960 essay dedicated to his brother, entitled "Philosophy and Theology," Barth clearly states that both philosophy and theology share a common devotion and are in service to the same truth, and that the supposed opposition of philosophy and theology is a misplaced abstraction.[35] In fact, when true to themselves, philosophy and theology are in the most profound cooperation as shared endeavors of fellow human beings. From philosophy, theology learns the love of the world, which means, among other things, that theology has the obligation to move beyond its critical task to an eventual point of construction and cooperation. This movement within Barth's own thinking can be seen in his shift from dialectics to dogmatics, a shift made possible by his study of Saint Anselm of Canterbury, in which Barth learned to appreciate the value of the analogical method for theology.[36] As Barth understands well, the difficulty is to avoid lapsing into a kind of naïveté that is forgetful of its earlier critical posture. Thus, still critical and distinct, but in Barth's theological shift from dialectics to dogmatics through the analogy of faith, Barth admits that theological thinking must also be constructive and cooperative.

For instance, to return to this 1960 essay by Barth, not only are philosophy and theology seen to be in fundamental cooperation by sharing a common truth, but also Barth admits that philosophy and theology are both to be understood as strictly human endeavors. As he writes:

> That in ever so different, indeed, opposing thought and speech just as of the philosopher so also of the theologian, we have to make it with the same human (also far too human) thought and speech. Thus on this point there can indeed yet be no serious judgment and separation between both of them, no incompatibility of their paths, no mild or wild astonishment of the one concerning the other to change something, seeing that everything takes place on one and the same plane, on which every still so radical confrontation includes in itself also a cooperation.[37]

Furthermore, both philosophy and theology encounter a related problem in that both are encircled by their own logic.

Still, in spite of these significant points of contact, more important for understanding Barth's concern with the problem of philosophical theology is not the convergence, but the divergence between philosophy and theology. On this point, Barth argues that the two are distinguished according to the direction of their thought. Philosophy is engaged in what Barth calls a "mighty elevation," moving from creation to God and then back again to its original starting point and primary interest;[38] whereas theology, on the other hand, is "a mighty act of condescension, which as such involves and entails an empowered act of elevation."[39] Theological thought begins with God and God's good purposes for creation. It is God's Word that reveals the truth of the human situation, and only by standing in that truth can one know the proper theological truth concerning God and humanity. "The theologian," Barth writes, "stands and falls with this sequence, in fact, with its irreversibility. With every attempt to reverse that sequence, pseudo-theology would begin."[40] As Stephen Sykes writes: "The theologian works in a descending order, from living creator to the creature; the philosopher, exactly the reverse. There cannot therefore be a 'Christian philosophy,' which is both properly philosophy and also Christian."[41] Of course, this is Barth's running critique of the "theology" of Friedrich Schleiermacher; namely, by beginning from the point of human experience, theology becomes nothing more than anthropology.[42] The freedom of God's Word is restricted by being predetermined by finite human understanding. In the case of Schleiermacher, one might say that he was not wrong, but neither was he a proper theologian.[43] This, then, is the key to understanding Barth's concern with philosophical theology.

For Barth, theology and philosophy are distinct though inseparable ways of thinking. Theology begins with the concrete act of revelation; philosophy with abstraction. Theology entrusts itself to the truth as revealed by God in history; philosophy to the capacities of human thought. To return to Barth's commentary on Paul's *Epistle to the Romans*, there Barth's theological critique of philosophy centered on the arrogance of philosophy; or if not arrogance, at least philosophy's failure to respect its own limits. Barth views this matter as a great irony, because in spite of the height of philosophical ambition, at its best, philosophy—at least from a theological perspective—can only give voice to the wrath of God, which is to say philosophy testifies to human ignorance and confusion. As Barth writes, the theological significance of philosophy is "that we can know nothing of God, that we are not God, that the Lord is to be feared." In this early phase of Barth's thinking, his criticism of philosophy is most harsh: "That God is not known as God is due, not merely to some error of thought or to some gap in experience, but to a fundamentally wrong attitude to life. Vanity of mind and blindness of heart inevitably bring into being corrupt conduct."[44]

What is at stake in Barth's concern with philosophical theology regards the proper attitude toward life, and whether that attitude corresponds either to God's revelation or to human vanity, blindness, and corruption. Certainly, this is a serious matter indeed. From a theological perspective, philosophy overextends itself, and as a result its truth becomes a lie and its ethic becomes the height of perversion. Concerning the ethics, Barth writes: "When the barrier between God and Man, the last inexorable barrier and obstacle, is not closed, the barrier between what is normal and what is perverse is opened." And on reason being made irrational, "Here is the final vacuity and disintegration. Chaos has found itself, and anything may happen. The atoms whirl, the struggle for existence rages. Even reason itself becomes irrational."[45]

It is here that the depth of misunderstanding of Barth's theological critique is most severe.[46] For while philosophy is indeed incomplete without theology, so too is theology served by the nature of philosophy's insight. In spite of the hyperbolic tone of his rhetoric, Barth's critique of philosophy is not a condemnation. Instead, philosophy exposes theology to the crisis of the human dilemma. By philosophy's shortcomings, the theological insistence on the primacy of the call of the Other is given its place and the theological task is set. Theology speaks from beyond, knowing full well the audacity, paradox, and even violence inherent to this claim. But when philosophy does its work well, there comes with it the realization that theology has no alternative. God's wrath is not the final word, nor does human knowledge exhaust the possibilities of human understanding. It is for this reason that Barth tames his critique so that the importance of the cooperation between philosophical and theological thinking might be more apparent.

Earlier reference was made to Barth's suggestion that theology learns from philosophy the love of the world. With this in mind, one might add that what philosophy learns from theology is the responsibility that this love is not without a cost. Thinking bears its fruit in the ethic it manifests. With philosophy alone, ethics is left open and indeterminate, like the emptiness of Kant's categorical imperative. Again, this is not a condemnation. Rather, it is the beginning of theological possibility, which means that what the Christian theologian would call *grace* begins where human comprehension ends, and that theological truth fills in the vacuity of philosophical knowledge. Philosophy and theology are not antithetical, but complimentary. The problem of philosophical theology, at least from Barth's perspective, is not the difference between the one and the other, but the fact that those differences are so often confused and boundaries are blurred.

BARTH'S "BENIGN NEGLECT" OF PHILOSOPHY

As a final testimony to this reading of Barth on the problem of philosophical theology, we can look to the correspondence between Barth and his theological colleague Rudolf Bultmann. In the beginning, there was little perceived difference between their theological projects. With time, however, the divergence of their paths emerged. As Bultmann clarified the existential component to his thought, Barth became more engrossed in the task of theological dogmatics. Bultmann was disappointed by Barth's reluctance to enter into dialogue with contemporary philosophy. For instance, in a letter from 1928 he writes to Barth:

> You have failed to enter into (latent but radical) debate with modern philosophy and naively adopted the older ontology from patristics and scholastic dogmatics. What you say (and often only *want* to say) is beyond your terminology, and a lack of clarity and sobriety is frequently the result . . . It seems to me that you are guided by a concern that theology should achieve emancipation from theology. You try to achieve this by ignoring philosophy. The price you pay for this is that of falling prey to an outdated philosophy.[47]

The problem with this rear-guard stance in Bultmann's mind is that Barth unwittingly allows a particular philosophy to go untested. As a result, it is Barth's theology that ironically becomes enslaved to philosophy. Even more it is a philosophy that Barth leaves unacknowledged and that remains uncritical.

Barth's response to this charge is to reverse it back onto Bultmann, but not after first admitting his distaste for what he takes as theological pandering to the philosophy of the day. Borrowing a phrase from Richard Rorty, Charles Marsh calls Barth's stance in relation to philosophy, a "benign neglect." Marsh explains, "[Barth] does not develop arguments against the Bultmannians, the Schelerians, the Gundolians, and 'all the philosophers'; instead, he suggests that the surest way of getting beyond, behind, around, or over institutionalized and time-honored theological problems is to simply start speaking about God in a new way." Barth confirms this reading when he writes to Bultmann: "I will not defend in principle what you call my ignoring of philosophical work . . . It is also a fact that I have come to abhor profoundly the spectacle of theology constantly trying above all to adjust to the philosophy of its age, and thereby neglecting its own theme." Again for Barth, the point of issue is the need to recognize limitations. For instance, he asks Bultmann whether it would be worthwhile "to spend the rest of my life acquiring an unambiguous terminology from the phenomenologists. What of *importance* would I really be gaining thereby?"[48] The answer to this question depends on how one perceives the "human possibility" of knowledge of God, or the range of human comprehension. Barth's position could be summarized as follows: If knowledge of God were a human possibility, then philosophy's reign would be complete and unrestricted, and the theological task would be redundant and therefore unnecessary.

If Barth is correct, philosophy's greatest accomplishment is precisely its failure to rise to the height of its aspiration. In this way the horizon of philosophical possibility is set as the boundary between philosophy and theology. The voice of theology, then, is distinguished by its origin beyond the human subject's capabilities, that metaphorical beyond that speaks more about the truth of desire than the truth of knowledge. Theology is made theological by what philosophy is not. In its relation to philosophy (as well as its relation to history, ethics, and religion), theology remains a critical endeavor. But as it speaks of its shared truth and to its common concern for humanity, it strives to give voice to a word that is not its own, which is the concrete truth of God's revelation, an inscrutable mystery that demands a constant watchfulness. In other words, the very possibility of theology rests strictly on the possibility and reality of God, which is not to say the knowledge of God's existence, but the faith that speaks desire. As Barth makes this point: "That is why when we asked how God does and can come to man in His revelation, we were compelled to give the clear answer that both the reality and possibility of this event are the being and action only of God, and especially of God the Holy Spirit. Both the reality and possibility!"[49]

Philosophical theology remains a problem for Barth, because if it succeeded, the cooperation between two discrete discourses would be collapsed into a mixed and totalizing discourse that was forgetful of the original difference that makes both philosophy and theology necessary human endeavors in service to the truth. Put simply, philosophical theology is a problem because it does not know which way to turn, whether to God or creation as the source of truth. As Marsh writes: "Barth's suggestion . . . is that the best response to the difference of the theologian and philosopher is simply to let both be what they are in their difference. Theology is a speaking about God on the basis of God's self-witness in Jesus Christ; philosophy is thought thinking itself and being on the basis of being."[50] Thus, in the end Barth's theology rests on an epistemological, and ultimately ethical, humility, urging both philosophers and theologians alike to accept their place, which together express the height of human longing coupled with the absolute distance of that longing from the theological truth of human possibility.

To summarize, Barth sees in philosophy an endeavor to test the limits of human understanding. Theology, on the other hand, speaks from a different source, derived not from the horizon set by knowledge, but from the Word of God spoken by faith. Philosophical theology is undesirable ethically, because it sets humans in the place of God by forgetting the infinite qualitative difference. It is resisted by theology, because it restricts the absolute freedom and transcendence of God by the standards of human knowing. Mixing what should be distinct discourses is a confusion and an indiscretion that leaves theology indistinguishable from the world and philosophy unaware of itself.

While there is much to commend in Barth's theological strategy of thought—most especially, his recognition of limitations and his insistence that a theo-logic of faith requires its own "grammar of signification"[51]—it also raises certain questions. Before proceeding, therefore, two points must be made concerning Barth's approach to the problem of philosophical theology and why it ultimately does not succeed in addressing the limitations of modernity that Barth correctly perceived:

(1) *Reversal does not equal overcoming.* Barth's corrective to the shortcomings of modern philosophy and theology was achieved through a reversal of priority, and this achievement is also its shortcoming. This strategy of reversal can be seen throughout Barth's career and explains why Barth's vision of cooperation is ultimately inadequate to the task of speaking to the shared concerns of both philosophy and theology in a pluralistic age. First, recall Barth's early concern with liberal modern theology's overconfidence in the power and range of human reason. It was this concern that was the inspiration for Barth's watershed theological commentary on Paul's *Epistle to the Romans.* It was also this concern that led to his critique of Schleiermacher's theology-turned-anthropology. Finally, this concern stands at the center of his critique of philosophical theology in the sense that what distinguishes philosophy from theology, and the reason why the two must never be confused or intermingled, is that philosophy is strictly a human endeavor, while theology begins and ends with the Word of God. Barth shatters this confidence in human reason by exposing its limitation in relation to the knowledge of God. Barth reminds philosophy that whatever it might achieve, theologically speaking, it is still lacking. Thus, Barth effectively reverses the modern emphasis on objective knowledge and self-mastery by substituting in its place such theological concepts as mystery, human vulnerability, and grace.

However, and this point will be elaborated in the following chapters, while Barth justifiably reduces humanity to size—and by this he is rightly considered as a forerunner to many of the themes common to postmodernity—he does this by insisting on the absolute autonomy and transcendence of God. In essence, *Barth replaces modern philosophy's grounding in human consciousness with his own theological grounding in the subject of God*—this is what is meant by the reversal of priority that was spoken of above. Such assurance, however achieved, has since grown suspect, for *it does not overcome the problems of representation, but only reverses them.* The question is no longer "How do we know what we know?" but rather, "How does God make himself known to us?" One stable foundation has been replaced with another. One cannot help but wonder at the continued viability of such an approach after the hermeneutics of suspicion and in the face of the increased global awareness that has only made more apparent the horrors of our time. Put simply, would not a broken humanity require a vulnerable God?[52]

(2) *"Benign neglect" does not translate into freedom.* This point is a reiteration of Bultmann's critique of Barth; namely, Barth's posturing of "benign neglect" toward philosophy does not achieve, as Barth hopes, the emancipation of theology from philosophy, but in fact only evidences an unacknowledged and uncritical philosophy. As previously noted, Barth's response to Bultmann was characteristic in the sense that he did not argue the point, but instead reversed the charge such that it was not him, but Bultmann, who was made to defend "the spectacle of theology constantly trying above all to adjust to the philosophy of its age." In short, one cannot make a discourse pure simply by asserting it to be so. Barth's refusal to engage seriously with the philosophy of his day not only leaves his theological critique of philosophy hollow, but also exposes the shortcoming of his critical theology, as it allows a particular philosophical perspective to go untested. Furthermore, the problem with such a naïveté is that it might easily lapse into a kind of fundamentalism wherein theological reflection is kept safe by its own version of the hermeneutic circle.[53] Not at all a genuine cooperation between philosophy and theology, Barth's thought instead reflects the assurance and expansive possibilities open to the trailblazer whereby a new path might be forged, but only along a circuitous route that leads back to the same. By Barth's own definition, dogmatic theology must always "begin again at the beginning," and as such, even as it works against the tradition it nevertheless remains predetermined by the modern philosophical search for foundations. From this we must conclude that theology is not freed from philosophy, but bound together with it by its very own efforts to resist, escape, or overcome.

Heidegger's Philosophical Critique of Theology

Roughly a contemporary of Barth, Martin Heidegger also sensed the crisis of modernity. Unlike Barth, however, for Heidegger this was not so much a moral crisis as a philosophical one. Philosophy had become entrapped in a modern, strictly epistemological mindset. Philosophy had been reduced to questions of knowledge, and as a result it had forgotten, left obscure, or confused its more fundamental task of asking the question of being.[54] In his classic early text *Being and Time,* Heidegger endeavored to reintroduce this most basic question according to the tenets of Husserlian phenomenology. However, in Heidegger's work, unlike Husserl's, phenomenology was used against modernity and the restrictions it placed on philosophy. That is to say, with Heidegger phenomenology effects the "destructuring of the history of ontology" so that the hidden ontological difference might be disclosed.[55] Philosophy's relation to its object is therefore a paradoxical one; it rediscovers the question of being as the task of philosophy by de-objectivizing it; it reorients the aim of philosophy by demonstrating the originary condition that makes thought possible in the first place; and finally, it retells the history of philosophy in order that history might be overcome.

When Heidegger writes that the human subject is a "being-in-time," therefore, he is not simply reminding humanity of its epistemological limitations; even more, he is venturing a claim as to its ontological nature. As he writes, *Dasein* is constituted by a *"constant unfinished quality,"* which means, among other things, that knowledge of oneself and others is always incomplete. What makes this most significant is not that it restates Kant's epistemological insights in a phenomenological idiom, but that it shows that phenomenology is unavoidably ontological: As long as *Dasein* is, it *"is always already its not yet."*[56] To be human is to be determined by a relationality beyond one's capacity to know and comprehend; to be in time is to be ahead of oneself as a *"being-toward-death."*[57] The appropriate task of philosophy, then, is to make this beyond known without reducing it to a concept, to think in such a way that one's concepts and questions are subjected to a constant critique befitting one's ontological (pre)determination.

To this point, there is little that separates Heidegger from Barth. Both affirm the task of thinking as a critical—that is, iconoclastic or de-objectivizing—endeavor. Both also agree that critique is in service to a greater or more fundamental calling. For Barth, this is the theologian's impossible obligation to speak the Word of God. For Heidegger, this is the fundamental task of the philosopher to ask the question of being. When thought through the problematic of philosophical theology, however, these similarities also reveal a difference that would determine much of the future of twentieth-century religious and philosophical thought.

DIFFERENTIATING PHILOSOPHY FROM THEOLOGY

According to Barth's perspective, the differences between philosophy and theology are according to the different directions of their thought. According to Barth, the importance of this difference is of an ethical nature. Theology humbles itself before a truth that it knows is beyond its comprehension. Philosophy, on the other hand, demonstrates the heights of human aspiration and the perversity of human relations that results when that aspiration passes over into sheer arrogance. Of course, theology is also victim to a kind of perversion and arrogance, which is why the theological examination of the relation between theology and philosophy eventually speaks of the need for cooperation. Ethics demands two distinct kinds of thinking. The one being philosophical, which begins from the knowledge of creation and through the method of abstraction, aspires to the knowledge of the beyond. The other being theological, which begins from God's Word revealed in history and through the method of interpretation, reaches down to the meaning of God's Word for humanity.

Heidegger, on the other hand, sees the differences between philosophy and theology in starker terms. For him, the opposition between philosophy and theology is no misplaced philosophical abstraction as Barth claims, but in fact provides insight into the very nature of thinking itself. Early in his thinking Heidegger argues that a radical divide between philosophy and theology exists through which the nature of thinking is given clarity. This divide reaches to the essence of thought, and accordingly, there are essential differences between philosophy and theology. This point is made in a lecture first delivered in 1927 entitled "Phenomenology and Theology," wherein Heidegger states, "Our thesis, then, is that *theology is a positive science, and as such, therefore, is absolutely different from philosophy.*"[58] At this still early stage of his career, we thus observe that Heidegger identifies the difference between philosophy and theology as the difference between thinking and science. Philosophy asks the question of being. As such, it is a thinking of an indeterminate origin and end. This is because being remains factually unknown and structurally unknowable. Theology, on the other hand, is the science of faith. Theology gives thought to faith. However, thought full of faith is not faithful to thinking and the uncertainty implied therein, but instead answers to a "God" who is the name of limit, a limit that encloses thinking in a circle of the same by knowing from the start both its beginning and its end. It is for this reason that Heidegger calls Christian philosophy a "square circle,"[59] and why he insists that if a "proper theology" were to be written, the word *being* would not appear.[60]

Robert Gall, author of *Beyond Theism and Atheism: Heidegger's Significance for Religious Thinking*, argues that Heidegger's statement regarding the possibility of a proper theology is a deliberately ironic one, and in fact, to the extent one takes Heidegger seriously, one becomes more deeply skeptical with regard to the possibility of theological thinking at all. Gall writes: "Heidegger, when 'properly' understood on such matters as truth, God (and gods), and 'faith', presents us with a unique voice and vision that cannot be co-opted into any sort of theology—be it negative, existential, dialectical or Thomistic—and indeed seriously challenges the viability of any 'theology.'"[61] Later in the work, Gall clarifies his argument: "We now have to ask whether theologians have attended to, or even can attend to, the matter at stake in Heidegger's thinking and remain theologians. For, first and foremost, the matter of concern for theology would seem to be faith. . . . Theology is the 'science' of faith, i.e., it gives systematic coherence and conceptual clarity to what is disclosed through faith."[62] In other words, according to Gall's interpretation, the more one is in sympathy with Heidegger, the less theological one would become. The consequence of Heidegger's thought, therefore, might be designated as a kind of de-theologization.

Key to this particular interpretation is what is meant by the term 'faith.' So long as one accepts Heidegger's definition of faith—e.g., "In faith rules certainty, that kind of certainty which is safe even in the uncertainty of itself, i.e., of what it believes in."[63]—then one might be led to the same conclusion as Heidegger concerning the limitations, and if Gall is correct, even the impossibility, of theology. Faith, according to Heidegger, is what "stands in the way of the questioning of being." According to Gall, this stopgap is the very thing that Heidegger's thinking resists: "What this means is that the self-certainty of the *ego cogito* that rules in modern metaphysics is not a revolt against the doctrine of faith, but a necessary consequence of it. . . . What this means is that theology, Christian theology, embodies the very thinking that Heidegger, following Nietzsche, finds questionable and is attempting to 'overcome.'"[64]

Of course, what this leaves unquestioned is the nature of faith. Heidegger's notion of faith is undoubtedly influenced by the fact that as a young theological student he was schooled in the Thomistic tradition.[65] However, if contemporary thought has learned anything from Heidegger at all, then it must question this notion of faith; we must read Heidegger against himself. In fact, according to Gall, the realization that all things are "question worthy" and "questionable" stands as Heidegger's greatest legacy: "It is a lesson Heidegger has undoubtedly learned from Nietzsche, who has made us *suspicious* of every assertion, every representation and every idol . . . as a manifestation of the will to power and an attempt to secure ourselves."[66]

With this in mind, who is to say whether faith can be likened to certainty, or belief, or doctrine, or any of these options? After *Being and Time*, what warrants speaking of faith as if it discloses an object of knowledge, a "what" to be scientifically explicated and exfoliated?

In other words, a certain kind of faith might indeed be governed according to the law of certainty, but as Luther, Kierkegaard, and perhaps Barth as well, have demonstrated, faith might just as well open the floodgates of uncertainty. In fact, these thinkers reflect a long-standing biblical tradition in which the link between faith and certainty would be utter nonsense, more symptomatic of an Enlightenment-like philosophical sensibility than that of a biblical theological perspective. Therefore, Gall's confidence that Heidegger gives "decisive criticisms" against the applicability of his thinking for theology rests on a profound misunderstanding of the nature of faith.[67] The historical fact of the matter is that Heidegger has been enormously influential for theological thinking and that perhaps he himself was least of all capable of grasping why.

This is to say nothing of Heidegger's understanding and appreciation of religion, which from his perspective is another matter from theology altogether. Thinking religiously opens possibilities that are unthought and unthinkable by theology. Such thinking is reserved to a kind of thinking that thinks meditatively rather than calculatively.[68] It is a quality of thought that allows itself to be determined by the radically indeterminate and indeterminable. This is in contrast to the theological rendering of religion that, according to Heidegger at least, purportedly strives to fix religion as an object of knowledge. If Heidegger is correct, then theology does not pertain to philosophy, just as faith should not be confused with knowledge. However, religion remains a distinct possibility as long as the problem of ontotheology is overcome.

THE PROBLEM OF ONTOTHEOLOGY

This leads from Heidegger's earlier, more "philosophical" or phenomenological works, to his later, more "thoughtful" or poetic works.[69] In this later work, Heidegger's early concern with hermeneutics becomes centered on the problem of ontotheology—specifically, how this problem, which Heidegger comes to realize is a historical inevitability of thought, can be overcome. However, what will be discovered is that Heidegger's strategy for overcoming ontotheology is surprisingly similar to Barth's preservation of theology. That is to say, Heidegger thinks philosophy serves its purposes best when it restricts itself to philosophy; likewise, theology best accomplishes its theological task when it does not pretend to be philosophical. Toward the close of *Identity and Difference,* the text in which Heidegger examines the problem of ontotheology most explicitly, he summarizes the problem of ontotheology as follows: "How does the deity enter into philosophy, not just modern philosophy, but philosophy as such?"[70] In other words, how is philosophy contaminated by theology, and theology by philosophy? This question is an outgrowth of a more fundamental question for Heidegger concerning the nature of thinking. As in the early essay "Phenomenology and Theology," Heidegger's primary concern is still in clarifying the essence of thought. At this later stage in his career, however, this clarification does not rest on a clear-cut divide between philosophy and theology. Heidegger now insists that thinking itself is constantly and necessarily threatened by the ontotheological problem, and thus, that both philosophy and theology are equally in danger.

What Heidegger seems to realize at this point is that what differentiates philosophy from theology is not a difference in essence, but of economy. Theology thinks through an economy of faith. Its chief danger to thinking is that the horizon of possibility is foreclosed by the limit concept of God. God is both the origin and end of theological thinking. To this Barth would agree. As Barth writes: "This event [of revelation] represents a self-enclosed circle. Not only the objective but also the subjective element of revelation, not only its actuality but also its potentiality, is the being and action of the self-revealing God alone."[71] The disagreement between Barth and Heidegger centers on their understanding of God. Barth speaks of God as a mystery, a mystery that is known only by means of revelation, whereas for Heidegger, God remains a critical concept predetermining the limits of humanity's creative capacity. Philosophy, on the other hand, at least when it attains to its utmost possibility, thinks through an economy of being, which means that thinking remains on a path of uncertain origin and destination.

Returning to Heidegger's *Identity and Difference*, the question regarding the essence of thought focuses in on the principle of identity (A = A). Heidegger's analysis begins with the principle of identity as the necessary postulate for Western rationality, and thereby demonstrates the predetermined history of Western thought as it establishes itself by its privileging of identity over difference. This history tells of the metaphysical demand for a unity of thought, which, according to Heidegger's analysis, culminates in the figure of Hegel. Hegel's dialectical method thinks of difference as that which gives movement, history, and substance to thought. Nevertheless, thought itself originates and is ultimately unified in the one universal idea of the absolute spirit. Difference is subsumed in identity.[72] From Heidegger's perspective, this privileging of identity over difference

covers or distorts the more fundamental truth concerning the principle of identity, namely, the truth of differences "belonging-together."[73]
This means that difference remains, that difference is both the substance and process of thought, and that identity is known in and
through differentiation.[74]

We may now return to Heidegger's question regarding the contamination of philosophy by theology, and vice versa. The answer
Heidegger provides is that philosophy comes to its limits and recognizes the abyss over which it stands. In order to give account of its
ungrounded ground, it makes an appeal to a logic not its own, and
thus, philosophy resorts to theology. When philosophy resorts to theology it is no longer philosophical, but ontotheological. Its identity has
become indistinguishable and its capacities for thoughtfulness have
become clouded over. Theology, on the other hand, seeks to know the
Supreme Being, which is by nature unknowable and ungraspable. In
order to make its faith secure, it speaks of God as if God belonged to
the order of knowledge; thus, God is made into a being among beings
and theology is transformed into metaphysics. What philosophy and
theology share in common that conjoins in the problem of ontotheology is that neither is content with its limited domain. As they seek
to know what is outside their respective economies of knowledge,
they each betray the very truth with which they are uniquely gifted.
The result is that theology, when ontotheological, keeps theology
from its desire by reducing God to a being among beings. Likewise,
philosophy fails in its most pressing desire—namely, the desire to
know—because the truth of its knowledge is only partial, but even
more, such partial truth is made untrue by what it conceals.

THE PROBLEM WITH "OVERCOMING"

Key to Heidegger's strategy of overcoming is the philosophical task of
differentiation. This strategy extends from Heidegger's earlier writings, in which he distinguished between philosophy and theology
according to the essence of thought, to his later, more critical writings, in which he recognized the threat of ontotheology as being
equally strong to both a philosophical and theological discourse. The
problem with Heidegger's position is that by the strength of his differentiation, he remains cut off from what might most forcefully call
his thinking into question. As one critic puts it, "Heidegger both
transgresses and is contained within the ontotheological determina-
tions of man."[75] Two points on this matter:

(1) *Heidegger's understanding of philosophical thought remains indebted to the theological tradition from which it emerged and from which it continues to differentiate itself.* First of all, there is the obvious matter of Heidegger's own debt to the Christian theological tradition, which seems apparent from two statements he made toward both the beginning and end of his career. First, in a letter to his friend Karl Löwith in 1921, he writes: "I am a Christian theologian."[76] Second, in an essay entitled "A Dialogue on Language" (1959), he writes: "Without this theological background I should never have come upon the path of thinking. But origin always comes to meet us from the future."[77] This latter statement was made in the context of Heidegger's dialogue with a Japanese thinker, in which the two explored points of intersection between Heidegger's long-standing interest in hermeneutics and Eastern philosophy. It was Heidegger's claim that he learned of hermeneutics through his study of theology, and that this interest stands in the background of his efforts in *Being and Time.* While this interest would be revisited, clarified, and expanded throughout Heidegger's career, the point of origin remains and might be said to have had a determinative influence in shaping the questions of Heidegger's ongoing inquiries, and consequently, in also prescribing his course of thought.

Indeed, the influence need not be thought of in such a straightforward and obvious manner. For not only are Heidegger's perduring philosophical interests linked to his early education in theology, but also the strategy of overcoming, which is of such importance to this present study, is in accordance with what might be considered a theological structure. As Frank Kermode has written, "The history of the rules and theory of interpretation—of hermeneutics as it used to be, before philosophy appropriated it—is closely linked with that of biblical exegesis."[78]

Or consider, for instance, the point already made on the differences between Heidegger and Nietzsche regarding the inversion of Platonism. Recall that Heidegger argues that Nietzsche's thought remains an expression of ontotheology because he fails to overcome the dualism that stands as the basis of the metaphysical tradition. Nietzsche merely pits a kind of antimetaphysics against metaphysics, thereby disrupting the balance of power, but certainly not escaping the dualism of which he was justly critical. In contrast, Heidegger presents his strategy of overcoming as a return to origins, not for the sake of the reestablishment of a foundation, but for the purpose of bringing the nature of the ontological difference to light. Thus, overcoming is achieved not through inversion, for that merely reifies the difference, nor through refutation, for that remains bound by a kind of dualism, but through repetition, by which the philosopher borrows from a tradition its means of overcoming. This strategy, I am suggesting, is indistinguishable from theological hermeneutics, regardless of Heidegger's own statements on the matter, for they are both thoroughly grounded in the concreteness of textuality. Both proceed from a given origin that contains all the necessary resources for thinking beyond it. Indeed, in this case the structural similarities between Barth's depiction of the interpretative task of theology as it speaks the Word of God and Heidegger's depiction of the differentiating task of philosophy as it identifies the ontological difference suggest an indebtedness on the part of the one for the other that makes suspect any attempts to keep the two apart. This leads into the second point.

(2) *This indebted nature of thought renders suspect the philosophical task of differentiation.* First, the question must be raised whether or not Heidegger's depiction of the philosophical task of differentiation is even an achievable goal. This question is increased in significance when considering Heidegger's own work, which has done so much to lead into the realization of the intersubjective nature of thought, and being. From his notion of the self as a "being-with-others," to his reflections on "sameness" without uniformity,[79] and finally, to *Identity and Difference,* wherein he makes the argument that differences "belong together," all of these suggest a fluid quality to identity that would seem to contradict notions of complete differentiation.

Furthermore, consider the work of Emmanuel Levinas, which, though taking the lead from Heidegger, would eventuate into one of the strongest and most passionate critiques of Heidegger. As Levinas writes in reference to Heidegger's presumed neutrality of thought in his brief intellectual autobiography: "*There is*—impersonally—like *it is raining* or *it is night.* No generosity which the German term 'es gibt' is said to express showed itself between 1933 and 1945. This must be said! Illumination and sense dawn only with the existing beings' rising up and establishing themselves in this horrible neutrality of the *there is.*"[80] These remarks will be discussed in fuller detail in the final chapter, but for now it is important to understand the perspective that leads Levinas to making this critique—his idea of the trace. From Levinas's view, the trace makes impossible the fulfillment of the desire for purity, which I have argued is one of the driving influences in Heidegger's critique of philosophical theology.

And because there are no "pure" actions or intentions, the notion of a pure differentiation is equally suspect.

However, this notion is not only suspect by virtue of its impossibility, but even more because of what such a desire for differentiation covers over. As John Caputo has argued in *Demythologizing Heidegger*, as Heidegger's thought became increasingly differentiated from its dual origin in both Greek philosophy and biblical theology, there was the simultaneous increase in his ethical insensitivity and political blindness.[81] Or from Ingraffia's perspective, Heidegger's attempt to differentiate his philosophy from theology is not the result of a neutral attempt at distinguishing the two, but rather exposes what can only be called an *antitheological bias* on the part of Heidegger. And this bias does not, as Heidegger proclaims, preserve the mutual integrity of both philosophy and theology, but instead subordinates the theological paradigm to the philosophical. In the process, the integrity of theology is distorted. Finally, therefore, rather than overcoming ontotheology, the effect of Heidegger's efforts at differentiation is instead the creation of a wholly new ontotheology.[82]

Conclusion

This leaves philosophical theology with strangely dissimilar antagonists. From the one side, Barth locates the problem in the transcendence of God. Theology is determined by the God who is wholly other, whereas philosophy is *limited* to the bounds of human knowledge and *limiting* by rendering what is other as the same. A theology beholden to philosophy loses itself in anthropology; thus, the freedom of God must be preserved from the arrogance of philosophy. From the other side, Heidegger locates the problem of philosophical theology in the difference between economies of thought. Philosophical thinking is a questioning that effects an opening; while theology, as the science of faith, restricts the mystery of faith to the order of the known.

What Barth and Heidegger share in common, and what will become the central problematic of this work, is their mistaken notion that the quality of thought is distinguished by its purity and, by extension, the claim that a philosophical theology would be either a logical impossibility (Heidegger) or an ethical undesirability (Barth). To claim that this is a mistake is not to suggest it is without its own utility or logic, but that it is short-sighted and ultimately betrays its final intentions of holding out thought for alterity. In other words, in order to preserve difference, both Heidegger and Barth turned their respective discourses inward in their efforts to distinguish a quality of thinking responsive to the other. Their success was also their failure, because the more they succeeded in differentiating their thought, the more cut off that thought became to what might effectively call their thinking into question. Heidegger's philosophical thinking finds its essence after philosophy realizes the overcoming of philosophy and the end of metaphysics, but the path from philosophy's origin to its end is a straight line uninterrupted by the complicating demands of theology. As Gall writes: "[W]hatever religious dimension we might discover in Heidegger, whatever direction it leads us in, it will not emerge along the track of theology, but rather from a turning away from theology."[83] In contrast, Barth speaks of theology as a language of crisis that corresponds to the permanent *krisis* that exists by virtue of the divine-human relation. In this way, a theological language is fundamentally an iconoclastic one. However, the language of the theological tradition is given privilege such that it alone is allowed to set the criteria for true theological reflection. In other words, theology provides for itself its own justification. Philosophy speaks philosophy. Theology speaks theology. And so long as each allows for the autonomy of the other, neither is implicated and purity is preserved.

To return to Kristeva's earlier description of the religious code of purity, the respective positions of both Barth and Heidegger will be shown to fall short of genuine dialogue, much like the biblical injunction of Holiness overlays overt human violence by the muted violence of prohibition. The danger of this understanding of the problem of philosophical theology will be more fully exposed in subsequent chapters, but for now what can be said is that Barth and Heidegger represent two sides of the same coin. With Barth, as has been demonstrated, theology begins in the crisis of the encounter between God and humanity through the event of revelation. As it seeks to give articulation to the Word of God, however, it recoils from the problems inherent in human attestation and settles in, instead, with the assurances offered by a dogmatic faith. Granted, this is an assurance that is rendered always uncertain by the transcendence of God, but the problem remains that this is a truth left open only to the initiated. Such a theology is self-affirming as it safeguards revelation from that which might more radically call it into question. In Kristeva's terms, this would be a discourse that witnesses to the abject, but only after it has been consecrated by the rubrics of faith.

With Heidegger, thinking begins where theology ends in the sense that philosophy proceeds by the step back from abomination to the sacred. In this way, philosophy follows a path that is uncertain and yet to be disclosed. Nevertheless, as this path proceeds, it too finds itself settling in according to its own question of origins. Philosophy, like theology, is faced with the constant threat of ontotheology. Its horizon of thought is not as unrestricted as one might believe; on the contrary, at its root is a certain commitment to a particular theological perspective, one from which it seeks to differentiate itself and to which it remains indebted. It should come as no surprise, therefore, that as Jacques Derrida seeks to think beyond the limitations of Heidegger, specifically with reference to religion, Derrida will deconstruct this false dichotomy between faith and thought by pointing to the duplicitous sources of religion, each of which presupposes the other.[84]

To conclude, the point that both Barth and Heidegger miss, which will become a pattern for those who follow in their respective paths of thought, is that philosophical theology is not the problem, but the symptom of a more fundamental condition. Try as they might, whether by a feigned cooperation or a predetermined differentiation, their efforts at overcoming will inevitably hand themselves back over to the more fundamental ontotheological condition. This condition is the very experience of abjection of which Kristeva speaks; and, as will be shown in the chapters that follow, it is an experience that by its very nature cannot be sidestepped, whether through theological consecration or the phenomenological reduction. What this means is that the nature and possibility of philosophical theology is still yet to be determined, because at this point in the analysis it remains fundamentally misunderstood—which is to say that the question of the conditions of philosophical theology is still yet to be addressed.

INTERLUDE 1

ON POLITICAL BOUNDARIES AND PROFIT

The United States suffers in its immigrations, which from within, challenge not only the idea of a national "organism," but also the very notion of confederacy. . . Furthermore, the cohesion of the American nation centered in the Dollar and God keeps troubling those for whom the future of men and women is centered in other values.

—Julia Kristeva, *Nations without Nationalism*

In the Communist world, we see failure, technological backwardness, declining standards. . . . Even today, the Soviet Union cannot feed itself. The inescapable conclusion is that freedom is the victor. General Secretary Gorbachev, if you seek peace, if you seek prosperity for the Soviet Union, if you seek liberalization: Come here to this gate! Mr. Gorbachev, open this gate! Mr. Gorbachev, tear down this wall!

—Ronald Reagan, Speech at the Brandenburg Gate, 1987

IT'S A QUESTION of strategy. Recall Saint Paul's admonition to be all things to all people.[1] Not simply an argument for the universality of the gospel, even more it was a proclamation of the missionary's strategy. This was a strategy that recognized the fluidity of language, the capacity for translation, and the means of travel. Nor was it simply a guise, the missionary masquerading as a native.

For Paul, rather, this was a statement of identity, a dynamic identity that knows itself not confined to any single self-conception—a borderland personality.

IN *Nations without Nationalism*, Julia Kristeva gives voice to the question that plagues those who are overly concerned with identity: "Whence do you speak?" The question regards perspective, origin, and place—for example, *Where* are your origins? *What* is the place of your perspective? *Why* your perspective of place? It also regards speech—for example, What language do you speak? From what land? And toward what ends? Kristeva's answer is a straightforward one: "I am a cosmopolitan." Not a proclamation of her sophistication, this answer is more of a stance, a way by which Kristeva positions herself. For Kristeva, in other words, to be cosmopolitan is to make a choice: "I maintain that in a contemporary world, shaken up by national fundamentalism on the one hand and the intensive demands of immigration on the other, the fact of belonging to a set is a matter of choice. . . . Thus when I say that I *have chosen cosmopolitanism*, this means that I have, against origins and starting from them, chosen a transnational or international position situated at the crossing of boundaries."[2]

Kristeva is well aware that one does not cross boundaries without difficulty. So why? Why subject oneself to such instability, such risk? Perhaps it is because one realizes that all other positions are merely compensations, that one stands before a crisis, and that to take shelter so as to preserve the self is a fundamental denial of one's responsibility. Not only that, but such efforts are destined to fail: "The values crisis and the fragmentation of individuals have reached the point where we no longer know what we are and take shelter, to preserve a token of personality, under the most massive regressive common denominators: national origins and the faith of our forebears. . . . It is a rare person who does not invoke a primal shelter to compensate for personal disarray."[3] To preserve the self is to maintain tokens of the past or to invoke borders from internal confusion. It is to divide oneself against oneself as a counterstrategy against one's feeling of always already being divided. It is to cut oneself off from the other, the enclosure of the self in a world where borders might be maintained, and thus, responsibilities denied.

Politically, this psychological dynamic is writ large in the investment of nations in their borders. There is much at stake in the control of immigration—most important, perhaps, is the case for a national identity, which is inseparable, of course, from the distribution of capital and the mediation of human relations. Who is to say who gets in and who stays out? And once within the supposed stable borders, and once a participant in the societal economic, on what right does a nation refuse its resources and deny its franchise? Finally, what is the ground of such inhumanity?

As a first answer to this all-important question, I offer the following account of an economic practice that is not without political implications. Eduardo Galeano, author of *Open Veins of Latin America,* notes, "International charity does not exist; it begins at home, for the United States as for everyone else." Galeano writes this as one on the underside of globalization, one from across the border in Latin America, one who has observed the structures of colonialism and the ongoing plunder of resources. In his critique of the International Monetary Fund, for instance, he speaks of formulas ensuring the access of "foreign capitals into an already scorched land."[4] These are economic formulas instituted by the IMF that capitalize on political borders. As a result, social unrest and increasing militarization drive up the market demand. It is a sinister plot couched in the rhetoric of the free exchange of capital, when in fact there is nothing free about a system based on radical inequality.

Symptomatic of this formulaic plunder is the strategy of "price dumping." Galeano tells the story of Union Carbide's takeover of the Brazilian-owned and -operated tape factory Adesite.[5] In this case, the U.S. manufacturer 3M was the culprit. In its efforts to control the Brazilian market, 3M progressively lowered its prices for Scotch Brand tape by 40 percent. Because its market stretched well beyond Brazil, 3M could afford to lose money in this particular market for a particular stretch of time. Adesite could not compete with such bargain basement prices. As a result, its sales dropped and its credit was cut off. Eventually, it was sold to Union Carbide, who together with 3M now controlled the entire Brazilian market. Together the two multinational corporations, with their sights set on the long term, agreed to divide the market by fixing their prices, which were a full 50 percent above the original price of tape. Short-term losses for 3M translated into significant long-term gains. But what may be a sound business practice to some may be financial blackmail to others.

I suppose it all depends on which side of the border one stands. But borders are not easy to decipher when speaking of capital. More and more often, money, resources, goods, and services pass from country to country with little resistance, almost innocently —as if the strategy of the transnational corporation were no different from the cosmopolitan. But nothing could be further from the truth. It is true that both cross boundaries. It is also true that both are matters of choice. The difference is that while one capitalizes on border control (such capitalization, in fact, is the very essence of its existence), the other speaks against it. One renders places indistinguishable through the commodification of a global culture. The other knows the discomfort of placing oneself at the crossing of boundaries, at the exchange of cultures, and the clash of incommensurabilities. Most simply, it is a strategy of competing loyalties. For the transnational corporation it wills one thing, and for that it more often than not succeeds. For the cosmopolitan, on the other hand, her loyalties are divided—a gratitude for her origins, but a defense against provincialism; a care for her own, but a realization that the web of relations stretches well beyond her capacity to know; and a language of one's homeland, but a voice that speaks on behalf of the other.

Thus the strategy of speaking against boundaries does not mean the naïve assertion of their nonexistence, nor the strong-willed endeavor toward their annihilation. Instead it means patiently, courageously, and sympathetically to scrutinize their implications. It means to think both critically and graciously. Such is the meaning of dwelling in the divide; such is the hope for justice.

2

THE PATH OF THEOLOGY
A STUDY OF DIETRICH BONHOEFFER

The relation of theology and philosophy requires a new clarification.
—Dietrich Bonhoeffer, *Act and Being*

IT IS A difficult thing to say about two figures who loom so large in the canons of twentieth-century theological thought, but neither Paul Tillich nor Rudolf Bultmann advance the present discussion regarding the divide between philosophy and theology in any significant manner.[1] Of course, both sought paths through or beyond the philosophical-theological impasse, but neither in ways that were not prefigured by Barth and Heidegger. Tillich's method of correlation, for instance, mediates the divide without ever truly questioning the supposed separation of faith and thought. Even while Tillich's method of correlation is driven by a genuine exchange between the structure of philosophical thought and the meaning of faith, the truth of the message of revelation remains absolute, unchanged, and unchanging. Likewise, Bultmann's method of demythologizing indeed shows a sincere appreciation for both Barth's new hermeneutic and Heidegger's fundamental ontology, but his thinking is little more than application, and his application remains essentially an effort of purification, trapped in a quest for essences.

The concern of this present text, however, is the possibility of a genuine philosophical theology—of a thinking that makes no appeal to either essences or dogma, but affirms its position as a mixed and implicated discourse. Contrary to Tillich, this means that the more natural step than his theology of culture, which still privileged the truth of the Christian message, would be the full embrace of a secular culture, or if not a secular culture, then at least a genuine embrace of a *multi*cultural reality. This is not to say that there is no longer a place for a kind of theological reflection rooted in the faiths of particular religious traditions, but that Tillich's attempts at tempering the philosophical impulse with the language of ultimate concern left the justification of his theology in need of more than the assurance of faith alone, something more akin to an aesthetic or pragmatic sensibility. Otherwise, to write of the anxiety of being while still clinging to a firm place to stand might strike some as a subterfuge, a crutch, or a slippery slope. Similarly, the limitations of Bultmann's demythologizing are important—most notably, as Jacques Derrida points out in his discussion of apophaticism, the fact that demythologizing, like negative theology, remains trapped in an onto-theo-logic by endeavoring in critique for the sake of saving the name of God.[2] Bultmann's critical posture, in other words, was just that—a posturing rather than a genuine commitment to the radical subjugation of the *kerygma* to the world.

The irony is that these two "existentialist" theologians rely on essentializing forms of thought and discourse. Therefore, their efforts at overcoming merely reinscribe the fundamental divide between faith and thinking, and thus leave us with the same predicament with which we began, namely, the desire for a purity of discourse and the fear of contamination.

Dietrich Bonhoeffer, on the other hand, while maintaining a critical stance toward the school of existentialist philosophers and theologians, was perhaps the least essentializing of all when it came to understanding the relation of philosophy to theology and when concerning the basis of action in the world.[3] It is for this reason that Bonhoeffer sought to develop a theological ontology—a task that both Barth and Heidegger agreed was an indiscretion at the very least, if not an utter impossibility. Nevertheless, this would be the very contribution Bonhoeffer makes to the problematic of philosophical theology. As the radical theologian Robert Scharlemann notes: "The question which Bonhoeffer raised, and raised almost as a solitary voice in Protestantism, is still worthy of attention. It is the question whether there is such a thing as a theological ontology . . . and, if so, how it differs from ontology otherwise."[4]

Two things in particular stand out from Scharlemann's statement: First, the idea that Bonhoeffer's might have been a solitary voice seems to indicate that the typical reading of Bonhoeffer strictly as a representative of neo-orthodoxy clouds the distinctiveness of his voice. As will be shown, while Barth's influence on the development of Bonhoeffer's theology was certainly formative, Bonhoeffer's critical stance toward Barth began almost simultaneously with this formative influence. Thus, it is a mistake to isolate Bonhoeffer's critique of Barth to his later famous remarks from the prison writings, in which he accuses Barth of failing to follow through on his original theological critique of religion. This is the famous passage that accuses Barth of "a positivism of revelation, which," as Bonhoeffer argues, "in the last analysis is eventually a restoration." The restoration Bonhoeffer is speaking of here is Barth's restoration of Christianity as a 'religion,' and as such, temporally and culturally bound to the "conditioned presuppositions of metaphysics, inwardness, and so on."[5] While this passage is certainly important for understanding what is at stake in the differences between Barth and Bonhoeffer—and perhaps even more so for its indication of the abyss that would come to divide the future of contemporary theological thought into its radical and conservative camps—it is important to note the often neglected fact that this critique has its history, one that explicitly begins at least as early as *Act and Being*.

Second, note that Scharlemann's comment is framed as a question. It is not the question of the nature of Bonhoeffer's theological ontology, but whether such a thing as a theological ontology is even possible. Why, we must ask ourselves, is this even a question? What is it about the nature of a theological ontology that raises the prior question of its possibility? To answer this question, we are thrust back into the ontotheological condition and the terms of the problem of philosophical theology as articulated by both Barth and Heidegger. While others left unquestioned the presumed divide between philosophy and theology, Bonhoeffer sought its dissolution by mixing together what was purportedly insoluble. It was as if Bonhoeffer realized from his earliest days as a theologian that a discourse that desires to speak the Word of God is always an unsafe one, and that the thinker who commits himself to the Other is driven to assume positions that could not be foreknown.

In this way, perhaps Bonhoeffer understood Barth and Heidegger better than they understood themselves. For instance, Barth's insistence that dogmatics was essentially an unsettling or "decentering" task was extended by Bonhoeffer beyond the confines of the Church's self-reflexive critique such that the world became the principle site and chief aim of theological thinking. So with Bonhoeffer, not only was the Church unsettled by the mystery of its faith, but that very faith was subjected to a world in which God's presence was lacking, hidden, or left obscured. Not only was the theologian assigned the task of interpreting and deciphering the Word of God, but now the cries of desperation from a broken and divided humanity demanded urgent action for which the theologian must answer. And more important than Barth's argument—which states that it is the direction of thought that distinguishes theology—is Bonhoeffer's theological inversion, which redirected theology to its life in the world. As he would write during his last days from the prison cell in Tegel: "During the last year or so I've come to know and understand more and more the profound this-worldliness of Christianity."[6] He continues to say that it is

> . . . only by living completely in this world that one learns to have faith. One must completely abandon any attempt to make something of oneself, whether it be a saint, or a converted sinner, or a churchman (a so-called priestly type!), a righteous man or unrighteous one, a sick man or a healthy one. By this-worldliness I mean living unreservedly in life's duties, problems, successes and failures, experiences and perplexities. In so doing we throw ourselves completely into the arms of God, taking seriously, not our own sufferings, but those of God in the world . . . That, I think, is faith; that is *metanoia;* and that is how one becomes a man and a Christian.[7]

Echoes of Heidegger's notion of *Dasein* as a "being-in-the-world," to be sure, but it is also an extension of Heidegger by Bonhoeffer's concrete expression of *Dasein's* moral culpability. By both his life's witness and his writings, Bonhoeffer reminds us that one's actions and one's thoughts are not completely one's own, for they implicate, and are implicated by, the other. He also reminds us that a thinking responsive to this intersubjective condition of thought and action must also know that the possibility of a purity of discourse is a troubling ideal—one, as Nietzsche explains, that betrays a desire for an escape, whether by mindlessness, dishonesty, or even brute acts of the will.[8]

Bonhoeffer's commitment to the "profound this-worldliness of Christianity" allows theology no such escape. On the contrary, Bonhoeffer establishes such a high standard of judgment by the thoroughness of his critique of modern theology, philosophy, and ethics, that what formerly appeared as satisfactory resolutions fell short of his demand for a thinking responsive to a "world come of age."[9] His work therefore demonstrates both a thoroughgoing critique and simultaneous revaluation of contemporary thought, with the standard of judgment being established by the former and the constructive challenge to the reader laid out in the latter.

In the pages that follow, this strategy of thought will be traced in two sections. The first, entitled "Against Idealism," centers on Bonhoeffer's early theological text *Act and Being* (1929). The second, entitled "Against Ethics," develops a critical line of thought drawn from Bonhoeffer's publication *Ethics*, which was written under the high pressures of his resistance activity to Hitler and during his subsequent imprisonment at Tegel. While much distinguishes the first section from the second, the force of the critique, characteristic of both, unites them in what should be seen as a cumulative and still evolving strategy of Bonhoeffer's. Key to understanding this cumulative strategy of Bonhoeffer's is appreciating his initial willingness to question the limits of philosophical and theological possibility as his predecessors had defined it. This means that Bonhoeffer's development of a theological ontology will be read as a deliberate transgression, one that questions and seeks to move beyond both Barth and Heidegger's ideal of a purity of discourse. It is for this reason that Bonhoeffer stands out as pointing a new direction and providing new possibilities for a "world come of age."

Against Idealism

Bonhoeffer's mature theology begins with his development of a theological ontology.[10] Building on the work of both Barth and Heidegger before him, Bonhoeffer's theological ontology was, at the same time, a critique of their limitations—most notably, a critique of their strategic disregard for the other in and of their respective discourses. In Bonhoeffer's mind such delimitation of thought was in fact evidence of the modern penchant for idealism, and as such, must be resisted with the same force and originality that characterized his predecessors. In short, Bonhoeffer realized the need for a strategy of thought that was otherwise than overcoming. This would be a strategy that might resist, counteract, and eventually move beyond the problem of philosophical theology and toward what he saw as the more urgent task of philosophical theology—the critical engagement with a world that was at war with itself.

The strategy Bonhoeffer develops is a systematic one: It includes his identification of idealism as the primary characteristic of modern thought; his explanation of idealism as both a philosophical and theological problem; and finally, his development of new resources for thought that might break open the self-imposed strictures of modern thought. He will call this latter strategem an "epistemology of revelation," which already suggests that the way beyond the philosophical-theological impasse is not achieved by the turning away or purification of the one from the other, but more complexly, by allowing the one to inform the other. In other words, Bonhoeffer makes clear that epistemology is not simply a philosophical problem. Instead, when attending to both philosophy and theology, epistemology is forced to expand its resources beyond experience and reason alone, even beyond the philosophical conditions that make experience and its intelligibility possible, to the point that theological possibility is set as the actual horizon of thought. What makes this most significant is that revelation is proven to be no mere flight of fancy, but in a way reminiscent to Kierkegaard's point in regard to the subjective quality of truth, it is a meaningful concept with actual philosophical consequence. Likewise with epistemology, it is not wholly self-determined; its concepts are not entirely its own. Instead, the philosophical quest for knowledge must admit the unknown and the unknowable. Even within the range of the known, philosophy must admit a complexity along the plane of immanence that is likened unto transcendence. The result: a reinvigoration and expansion of modern philosophical thought by the inclusion and employment of theological concepts; and vice versa, a concretizing of modern theological thought by the affirmation of the world come of age.

BONHOEFFER'S "THEOLOGY OF SOCIALITY"

To say that Bonhoeffer's mature theology begins with the development of a theological ontology is not to diminish the central importance of Bonhoeffer's "theology of sociality."[11] In fact, it is precisely his appreciation of the social dimension of life that impels and gives resources to his critique of idealism. Clifford Green, more than anyone, has drawn attention to this dimension of Bonhoeffer's thought. Of the importance of sociality, Green writes: "Bonhoeffer sees all human life as essentially social, that he develops a theological phenomenology of the human person in relation to other persons, and to various types of corporate communities and institutions, and that he interprets the Christian gospel within this matrix."[12] According to Green, Bonhoeffer's theology of sociality should be read as offering an alternative to the dead end of epistemological skepticism:

> Aware of the theological problems that derive from the impact of Kant and post-Kantian epistemology, he [Bonhoeffer] does not seek a breakthrough via an alliance with neo-Kantianism or existentialism, as his older contemporaries in the dialectical theology of the 1920's were doing

at the time. It is rather with sociological categories that he tries to develop a new conceptuality for dealing with theological subjects such as transcendence, Christology, faith, justification, and so on. Not the context of epistemology, but human sociality, holds theological promise.[13]

Green continues: "By definition, the relationship of knowing does not bring the knowing subject into the social sphere; knowing does not involve the whole being of the knower as person. . . . In opposition to idealistic-epistemological thinking, Bonhoeffer asserts that *human reality is encountered in the social sphere.*"[14] Or as Bonhoeffer himself writes in *Sanctorum Communio, "The transcendence of the You says nothing at all about epistemological transcendence.* This is purely ethical transcendence experienced only by those facing a decision."[15]

In spite of the rather hyperbolic tone both Bonhoeffer and Green employ on this point, it would be difficult to overestimate the importance of this innovation by Bonhoeffer. Like Barth and Heidegger before him, Bonhoeffer was seeking a language of transcendence that was neither reductive nor essentializing. Yet where Barth and Heidegger failed by turning inward in the clarification of their respective positions, Bonhoeffer's theology of sociality suggests an excessive expenditure of identity, a self that is inseparable from the infinitely complex web of social relations. This innovation, according to Green:

> . . . signaled a completely new context and approach for theological thinking. While aligning himself with the new theological movement of Barth and his early colleagues, Bonhoeffer criticized and went beyond them. He saw their theological renovation inhibited by a preoccupation with *epistemology* characteristic of modern European philosophy. . . . The influence of epistemologically-oriented philosophy in theology was more effective in polemics than in new constructive thinking. Bonhoeffer, consequently, wanted to move theology to a world of persons, communities, historical decisions, and ethical relationships.[16]

If Green is correct, Bonhoeffer was both aligned with and critical of the contemporary currents of thought seeking to overcome modernity and its "preoccupation with *epistemology.*" He accomplishes this by affirming the gesture toward transcendence that is characteristic of both Barth and Heidegger, while at the same time critiquing their delimitation of transcendence to the terms of either theology or philosophy. Bonhoeffer's approach, instead, was to employ the terms of sociality and thereby create new resources for thought that simultaneously affirms both an immanent transcendence and a transcendent immanence.

With this in mind, we might now turn to *Act and Being*, in which Bonhoeffer's complex relation to and understanding of his philosophical and theological predecessors is most explicitly engaged.

SEEKING AN EPISTEMOLOGY OF REVELATION

Bonhoeffer begins *Act and Being* with the following observation: "The most recent developments in theology appear to me to be an attempt to come to an agreement about the problem of act and being."[17] When making this observation, he has in mind Barth, Bultmann, and Heidegger, among others. For instance, Bonhoeffer accuses Barth of a "critical reservation,"[18] which Bonhoeffer understands as a kind of theological foundationalism; Bultmann, of the wish to liberate humanity from its self-delusion; and Heidegger, of delimiting the ontological difference to terms of existence. For Bonhoeffer, these diverging problems coalesce in the struggle with and against idealism. As he writes: "At the heart of the problem is the struggle with the formulation of the question that Kant and idealism have posed for theology. It is a matter of the formation of genuine theological concepts, the decision one comes to between a transcendental-philosophical and an ontological interpretation of theological concepts." And soon after, this struggle against idealism is clarified as a matter of epistemology. "The meaning of epistemology," he writes, "is anthropology. Wherever the capacity of human beings to know is attacked, nothing less than being human itself is at stake, which is the reason why, ever since Descartes, the passion of philosophy has burnt so strongly here."[19] Therefore, the problem of act and being, which Bonhoeffer introduces as a question regarding a proper epistemology, is in fact a question concerning the status and nature of the human being. Where confusion reigns, self-knowledge is left in abeyance, but this does not mean that desire for such knowledge is foreclosed. Rather, so Bonhoeffer seems to be suggesting, it is this very confusion, the very question regarding its possibility that gives epistemology its urgency.

In this respect, Green might be guilty of overstating his case when he argues that the consequence of Bonhoeffer's theology of sociality is a turning away from epistemology. Bonhoeffer is indeed critical of the reign, and even tyranny, of epistemology in modern philosophy, but this critique does not excuse the theologian from the problematic. Instead, theology must actively seek its own contribution by speaking of a kind of knowledge that opens possibilities other than those strictly determined by the terms of the self. As Bonhoeffer insists: "The concept of revelation must, therefore, yield an epistemology of its own."[20] Or as Wayne Whitson Floyd writes in the introduction to the text: "*Act and Being* is a theologian's proposal of that *certain* way in which to read theology's investments in the continental philosophical tradition, rather than merely turning its back when the relationship had become problematic, as seemed to Bonhoeffer to be the case with the rise of dialectical theology. . . . To be sure, Bonhoeffer's willingness to think along with philosophy, indeed, to see a congruity between the philosophical and theological tasks, is striking."[21]

At least at this point, then, the question concerning epistemology and the possibility of a theological ontology is the discernment of a way of thinking that in the end is not completely self-directed and self-enclosed. As suggested before, this concern of Bonhoeffer's is consistent with Barth and Heidegger to the point that it is accurate to see his efforts as aligned with theirs. With Barth, for instance, revelation holds the key to overcoming the tyranny of epistemology by exposing the Church to the hidden mysteries of faith. Nevertheless, theology remains a self-enclosed circle beginning and ending in the God whose grace signals a transcendent truth known only through faith. With Heidegger it is not faith per se that unveils the truth of being, but a quality of thought that could be called religious. In this way, the thinker is more akin to the poet than the philosopher, making strange use of language such that one is made conscious of one's dwelling in the abyss. Even here, however, the self-enclosed circle remains. Of decisive importance, therefore, is not the will toward escape, but a more interesting engagement through the asking of important questions.

TOWARD A THEOLOGICAL ONTOLOGY

To reiterate, Bonhoeffer's critique of both modern theology and philosophy begins with appreciation. While "absolute idealism" stands as a constant threat to those who accept the reign of epistemology, Bonhoeffer also affirms the positive value of "genuine transcendentalism" (e.g., Kant's critical philosophy and Barth's dialectical theology) and "true ontology" (e.g, Heidegger's fundamental ontology). As he writes in reference to Kant: "Genuine transcendental philosophy, such as that which Kant tried to develop . . . must be distinguished from the concept of transcendentalist philosophy as understood by post-Kantian idealism." What distinguishes the former from the latter is that genuine transcendentalism acknowledges transcendence as being integral to thought, both as its condition and its limit. As Bonhoeffer explains, "It is *retrospective* in that thinking, *qua* thinking, lays claim to a meaning which it cannot give to itself—in that such meaning is in reference to the logos of transcendence. The reference is *prospective* in that thinking, *qua* relation, is in reference to objects, coming up against something transcendent." He continues, "One may speak of genuine transcendentalism so long as the resistance of transcendence to thinking is upheld, that is to say, so long as the thing-in-itself and transcendental apperception are understood as pure limiting concepts, neither of which is entangled in the other. In knowing, human Dasein knows itself to be suspended between two poles that transcend it."[22]

As with genuine transcendentalism, the same might be said of ontology. At its best, true ontology acknowledges "the primacy of being over against consciousness," which is to say that while consciousness is the condition of thought, it is neither exhaustive of thought's possibilities, nor can it account for the origin of thought. Bonhoeffer writes: "Thought does not, therefore, produce its world for itself. Rather, it finds itself, as Dasein, in the world; in every instance, it is already in a world just as, in every instance, it is already itself. Dasein is already its possibility, in authenticity or inauthenticity."

When speaking of "true ontology" Bonhoeffer has Heidegger's *Being and Time* in mind. Bonhoeffer praises the innovation of Heidegger's *Being and Time*, calling it "the bluntest reversal of phenomenology thus far," noting especially Heidegger's innovation in the interpretation of being in terms of temporality. Further, Bonhoeffer credits Heidegger with the unique distinction of "succeeding in forcing together act and being in the concept of Dasein."[23] What this means is that Heidegger's realization of the historicity of being leads *Dasein* beyond itself in the questioning of its ontological structure. Thus, it might be said that a genuine ontology has the possibility of transcending epistemology.

With genuine transcendentalism and true ontology, therefore, there is both the epistemological recognition of limitations and the ontological realization of the self in relation. The problem, however—and this is where Bonhoeffer parts company with both Barth and Heidegger—is that neither allows adequate concepts for a true theological ontology. As Floyd writes: "*Act and Being* evidences Bonhoeffer's emerging practical concern to find for theology a methodology adequate and proper to its unique subject matter."[24]

With transcendentalism, for instance, its logic is left open to a "profound contradiction," which Bonhoeffer describes as follows:

"[T]he I is being-already there. It is both the very process of attainment and its precondition, and as such the I logically *precedes* thinking. But inasmuch as everything about the I is constituted by
thought, *thinking precedes the I.*"[25] Furthermore, not only does
transcendentalism contradict itself, but also the relief it promises
through practical reason is shown to be without a ground on which
to stand. It is completely empty of content and thereby unable to
meet the critical demands of the existent subject. Transcendentalism
is utterly incapable of accounting for itself on its own terms; thus,
Bonhoeffer concludes that it fails to reconcile the problem of act and
being precisely because it is unable to reconcile the one with the
other. In other words, from the perspective of transcendentalism,
being signifies the beyond; as such, it remains forever incomprehensible and out of reach—one might even say, utterly out of touch.
Meanwhile, life in the world is guided exclusively by the act of practical reason, which when severed from its basis in an entire system of
thought that manifests an almost unconditional and unconditioned
(pre)commitment to the theological and philosophical principles of
God, freedom, and immortality, is rendered completely incapable of
critique. When such is the case, practical reason becomes nothing
other than the justification of self-interest. Put simply, transcendentalism presents the mutually exclusive alternatives of either negation or affirmation, both of which are symptoms of idealism, which
Bonhoeffer believes to be the great failing of modern thought.

True ontology fares no better in Bonhoeffer's assessment. That is
because the preunderstanding of being, which allows the self to know
itself, means that "the concept of being remains self-contained. . . .
It is decisive for the existential analysis of Dasein that finitude is
conceived to be closed in. *Being enclosed* is something that can no
longer be separated from finitude." For Bonhoeffer, the problem with
ontology is that it leaves no room for revelation, and thus, it cuts off
theological possibility as it gives way to its own distinctive form of
philosophical idealism. For Heidegger in particular, Bonhoeffer would
see this tendency toward idealism to express itself as "a consciously
atheistic philosophy of finitude," in which the attempt to come to
terms with being seemingly requires being to become self-enclosed.[26]

To break free from this self-enclosed circle that ultimately characterizes both transcendentalism and ontology, Bonhoeffer, like Barth
before him, turned to a third option of revelation. At times even,
when speaking of revelation in *Act and Being*, Bonhoeffer sounds as
though he is in complete agreement with Barth.[27] Nevertheless, he
also detects in Barth a fundamental limitation; namely, Barth thinks

of revelation only in terms of act according to the rubrics of transcendental philosophy. "Thus," according to Bonhoeffer, "the problem of transcendental philosophy, discussed at the beginning, presents itself anew. God recedes into the nonobjective, into what is beyond our disposition. . . . God remains always the Lord, always subject, so that whoever claims to have God as an object no longer has *God*; God is always the God who 'comes' and never the God who 'is there' (Barth)."[28] Bonhoeffer sensed that Barth's success in recovering theology from modernity came at a high cost. Bonhoeffer described this cost as the disjunction between transcendentalism and ontology, which is to say the radical transcendence of Barth's wholly other God left God's relation with the world unclear and incomprehensible.

As a critical statement of the fundamental limitations of knowledge, Barth's theological appropriation of transcendental philosophy is important, but fails to recognize that like the genuine transcendentalism that can be of service to a theological understanding, so too is there a genuine ontology that effectively limits knowledge and thereby makes room for faith. Had Barth been more in conversation with contemporary currents in philosophical thought, there would have been an alternative conceptual language from which he could draw to interpret the meaningfulness of the Christian faith. The irony then is that the more Barth tried to safeguard the critical task of theology, the more dogmatic his theology would become. As such, it remains an essentially "modern" endeavor by perpetuating the very epistemological problem he meant to overcome.

So while the subject of God's transcendence was of decisive importance in Barth's critique of modernity, it also, as was argued in chapter 1, remained trapped within the modern epistemological problematic as the autonomy of God became the substitute and reversal of philosophical subjectivity. Even after Barth moved from a dialectical theology to a dogmatic theology, and even after he speaks of the cooperation that should exist between philosophy and theology, he still remains committed to two distinct ways of thinking. In Bonhoeffer's terms of analysis, Barth might make use of ontological language, but never in such a way that this would redirect the thinking of theology. This is the point of disagreement between Barth and Bultmann, and ultimately why Bonhoeffer, rather than Barth, stands as the figure who advances the prospect of philosophical theology. In Marsh's words: "Bonhoeffer wants to account for the inner rhythm of the world's worldliness in a more nuanced, more indigenously attuned way. Bonhoeffer holds that there need be no decision between God and the world."[29]

To repeat, what this means is that Barth's critique of modern theology fails to overcome the Enlightenment notion of the self-secure ego; Barth merely replaces it with God. It is not the human, but the divine ego that stands as the ground and arbiter of knowledge. Again, Marsh makes this point clear: "Nowhere more clearly do we see Barth struggling to get beyond the nineteenth century and all the while remaining in its firm grasp; for while rejecting the priority of the self-reflective human subject in knowledge of self, world, and God, he emphasizes instead the preeminence of the self-reflective divine subject, a notion still deeply ingrained in the transcendental tradition's conceptual repertoire." Marsh continues: "Barth's view puts divine self-possession in opposition to human self-possession and assumes that one must choose one or the other. Self or divine possession, theological presumption or faithfulness to the first commandment— no other options seem available."[30] This notion of Barth's efforts "to get beyond" while still remaining "firmly within the grasp" of modernity is one of Bonhoeffer's early concerns, and it is perhaps why Barth's theological strategy of epistemological reversal was ultimately seen by Bonhoeffer as ineffectual, if not entirely counterproductive. Bonhoeffer wastes no time in making this point in *Act and Being*, opening the first paragraph with his accusation against Barth of a "critical reservation," in which he "seeks to hold on to the freedom of God's grace and thereby to provide a foundation for human existence."[31] From Bonhoeffer's perspective what was needed was not simply Barth's theological inversion of modernity, which still spelled fundamentally the same self-contained epistemology, but a genuine reconciliation of the problem of act and being—a kind of thinking released from the self and its consuming interest in identity and self-certainty, a theology risking the questions of ontology, and an ontology that still makes room for faith.

Bonhoeffer's theological ontology, in other words, is a struggle with and against the modern sensibility, but in such a manner that his critique does not rest on the foundation of knowledge that he himself is questioning. He is not replacing one proposition with another, nor a set of assurances for faith. Neither is he relying on a clarity of identity in order to reveal or unveil the truth of difference, the limitations of knowledge, and the openness toward the other. Instead, Bonhoeffer manages to speak from at least two positions at once—voicing appreciation for Heidegger's temporalization of being, while at the same time echoing Barth's reflection on revelation; criticizing modern epistemologies that are closed in on themselves, while at the same time recognizing how often such criticisms fail to break free from the premium on knowledge.

By advancing a theological ontology, Bonhoeffer brings together what was previously thought to be mutually exclusive, but in such a way that it is neither simply cooperation, as in Barth; nor correlation, as in Tillich; nor interpretation, as in Bultmann; nor differentiation, as in Heidegger. Instead, with Bonhoeffer there is the advance toward a genuine and mutual interrogation such that theology and philosophy are transformed by realizing the fluidity of the boundary in between. And, as is well documented in reference to Bonhoeffer, this was not simply of theoretical interest for him. The fact that his thinking and writing were driven by this early realization is given even greater clarity by the witness of his life and the scrutiny under which he held his own actions and involvements.

The task is to bring together act and being, not in such a way that one is subsumed in the other, nor in such a way that one is bound off from the other—instead, so that both realize themselves as coimplicated, intermixed, and mutually absorbed in the other. In this way, theology fears not speak the language of ontology; in fact, it discovers it as a fundamental task even as the ontological question is broadened and revamped so that its terms are not strictly self-prescribed. Neither must ontology resist the language of theology; otherwise, its restriction of difference to existence alone oversteps the bounds that it means to preserve (e.g., a totalitarian immanence) by delimiting the possibility of being otherwise. Bonhoeffer himself accomplishes this aim by speaking of the self in terms not limited to the self, but also in terms of sociality with the language of the "I and Thou." Bonhoeffer moves outside the philosophy of consciousness by suggesting a being that is determined not by the ego alone. He also moves beyond Barth and Heidegger, because for Bonhoeffer, the ego is not swallowed up. Rather, the self discovers itself as a responsible and thoughtful subject in relation with others. This is a theological relation that joins one to the world, as to Christ, the being-for-others, who witnesses to the obligation for the world.

Against Ethics

I have suggested that Bonhoeffer stands apart from his theological contemporaries because of his willingness to forgo appeals to identity. In terms of chapter 1, this means he abandons the desire for a purity of discourse and accepts the contamination of act and being. In his early work, this comes to expression in his critique of idealism and his reconfiguration of epistemology from a more comprehensive perspective. Later, as Bonhoeffer is increasingly drawn into a politics of resistance, his writing gravitates more toward the ethical, toward a seeking out of purposeful action in a world without assurances.[32] This is an ethic of expenditure and obligation, one that shares much in common with Kierkegaard's "teleological suspension of the ethical" in that it is a complete abandonment to the will of God.[33] It manifests a profound concern and sorrow with a culture of lost ideals. But this is not to be confused with nostalgia. Indeed, where others saw only loss and decay, Bonhoeffer found cause for celebration: "Here is the decisive difference between Christianity and all religions." Bonhoeffer writes:

> Man's religiosity makes him look in his distress to the power of God in the world . . . The Bible directs man to God's powerlessness and suffering; only the suffering God can help. To that extent we may say that the development towards the world's coming of age outlined above, which has done away with false conceptions of God, opens up a way of seeing the God of the Bible, who wins power and space in the world by his weakness. This will probably be the starting-point for our "secular interpretation."[34]

Bonhoeffer was the rarest of persons—a martyr who was driven by his love for the world.

BONHOEFFER'S CRITIQUE OF ETHICS

Perhaps the closest contemporary comparison to Bonhoeffer's *Ethics*, at least in terms of Bonhoeffer's critique of ethics, would be John D. Caputo's work entitled *Against Ethics*. To be against ethics or to deconstruct ethics, Caputo writes, "is to own up to the lack of safety by which judging is everywhere beset. The thing that concerns me . . . is the loss of the assurance, the lack of the safe passage, that ethics has always promised. Ethics makes safe. . . . It clarifies concepts, secures judgments, provides firm guardrails along the slippery slopes of factical life." Before one mistakenly thinks that this critique of ethics is an excuse for indifference, Caputo reminds the reader: "Undecidability does not detract from the urgency of decision; it simply underlines the difficulty."[35] Such undecidability in fact makes one's obligation even more pronounced. That is because one cannot rest assured in the confidences that generalizable rules and universal principles allow. Instead, one is obligated to think, to assess, to become involved and implicated in the values one holds and the decisions one makes. In this way, to be "against ethics" is to be driven by a fundamentally positive *ethical* imperative; to recognize ethics as a problem is to begin to affirm its real possibility.

Likewise, Bonhoeffer's *Ethics* (a work that was left incomplete at the time of Bonhoeffer's execution, but one that, according to his friend Eberhard Bethge, Bonhoeffer considered to be "the beginning of his actual life work"[36]) begins with a critique of ethics:

> The knowledge of good and evil seems to be the aim of all ethical reflection. The first task of Christian ethics is to invalidate this knowledge. In launching this attack on the underlying assumptions of all other ethics, Christian ethics stands so completely alone that it becomes questionable whether there is any purpose of speaking of Christian ethics at all. But if one does so notwithstanding, that can only mean that Christian ethics claims to discuss the origin of the whole problem of ethics, and thus professes to be a critique of all ethics simply as ethics.[37]

Similar to his critique of idealism in *Act and Being*, Bonhoeffer's chief concern with ethics is that it overextends its bounds of knowledge. Ethics, like idealism, becomes no more than self-knowledge. It is humanity's attempt to overcome its disunion by thought. The result is that humanity cuts itself off from the true source of knowledge, which Bonhoeffer understands theologically to be the will of God.

This critique of ethics is most formidable in part 3 of the work, entitled "Ethics as Formation." Here Bonhoeffer surveys the full range of ethical options in order to expose their inadequacies. This is an urgent and pressing task, according to Bonhoeffer, because if left to ethicists alone ethics would appear as "the most superfluous" of all questions. This is a serious claim to make against ethics when one is writing in the heart of Germany in the midst of World War II, imprisoned for political treachery and living with the imminent threat of execution. Bonhoeffer explains: "The reason for this is not to be sought in any supposed ethical indifference on the part of our period. On the contrary it arises from the fact that our period, more than any earlier period in the history of the west, is oppressed by a superabounding reality of concrete ethical problems." In this period, Bonhoeffer writes, "there are once more villains and saints, and they are not hidden from public view. . . . But the villain and the saint have little or nothing to do with systematic ethical studies."[38] Put simply, Bonhoeffer's critique of ethics is a demand for the concrete relevance of thought. When the world is facing a "superabounding reality of concrete ethical problems," what it needs is an equally concrete analysis of its situation, and too often what it gets are pre-fabricated systematical theories.

As for the specific systematic ethical theories that Bonhoeffer has in mind, he lists the following:

(1) *The Moral Theorist:* This person stands as the very embodiment of an Enlightenment ethic. Against such a stance, Bonhoeffer writes: "One is distressed by the failure of *reasonable* people to perceive either the depths of evil or the depths of the holy. With the best of intentions they believe that a little reason will suffice them to clamp together the parting timbers of the building." And further: "With the concepts he already has in mind he is unable to grasp what is real and still less able to come seriously to grips with that of which the essence and power are entirely unknown to him."[39] Like Martin Luther King Jr.'s challenge to the ministers of "genuine good will" in his famous "Letter from Birmingham City Jail,"[40] in Bonhoeffer's critique of the moral theorist, he is arguing for the need for thought to be wed with action, like King's claim that love is incomprehensible apart from justice. In other words, the dispassionate reflection of the ethical forces at work in society is not the same as *being* ethical.

(2) *The Ethical Fanatic:* On the opposite side of the spectrum from the moral theorist is the ethical fanatic. "The fanatic," Bonhoeffer writes, "believes that he can oppose the power of evil with the purity of his will and of his principle."[41] The fanatic is simple-minded, convinced that the matter of ethics is straightforward. It is not long, however, that the complexity of the given situation becomes overwhelming. Traps are set and the fanatic rushes headlong into them.

(3) *The Good Conscience:* Bonhoeffer describes the third position as the person with a conscience. This is certainly not a bad thing in itself. However, when confronted with the clash of incommensurates, it is impossible for the purity of conscience to be preserved. That is because it is not always the decisions between good and evil or truth and falsity that demand one's attention, but more often the decisions besought by competing goods and grades of truth. To the person most interested in keeping a clear conscience this often leads to despair and inaction. Bonhoeffer's advice to such a person: "A man whose only support is his conscience can never understand that a bad conscience may be healthier and stronger than a conscience which is deceived."[42]

(4) *The Dutiful:* Bonhoeffer is critical of the dutiful for their fundamental denial or displacement of responsibility. The dutiful are deceived by convincing themselves that so long as they follow the law or obey commands, they have fulfilled their ethical obligation. The classic indictment of this position comes from Hannah Arendt's coverage of the trial of Adolf Eichmann in Jerusalem. Eichmann had

been accused of crimes against humanity for the role he played in the Jewish Holocaust. His repeated response to the charges against him was like a refrain: "Not guilty, in the sense of the indictment." His closing comments as summarized by Arendt: "His hopes for justice were disappointed; the court had not believed him, though he had always done his best to tell the truth. The court did not understand him: he had never been a Jew-hater, and he had never willed the murder of human beings. His guilt came from his obedience, and obedience is praised as a virtue. His virtue had been abused by the Nazi leaders."[43] With the example of Adolf Eichmann in mind, what can be said about the problem with the dutiful is that they fail to recognize their freedom. Or perhaps in the case of Eichmann, their freedom is a burden too great to bear. In its place is substituted a mindless, thoughtless obedience, with no concern for whom this obedience might serve and what harm it might do. As Bonhoeffer writes: "The man of duty will end by having to fulfill his obligation even to the devil."[44]

(5) *The Self-Willed:* These are those convinced of their own absolute freedom. However admirable these people might be for their willingness to recognize the complexities of existence and to accept their own personal responsibility, they still, according to Bonhoeffer, end in tragedy. As Bonhoeffer writes: "He will easily consent to the bad, knowing full well that it is bad, in order to ward off what is worse, and in doing this he will no longer be able to see that precisely the worse which he is trying to avoid may still be better. This is one of the underlying themes of tragedy."[45]

(6) *The Virtuous:* Finally, there are those who take refuge in their own private virtue. Guiltless of wrongdoing, they nevertheless fail to commit themselves to the positive forces of good. They are those who stand at a safe distance from whatever might infringe upon their personal purity. They are the hypocrites. In their "voluntary renunciation of publicity," they think they have measured up to the demands of the ethical, but their blamelessness, according to Bonhoeffer, is their own undoing in an age that desperately cries out for justice.[46]

On the one hand, Bonhoeffer states, one should not frown upon these various ethical positions, for they are together "the achievements and attitudes of a noble humanity." On the other, they are all quixotic in nature. One might sympathize with their efforts; however, one must also understand that they are ultimately misguided. As Bonhoeffer writes: "That is how it looks when an old world ventures to take up arms against a new one and when a world of the past hazards an attack against the superior forces of the commonplace and mean."[47]

If indeed the world has come of age, as Bonhoeffer suggests, the ethical reasoning must adapt accordingly. No longer will the old assurances and tactics meet the new challenge of a world that has witnessed holocausts, that has seen a nation turn against its own people, that has watched the heights of civilization and culture collapse in total warfare, and that has advanced technology to such a degree that for the first time in history the destruction of the world is a realistic possibility. The new ethic must launch an attack on the old ethics; or, according to Bonhoeffer's famous phrase, it must "replace our dusty swords with sharp ones."[48] The question is, *how?*

RECOURSE TO DOGMA

Bonhoeffer's answer, unfortunately, is a dogmatic one. One cannot help but wonder how—if he would have had the time to complete this work in ethics, which he considered to be only the beginning of his life work—he himself would have forged a new path in ethical thought, one that would have met his standard of a "non-religious" interpretation, a true embrace of secularity as the arena in which the believer must work out his or her faith. As it stands now, the dismantling of ethics that Bonhoeffer accomplishes is itself undone by the restoration of a Christian ethic that reifies many of the same patterns of which he was critical.

His Christian ethics, therefore, while still valuable for its critique of ethics, resolves itself in a reassertion of dogmatic certainty. In other words, with Bonhoeffer's ethics it could be said that Barth's radical orthodoxy comes full circle from the primacy of revelation, to the critique of self-knowledge, and back again to the truth as revealed and resolved in the Christian gospel. How, Bonhoeffer asks, does one achieve the new ethic demanded by the world come of age? His answer is through the combination of simplicity and wisdom. Simplicity is defined as fixing one's eyes solely on the simple truth of God. Through simplicity, Bonhoeffer claims, one is set free from the problems and conflicts of ethical decision. Wisdom, accordingly, is defined as seeing reality as it is, as the ability to see the essential nature of things, to see in Jesus Christ the reconciliation of the world and God. The result is an idealized vision of the harmony achieved through faith. Its defining characteristics are the following: (1) The world is realized to be inseparable from God, and God is unimaginable apart from the world; (2) Humanity might be affirmed in its weakness, doubt, fear and insecurity; (3) Success as the sole standard for truth and goodness is supplanted by the concrete reality of divine justice; (4) Death is overcome; (5) Humanity is formed in the living witness of Christ; and (6) Ethics moves away from abstract, overly systematic formations, toward an ethic that is entirely concrete.[49] The goal of ethics, therefore, is not "to develop a programme for shaping or formation of the Western world. What is intended is rather a discussion of the way in this Western world the form of Christ takes form."[50]

In Bonhoeffer's defense it should be said that the form of Christ that he speaks of is the witness of Christ as a being for others. Throughout his works, Bonhoeffer is critical of the ego that sets itself up as the arbiter and full range of knowledge. This critique extends as well to Barth's theological reversal of modern Western philosophies that depicts God in the place of Descartes's *ego cogito*. Thus, Bonhoeffer's argument for Christ serving as the renewal of ethics in the Western world is not the same as the reestablishment of Christendom. Instead, it is only through the Church's confession of guilt that the possibility for renewal and justice might be achieved.[51] Finally, Bonhoeffer admits in the closing lines of part 3 that justice is incomplete so long as exclusion, oppression, or suffering of any sort persists.[52] This articulation of Christian ethics, therefore, could be considered as an anticipation of the narrative or virtue theory ethics that would be formulated a generation after the time of Bonhoeffer.[53] As such, it would be more akin to ethical communitarianism than theological triumphalism.

BONHOEFFER AS A "POST-LIBERAL THEOLOGIAN"?

Even still, such a position is not without its own problems. Consider, for instance, Bonhoeffer's similarities with Stanley Hauerwas's narrative theology or Alisdair MacIntyre's virtue theory.[54] First, they all share the common recognition of modernity's failed attempt at finding a secure foundation for ethics in reason alone. Their common project can be described as the attempt to speak of ethics without foundations. In this way, they propose either the path of faith or tradition in the place of the Enlightenment's trust in rationality. They also affirm the historically conditioned as opposed to the quest for essences or universals. Evidence of this in Bonhoeffer is when he speaks of the concrete revelation of God in Christ through history. For Hauerwas, that revelation itself has a history and forms a community. As he writes: "The nature of Christian ethics is determined by the fact that Christian convictions take the form of story, or perhaps better, a set of stories that constitute a tradition, which in turn creates and forms a community."[55]

Second, all three thinkers are opposed to the privatization of ethics. Ethics, instead, is described as a lived tradition determined by and embodying concrete values and sets of beliefs. For this reason, ethics cannot simply be reduced to emotivism, which is no more than the valorization of personal preference. Nor is it enough simply to call for greater personal accountability. That is because the ramifications of ethics extend beyond the self alone, because the self is by nature social and historical. The self, when considered from this position, is realized to be always already "storied," qualified, and/or conditioned. Again, in the words of Hauerwas: "The very notion that we are 'choosing' or 'making up' our morality contains the seeds of its own destruction, for moral authenticity seems to require that morality be not a matter of one's own shaping, but something that shapes one. We do not create moral values, principles, virtues: rather they constitute a life for us to appropriate."[56]

A further implication of this critique of modern ethical theory and the privatization of ethics is that the understanding of freedom is transformed. Freedom is not to be thought of as an end in itself, because such an understanding of freedom is both self-contradictory and counterproductive. It is self-contradictory because the exercise of freedom necessarily infringes on the freedom of others. "In fact," Hauerwas writes, "there is *no* morality that does not require others to suffer for our commitments. But there is nothing wrong with asking others to share and sacrifice for what we believe to be worthy. A more appropriate concern is whether what we commit ourselves to is worthy or not." To understand freedom as an end in itself is also counterproductive, because it does not allow for a meaningful interpretation and guide for human relationships. Freedom, when thought of as an end in itself, or as the chief value of ethical theory, extends only to the rights of individuals—a good place to begin, perhaps, but ultimately inadequate for the formation of community and the shaping of values. In Hauerwas's words: "Our stress on freedom and its ethical expression renders us incapable of accounting for certain activities which seem central to the human project."[57] One example Hauerwas gives is concerning parents' decision to have a child. From the perspective that considers freedom as its chief value, the decision to have a child would in fact be immoral, because it would be the imposition of the parents' will and desire on that of the child. In this respect, modern ethical theory is shown to be inconsistent with itself, as it presumes certain cultural practices as laudatory, while the consequence of its reflections would suggest otherwise.

MacIntyre makes a similar diagnosis. His claim is that the Enlightenment project has failed and that its failure was in fact predestined by the very nature of the project itself. He points to Nietzsche as the one who most fully exposes the "conceptual incommensurability" of liberal individualism. In the wake of rationality and its failed attempt to secure objective knowledge, Nietzsche leaves us with the arbitrary will to power as being the only apparent alternative. According to MacIntyre, however, there is another path, which is Aristotelian virtue theory, and which affords a coherent notion of the good according to practice and tradition. The choice is between the chief value of freedom and the consequence of relativism, or virtue theory and the possibility for coherence.

To the extent that one reads these ethical projects as critical endeavors, they are to the point in their common claim regarding the inadequacy of modern ethical thought. Nevertheless, without fail, their proposed solution to this contemporary ethical quandary betrays nostalgia for an idealized vision of the past. With Bonhoeffer, for instance, he would speak of the New Testament as "the world of recovered unity."[58] This view is difficult to maintain in the face of the obvious disparity contained within the New Testament itself, not to mention the history that lies behind the process of canonization, and the century-long battles fought by the early Church on behalf of determining orthodoxy. With Hauerwas, in spite of his appreciation of the historically conditioned—e.g., "every ethic requires a qualifier"—he has no qualms in claiming narrative as *the* "fundamental way to talk of God."[59] Furthermore, "nonviolence," Hauerwas writes, "is not just one implication among others that can be drawn from our Christian beliefs; it is at the very heart of our understanding of God."[60] One might certainly appreciate the value of this particular reading of the Christian story, but herein also lies the fundamental limitation of the narrativist position; namely, Hauerwas has cut himself off from an entire history of Christianity that testifies to alternative systems of values and sets of beliefs. His Christian ethics, in the end, is a kind of tribalism. To be sure, it has the potential to be a potent countercultural force, and one can certainly recognize resonances of the New Testament communitarian ideal at work. However, to be true to such a stance the qualifier "Christian" must be further qualified to the point that what remains is the substitution of the autonomous individual—of which Hauerwas is rightly critical—with the autonomous community. While this might serve as a needed corrective to the shortcomings of modern ethics, at its base there remains a recourse to dogma that still separates the initiated from the uninitiated, or those within a tradition from those outside.

Conclusion

To conclude this discussion of Bonhoeffer, his attempt at articulating an ethic in response to the "world come of age" ultimately relies upon his depiction of the Christian faith as a unity—albeit one that has to be recovered because it has been either forgotten or corrupted. Trusting in this depiction requires an act of faith on the part of the reader. While it might prove useful as a potent critical lever by which to compare and contrast the ideals of justice and love with the realities of a broken and divided humanity (as was demonstrated in the case of his theological predecessor, Barth), Bonhoeffer's recourse to dogmatism was simultaneously both its strength and its limitation. That is to say, it effectively reverses the modern tendency toward philosophical and theological idealism and also exposes the various shortcomings and contradictions in contemporary ethical thought. However—and this is the problem—it does so only by virtue of its own confidence in its tradition's idealized past. As was stated in reference to Barth in chapter 1, reversal does not equal overcoming; and in the case of Bonhoeffer, it might be said that the potency of his critique does not pardon the blindness of faith.

As Bonhoeffer stated in another context referring to the need for a *nonreligious* interpretation of scripture, his admission of the incompletion of justice or his critique of contemporary ethics might serve well as an alternative starting point for a new ethic for a world come of age. In contrast to Bonhoeffer's depiction, however, this starting point cannot also be considered the solution to the problems and uncertainties that we face. We must admit that it is still unclear where this path might lead, and whether in fact as well as in theory it might allow for a genuine opening up of the self toward the other in such a way that the self is stripped of its confidences, theology of its dogmatism, and philosophy of its essences.

3

THE PATH OF PHENOMENOLOGY

A STUDY OF EDMUND HUSSERL

It can be said that every philosophy is an interpretation of the history of philosophy, an explication of its contradictions, and a justification of its possible unity by the suprahistorical sense of the philosophical activity or the philosophical intention.

—Paul Ricoeur, *Husserl: An Analysis of His Phenomenology*

Philosophy as science, as serious, rigorous, indeed apodictically rigorous, science—the dream is over.

—Edmund Husserl, *The Crisis of European Sciences and Transcendental Phenomenology*

So FAR this text has described a bifurcated path that marks twentieth-century thought. On one path stands the quest for pure thought, unadulterated by faith, and not necessarily implicated in the consequences of its journey. On the other stands the search for a theology that refuses a common language, a peculiar discourse that gives voice to a Word from afar. Each path might very well lead to a truth that is spoken both critically and thoughtfully; nevertheless, it is a truth preserved, when all around there is the stench of God's absence. It is the argument of this text that no matter how coherent or alluring, both paths are fundamentally misguided. The question that must be asked of both the theologian and the philosopher, then, is whether there is a kind of thinking that thinks otherwise—one that values the question of truth's value over the need for its preservation? This is the question that Bonhoeffer begins to ask before his untimely death. As was shown, however, Bonhoeffer himself never arrived at a genuine reconciliation of philosophy and theology. Instead, when pushed to the limit, his theological ethics appeals to revelation as though the unity attested to through faith somehow trumps the disunity of a divided civilization. Is our history a history doomed to repeat itself? Or might a better understanding of the historically constituted and ethically subjected self lead beyond the desire for purity to a recognition of the responsibilities of freedom—to a freedom conditioned and made possible only by relations in time?

The following two chapters will deal with this latter possibility through an examination of the philosophical path of phenomenology. In the course of this analysis the galvanizing figure will be Heidegger. Heidegger, of course, was a student of Husserl's, and it was Husserl's phenomenological method that gives direction to Heidegger's early philosophy. At the same time, Heidegger is often the key thinker credited with transforming phenomenology. Therefore, in the examination of the philosophical side to the problem of philosophical theology, one must speak of both Husserl and Heidegger and how together they bequeathed a complex legacy to the generation of thinkers who followed. Furthermore, this complex legacy can be analyzed theoretically and more historically and/or biographically as the relations between these two figures fragmented and eventually dissolved, which in a way can be seen as a parallel to the fragmentation and dissolution of Western Europe during this same period.

Before turning directly to Husserl, however, a word needs to be said on the guiding thematic of this chapter; namely, that of history, and more specifically, the structure of the historical "development" of ideas. As will be demonstrated in the pages that follow, Husserl's description and explanation of phenomenological philosophy underwent a series of transformations or revolutions. A lens by which one might understand this "development" within Husserl's thought is according to Thomas Kuhn's well-known work, *The Structure of Scientific Revolutions.* Kuhn argues against the long-standing misinterpretation of the history of science in which scientific advancement is understood as a story of "development-by-accumulation." According to this misinterpretation, "Scientific development becomes the piecemeal process by which these items [scientific theories and/ or empirical facts] have been added, singly and in combination, to the ever growing stockpile that constitutes scientific technique and knowledge." As a result, the task of the historian of science is twofold: "On the one hand, he must determine by what man and at what point in time each contemporary scientific fact, law, and theory was discovered or invented. On the other, he must describe and explain the congeries of error, myth, and superstition that have inhibited the more rapid accumulation of the constituents of the modern science text."[1] In contrast to this straightforward theory of scientific "development-by-accumulation," Kuhn focuses instead on the role of revolution in the inauguration of new scientific paradigms. Science is not advanced simply through the testing of hypotheses, the accumulation of facts, and the development of theories. Rather, any given science reaches its breaking point when the field of its explanatory power is besought by incommensurabilities and anomalies. Furthermore, this breaking point is not overcome, but only extended by the further increase in knowledge. Accordingly, a revolution in science means to start over again at the beginning; it means that there is a consequent shift not only in the supporting evidence, but more importantly, in the very problems and standards of philosophical scrutiny. In other words, in addition to the *quantitative* advancement, which historians of science have emphasized almost exclusively, is the qualitative transformation, which is the effect of a paradigm shift.

As for the definition of a scientific paradigm, Kuhn writes that paradigms "provide models from which spring particular coherent traditions of scientific research. . . . Men whose research is based on shared paradigms are committed to the same rules and standards for scientific practice." Also, that a paradigm is the "fundamental unit for the student of scientific development, a unity that cannot be fully reduced to logically atomic components which might function in its stead."[2] Finally, then, a history attendant to the role of paradigms in the making of meaning would be a history that admits the importance that crises play throughout history in setting history on different paths that cannot be explained by the historian's appeal to linear progression.

In the analysis of Husserl that follows, perhaps one could say that what is most interesting is the way by which history might even reverse itself—not in such a way that the philosopher goes back in time to recover a philosophy of the past, but rather in the phenomenological discovery of time and the consequent philosophical crisis this discovery introduces. Another point of interest is regarding the larger concern of the work as a whole in which the path of phenomenology leads to the discovery of history, and how history leaves philosophy without a stable ground on which to stand. As Husserl writes in the closing of his career, "the dream is over," which means, among other things, that the desire for purity that keeps the discourses of philosophy and theology apart gives way to new questions and new standards for thought—in short, a new paradigm that makes possible a genuine philosophical theology.[3]

Specifically, this means that Husserl's scientific ideal for phenomenology eventually gives way to an even more radical philosophical grounding in the crisis of history. This phenomenological "discovery" of history cannot be accounted for simply through an appeal to the historical unfolding of ideas that were latent from the beginning; but rather, it is the very transformative, or more precisely, revolutionary effect of history on Husserl's understanding of phenomenology that circles philosophy back toward its mixed origins. The seriousness of this crisis for Husserl's understanding of phenomenology has been suggested by Ricoeur, when he writes in reference to Husserl: "One can certainly contest the possibility of a philosophy with two sources— the cogito and God. That is to say, one can deny the possibility of holding at one and the same time a philosophy where subjectivity is the reference pole of all that can be thought and a philosophy where being is the reference pole of all that exists. However, to fail to recognize the structure of Cartesianism is to produce a philosophy other than Descartes's and not to radicalize Cartesianism."[4]

Insofar as Husserl's stated intentions, most especially in the *Cartesian Meditations*, were precisely to radicalize Cartesianism, Ricoeur is suggesting that Husserl's neglect of the idea of the infinite shows his phenomenology to be fundamentally misguided and that, consequently, it completely missed its mark. Our interest, however, has less to do with either the "success" or "failure" of Husserl and more to do with Ricoeur's suggestion that phenomenology, when properly understood, is a philosophy of mixed origins, not only pertaining to the self-explication of the ego, but also pertaining to God. Speaking as a phenomenologist himself, this suggestion by Ricoeur seems to be a complete heterodoxy. But even Husserl, the most ardent advocate of the purity of the scientific ideal of phenomenology, would come to a like recognition by the end of his writings.

As for this chapter itself, the purpose it serves for the understanding of the problematic of philosophical theology is that it demonstrates the necessary complicity of phenomenology in history and, accordingly, the impossibility of a philosophy to stand completely on its own. As phenomenology circles back toward the history of its own making, it also moves forward to the opening of philosophy toward theology. This present chapter, therefore, will lead directly into chapter 4, where the phenomenological and theological traditions meet.

The Beginning of a Philosophy "Not Yet Begun"

There is general confusion and disagreement regarding the proper legacy of Husserlian phenomenology.[5] As Paul Ricoeur wrote: "Husserl abandoned along the way as many routes as he took. This is the case to such a degree that in a broad sense phenomenology is both the sum of Husserl's work and the heresies issuing from it."[6] Matters are not helped, of course, when the initial chosen heir and successor not only offers a revisionist account of the aims of phenomenology, but also cuts off personal relations.[7] Indeed, Heidegger's dedication to Husserl in the opening of *Being and Time* could be considered one of the great ironies of contemporary philosophy. For while it is generally recognized that this monumental early work of Heidegger's was deeply indebted to Husserl and greatly informed by the phenomenological method, it also stands as a turning point in contemporary thought, away from the descriptive, scientific ideals of Husserl and toward the philosophies of existence and the question of being. As Dermot Moran, author of the recent work *Introduction to Phenomenology* writes: "After the publication of Heidegger's *Being and Time* (1927), phenomenology came to be understood almost exclusively in terms of the *combined* contribution of both Husserl and Heidegger." Moran continues by speaking of "Husserl and Heidegger as, respectively, [the] founder and transformer of phenomenology."[8] Ricoeur makes a similar observation when he argues that Heidegger's philosophical hermeneutics effects a "subversion" of Husserl's phenomenology. "In this way," Ricoeur writes, "Heideggerian and post-Heideggerian hermeneutics, though they are indeed heirs to Husserlian phenomenology, constitute in the end the reversal of this phenomenology to the very extent indeed that they also constitute its realization."[9] Therefore, while it might be the case that Heidegger's fundamental ontology was a logical outgrowth of Husserl's phenomenology, phenomenology would prove to be hardly a uniform path. Yet another irony, therefore, concerns Husserl's abiding concern with the crisis of modern philosophy, which from early on he understood as the problem of relativism and the failure of philosophy to achieve the objectivity for which it aspired.[10] The outcome of his lifelong project to provide a unity to thought, however, would prove instead to fuel a generation of domestic squabbles.

THE QUESTION OF HISTORY

Perhaps chief among these squabbles was the relation of phenomenology to history. Regarding Husserl in particular, there are at least three questions that must be asked concerning this relation: (1) What is Husserl's stance toward history; specifically, what value does the history of philosophy have for the philosophical thinker, and how should the philosopher understand the course of history? (2) To what degree does Husserl's philosophy show an appreciation and understanding of historicity; specifically, are philosophical concepts historically constituted and historically determined, or do they stand outside of history? (3) What historical purpose does philosophy serve? These questions are even further complicated by the fact that in the course of Husserl's long career, his position on these matters would undergo a decided shift in accordance with his ongoing reinterpretation and redescription of phenomenology—from phenomenology as a *descriptive science,* to *transcendental subjectivity,* to his last period that speaks of a philosophical, historical, and cultural *crisis.*[11] Perhaps more than any other factors, it is both the imprint of history on Husserl's life and thought and his growing appreciation of the historicity of meaning that best accounts for these changes in his understanding and his description of philosophy. That is to say, history impresses or imposes itself on Husserl in such a fashion that it becomes impossible for him to maintain what was an essentially ahistorical understanding of philosophy.[12]

Husserl's early perspective on these matters can be seen in an essay written in 1911 entitled "Philosophy as Rigorous Science." In this essay, Husserl contrasts phenomenology with Wilhelm Dilthey's *Weltanschauung* (i.e., "worldview") philosophy.[13] Husserl's main objection to Dilthey was not concerning the accuracy of his cultural analysis, but instead, whether such an analysis should rightly be called a philosophy, or more precisely, whether it meets the demands of a scientific investigation.[14] Dilthey's response to such a critique would be regarding its value for lending understanding to life in the world. Philosophy, according to Dilthey, like all other forms of cultural life, is a product of history and relative to a given culture. There is no universal standard by which to assess one life-world compared with another, nor is there an uncontested point of origin.[15] For Dilthey, it is lived experience, not the natural sciences, which provides the primary category of intelligibility. That is because lived experience incorporates both the outer and inner experiences that determine the natural and human sciences, respectively. In other words, the sciences are a second-order, interpretative endeavor that stand in need of some form of accountability, justification, or, more precisely, worldview. The worldview functions as an overarching perspective or framework. It provides the context by which the knowledge, will, and emotions with regard to the world are made both meaningful and valuable.

For Husserl such a perspective fails to overcome the travails of relativism.[16] It is a kind of historicism that remains trapped in its own history, and, as Husserl writes, "if consistently carried through, carries over into extreme sceptical subjectivism." Furthermore, it is a contradiction in the sense that in order for one to speak of one world-view in relation with another, one must presume a common frame of reference. "It can," Husserl writes, "as historical science in no way prove even the affirmation that up to the present there has been no scientific philosophy; it can do so only from other sources of knowledge, and they are clearly philosophical sources."[17] Put otherwise, the cultural criticism that is characteristic of Dilthey's work is only the first step in philosophy. But to stop there would be to end in "nonsense," because one has not disproved the objective validity of the philosophical method in general, but instead, has only served the proper ends of philosophy by exposing a particular perspective that does not meet philosophical standards of clear and distinct knowledge. Again, in Husserl's words: "If criticism has proved that philosophy in its historical growth has operated with confused concepts, has been guilty of mixed concepts and specious conclusions, then if one does not wish to fall into nonsense, that very fact makes undeniable that, ideally speaking, the concepts are capable of being pointed, clarified, distinguished, that in the given area correct conclusions can be drawn."[18]

The distinction between Dilthey and Husserl is the different understanding of history that emerges from their respective "philosophies." Put most simply, for Dilthey philosophy is a product of history. For Husserl, on the other hand, at least in this still early stage in the development of his phenomenology, history is a product of philosophy, or perhaps more accurately, history presupposes philosophy. Furthermore, for Dilthey history testifies to the diversity of philosophical frameworks and the differences between worldviews. For Husserl history only reveals the unscientific nature of philosophies of the past. As such, history is useful only insofar as it helps the philosopher avoid the missteps of previous generations of philosophical thinkers, or only insofar as it reiterates the point that up to now there has not been the realization of a genuinely scientific philosophy. Quentin Lauer, in his introduction to the essay by Husserl, voices Husserl's position as follows: "Philosophy is as yet not merely an incomplete or imperfect science, it simply is not science at all; there is no objectively valid philosophical 'system'; there are only philosophical 'tendencies,' which do not add up to 'philosophy.'"[19]

Jacques Derrida, in his essay, "'Genesis and Structure' and Phenomenology," suggests that the reason for Husserl's strong critique of Dilthey's *Weltanschauung* philosophy is that it too closely resembled Husserl's descriptive phenomenology. Dilthey so resembled Husserl, in fact, that one could read Husserl's critique as an attempt to convince himself that phenomenology was not just a reiteration of Dilthey, that there was indeed something radically new in phenomenological philosophy. As Derrida writes: "If Husserl attacked Diltheyism with such violence, it is that he found in Diltheyism a *seductive* attempt, a tempting aberration."[20] Derrida describes this temptation as historicism's confusion of actual truths of fact with the pure truths of reason. Therefore, according to Derrida's analysis, what is at stake in Husserl's critique is precisely the question of purity and whether the philosopher will allow pure truth to be compromised by the facts of history.[21] The reason why this might pose a temptation is because of its allure of comprehension, that is to say, its ability to systematically unify particular historical facts into a coherent whole. Even still, for Husserl, regardless of whether Dilthey successfully unifies history into a systematic whole or not, historicism is still unable to get beyond its own historical limitations as an empirical science of facts, thus it must not be considered truly philosophical. As Derrida explains: "History does not cease to be an empirical science of 'facts' because it has reformed its methods and techniques, or because it has substituted a comprehensive structuralism for causalism, atomism, and naturalism, or because it has become more attentive to cultural totalities. Its pretension to founding normativity or a better understood factuality does not become more legitimate, but only increases its power of philosophical seduction."[22]

THE SCIENTIFIC IDEAL

To repeat, Husserl distinguishes between phenomenology and Dilthey's *Weltanschauung* philosophy because Dilthey's historicism fails to meet the scientific demands of philosophy. The fact that no philosophy throughout the history of philosophy has ever met this demand, from Husserl's perspective, does not invalidate his critique. Which is to say, Husserl refuses to allow history to relativize philosophical reason, even when the history of philosophy itself testifies to the unreasonableness of this demand.

This addresses the first question regarding Husserl's stance toward history. For Husserl this is a rather straightforward point beginning from the perspective that philosophy aspires to meet the demands of a rigorous science. In relation to the scientific demand for radicality, systematicity, and universality, philosophy does not meet, nor has it ever met, the standard.[23] It is for this reason that the essay begins with the failure of philosophy to meet this scientific aspiration. On the aspiration itself, Husserl begins the essay with the following: "From its earliest beginnings philosophy has claimed to be a rigorous science. What is more, it has claimed to be the science that satisfies the loftiest theoretical needs and renders possible from an ethico-religious point of view a life regulated by pure rational norms." On the failure of philosophy, however, he writes: "During no period of its development has philosophy been capable of living up to this claim of being rigorous science." Husserl continues: "Thus philosophy, according to its historical purpose the loftiest and most rigorous of all sciences, representing as it does humanity's imperishable demand for pure and absolute knowledge . . . is incapable of assuming the form of rigorous science." Then, to conclude this point: "I do not say that philosophy is an imperfect science; I say simply that it is not yet a science at all, that as science it has not yet begun."[24] History, in other words, offers no positive proof of the possibilities of philosophy, because from a properly scientific perspective philosophy "has not yet begun."

Therefore, those who relegate philosophy to a lesser status do so only from a misinformed perspective of the true possibilities and objectives of philosophy. They have confused the history of philosophy with its essence. This, then, begins to address the second question regarding phenomenology's relationship to history, which is the more complicated issue of historicity. It is on this matter that Dilthey's historicism and Husserl's descriptive phenomenology should be sharply distinguished. One is not the outgrowth of the other. On the contrary, *Weltanschauung* philosophy is in fact only philosophical in the sense in which philosophy has been historically misinterpreted and misapplied. As Husserl writes:

> Thus *Weltanschauung* philosophy and scientific philosophy are sharply distinguished as two ideas, related in a certain manner to each other but not to be confused. Herein it is also to be observed that the former is not, so to speak, the imperfect realization of the latter. For if our interpretation is correct, then up to the present there has been no realization at all of that idea, i.e., no philosophy actually in existence is a rigorous science; there is no "system of doctrines," even an incomplete one, objectively set forth in the unified spirit of the research community of our time.[25]

This concerns Husserl's point that the scientific validity of philosophy cannot be grounded in history; rather, the relationship should be
reversed. The former leads to philosophical skepticism and cultural
relativism, while the latter provides the only means for the possibility of an objective knowledge of essences. It is for this reason that
Husserl can on the one hand affirm the failure of philosophy throughout history, while on the other, still speak of the need for a scientific
philosophy to be given priority. That is because a scientific philosophy is not based in history, but is a pure and absolute philosophy. As
Husserl claims, "It is not through philosophies that we become philosophers."[26] In this way, according to Husserl's early understanding,
phenomenology is *purely* and *absolutely* ahistorical.

THE "SPIRITUAL" URGENCY

One final point of difference between Dilthey and Husserl should be
made before moving on. In Husserl's mind, the making of philosophy into a "rigorous science" is no mere practical concern, but "the
spiritual need of our time." This spiritual need he defines as "doing
justice to validity and invalidity according to the alleged norms of
absolute validation." According to Husserl, only science can meet
this need. "And so," he writes, "whatever be the direction the new
transformation of philosophy may take, without question it must not
give up its will to be rigorous science. Rather as theoretical science it
must oppose itself to the practical aspiration toward *Weltanschauung*
and quite consciously separate itself from this aspiration."[27] Therefore,
for philosophy to become a science, it must purify itself from the
practical concerns of life in the world, and from the demand made by
some of philosophy that it make its relevance more apparent. This
would be a radically new philosophy; its ideal would be to be completely liberated from the prejudices and biases of the past, and also
liberated from the prevailing scientific outlook of the present. This is
what it means for phenomenology to be a "pure" or "eidetic" science,
as opposed to being merely "factual." As Moran writes: "Husserl
designates phenomenology as a 'pure' science, by which he means,
following Kant, one stripped of all empirical content, one which provides essential knowledge of the invariant structures at work in all
knowing, perceiving, imagining, and so on, irrespective of what goes
on in the actual world, irrespective of the existence of that world."
This is the famous phenomenological *epoché*, the suspension of the
natural attitude. All things must be put in brackets, even the most
basic attitude regarding existence as such. Again, in Moran's words,

"The science of essences has nothing to do with actual existence, but moves in the sphere of pure possibilities. Eidetic sciences have nothing factual about them, while on the other hand, every factual science depends on eidetic insights."[28] Phenomenology works independently of questions of existence or nonexistence. This is a phenomenology "without," or "otherwise than," being. [29] Only in this way might philosophy finally become "a science of true beginnings."[30] Only in this way might philosophy begin to fulfill its true historical purposes.

Certainly not for the faint of heart, this philosophy is more like a spiritual exercise or a vocation. As Rüdiger Safranski, a biographer of Heidegger, writes: "Phenomenology aspired to be more than just a school of thought; it therefore called itself a movement. It aimed not only at the restoration of strict scholarship in philosophy . . . but also at the reform of life altogether under the aegis of intellectual honesty."[31] And from Moran, this spiritual dimension to the movement of phenomenology is spelled out even more explicitly: "Husserl saw himself as founder of an entirely new discipline, a self-styled 'radical beginner,' engaged in the constant act of radical founding. He frequently cast himself in the role of pioneer, an explorer in the new domain of consciousness, a Moses leading his people to the new land of transcendental subjectivity."[32]

Phenomenology within the History of Philosophy

It is within this context that one can better understand and appreciate Heidegger's early efforts to distinguish phenomenology from theology.[33] In one respect, this 1927 essay by Heidegger can be seen as an extension of the Husserlian project. Like Husserl, Heidegger begins from what he considers to be the essence of philosophy. That is to say, both philosophy and theology spring from their own source. In addition, Heidegger shares with Husserl the opinion that phenomenology is an arduous task, one that is yet to be realized. At the same time, theology is renewed with each generation as faith stands as the data to be interpreted, clarified, and applied according to the practical concerns of those who believe. In contrast to Husserl, however, Heidegger has reinterpreted the task of philosophy. That is to say, philosophy is not to be thought of as a rigorous science, but as the question of being. And it is theology, not phenomenology, which should be likened to science.[34]

In spite of this difference, Heidegger still shares much in common with Husserl. Most importantly, Heidegger, like Husserl, reads history as the failure or inadequacies of the philosophies of the past. Evidence

Being and Time, which begins with what Heidegger terms the "destructuring of the history of ontology."[35] According to Heidegger, history only tells the tale of the forgetfulness of being. In addition, however, Heidegger also allows for a positive appropriation of historicity in the sense that *Dasein* is a historical subject, constituted as a self in its constant relation to its past, present, and future. It is for this reason that science no longer stands as the ideal for the philosopher in Heidegger's mind. Science speaks of a certain or absolute knowledge for which the self as a being-in-time cannot attain. Even the scientific knowledge that is available is relativized by its necessary presupposition of being. Furthermore, the question of being is of a certain nature that it demands fundamentally different criteria of assessment and validation. Phenomenologically speaking, its mode of givenness must be attended to accordingly. As such, the language of science might be inadequate to the task of properly responding to the question of being.

THE RIFT BETWEEN HEIDEGGER AND HUSSERL

In other words, Heidegger's fundamental ontology stands as a rupture within the history of phenomenology. It could even be said that Heidegger's rediscription of the task of philosophy gives history to phenomenology, which is to say that it opens phenomenology to the question of history. It is in this sense that Heidegger, though himself a student of Husserl's, sets Husserl on a path in which the problem of philosophical theology is made apparent. As Husserl reintroduces and redescribes the task of phenomenology, he becomes increasingly drawn into a philosophical path that was not of his own making. If Moran is correct, Heidegger effectively transformed phenomenology by historicizing it.[36] Thus, as Husserl takes history more into account as his thinking develops, it will be demonstrated that this historicized phenomenology is in effect an effort at overcoming history—or in terms of chapter 1, an effort driven by the desire for purity and the fear of contamination. Husserl's philosophical project was united by the hope to restore the ideals of a truly scientific philosophy, which he believed would lead to an objective knowledge of essences. However, in large part due to Heidegger, the path to the achievement of this ideal would be forced to travel a circuitous route through history, and along the way, not only phenomenology in general, but also Husserl's own thinking would be transformed.

This rupture between Heidegger and Husserl has its own story, one that begins as early as 1919, when Heidegger first spoke of the "worlding" of experience.[37] "Worlding" was Heidegger's way of giving expression to the fundamental relatedness between the world and the knower, a kind of relationality that was of a different order from perception, and that suggested that thinking is a performative—not simply a descriptive—act. The significance of this first neologism of Heidegger's is that it also announces his first public break from Husserl, specifically with regard to the primacy Husserl gives to the theoretical, or the value of philosophy understood strictly as a descriptive science. In other words, for Heidegger, the usefulness of phenomenology is that it allows for a kind of "de-experiencing," so that the thing itself might appear in all its complexity. The breach between the subject and object is overcome by an antecedent unity of being. Phenomenology, when accepted as a method for uncovering the world, reverses the "progressive destructive infection of the environment by theory;"[38] it uncovers a realm of being prior to description. Thus, while Husserl also pursued phenomenology as a way to overcome the subject-object divide, his methodology develops into what some would consider a recovery of transcendental idealism. Heidegger, on the other hand, made use of phenomenology in order to rebel against precisely such transcendental idealism.[39]

There are several reasons why Husserl might have been slow to realize the extent of the rift between his own project and that of Heidegger's. First of all, there is some truth to Heidegger's statement regarding Husserl's "mission of being 'the founder of phenomenology.'"[40] Husserl indeed took great satisfaction in having attracted to his "movement" many of the finest minds of the new generation of philosophical thinkers. Perhaps his investment in what he considered to be the overarching project of the renewal of philosophy blinded him to the differences between himself and his students. Also, it was not until 1927 that Heidegger's *Being and Time* was published and began to cause a stir among its contemporaries. Finally, even as late as 1928, Husserl had supported Heidegger as his successor to the chair of philosophy at the University at Freiburg. It was only at this time that Heidegger's tone of philosophy underwent a decided shift in lectures such as his inaugural lecture, "What is Metaphysics?" and his series of lectures from 1929–30, "The Fundamental Concepts of Metaphysics." Safranski describes this shift in tone as follows: "The temperature is rising. . . The cool, almost engineered fundamental ontological descriptions are now expressly put under an existential pressure."[41]

While the "existential pressure" is important, it is not all that contributed to Heidegger's new tone. This is also the time in which

Heidegger is beginning to speak of the thinker as a poet. The significance of this, as Heidegger states in his essay "What are Poets for?" is that in a time of cultural and religious destitution, it is the poet who is most able to "utter the holy," it is the poet who tells of the loss of the gods, and it is the poet who exposes us to the emptiness that our technological civilization has engineered us to deny.[42] Therefore, to say that Heidegger's tone of philosophy undergoes a decided shift toward the more existential and poetic is also to speak of his thinking becoming more cognizant of the loss and decay of Western civilization.

A NEW (CARTESIAN) STYLE FOR PHENOMENOLOGY

Perhaps more than anything else, it was this new tone that separated Husserl, the "founder" of phenomenology, from Heidegger, the "transformer" of phenomenology. This is not to suggest that there were only stylistic differences that hid a kind of substantive agreement between Husserl and Heidegger. On the contrary, it was precisely Heidegger's emphasis on the style or tone of philosophy, which Heidegger had learned from his study of Nietzsche, that would prove to be his greatest ingenuity as he reinterprets the history, and redefines the task, of philosophy. Therefore, while Husserl remains committed to an old style of philosophy in his efforts to develop a transcendental phenomenology, Heidegger upsets the balance by such things as his philosophical appropriation of poetry—whether it be the poetics of the pre-Socratics, the Christian mystic, the Japanese philosophical tradition, or German literature[43]—by his proclamation of the end of philosophy, and by his efforts at overcoming metaphysics.

During the same span of time when Heidegger was developing an international reputation in the wake of the publication of *Being and Time,* Husserl's own work came to a point of crystallization in a series of lectures introducing the French-speaking world to transcendental phenomenology, which were given in Paris at the Sorbonne in 1929. These lectures were eventually elaborated and published by the title of *Cartesian Meditations* (1931). In this work Husserl shows that he was certainly not naïve with regard to the importance of style for philosophy. On the contrary, it was because he was invested in and committed to a certain style of philosophy that he resisted the shift in style inaugurated by Heidegger. For instance, it is interesting to note Husserl's introductory comments on the importance of Descartes in the history of philosophy. "Descartes, in fact," writes Husserl, "inaugurates an entirely new kind of philosophy. Changing its total style, philosophy takes a radical turn: from naïve Objectivism to transcendental subjectivism."[44] Husserl is clear that it is to Descartes's credit that he is responsible for this shift to transcendental subjectivism, but as has already been shown, Husserl also makes the case that philosophy has yet to begin. In fact, as Quentin Lauer demonstrates, Husserl regarded the Cartesian revolution as only the second of four revolutions in philosophy—the final and most radical of these being the phenomenological revolution.[45] Descartes successfully turns philosophy toward the subject, but his is a philosophical subjectivism that is still incomplete because it maintains a fundamental dualism between the self as a thing that thinks and the object of thought. Likewise with Kant's "transcendental" revolution in philosophy, his insistence on the divide between the noumenal and the phenomenal prevented Kant from seeing his "Copernican revolution" to its logical end. As Lauer writes: "Kant had recognized the necessity of a transcendental subjectivity if ever philosophy was to escape the Humean dilemma, but he destroyed the purity of this subjectivity by his concession to transcendence under the guise of the 'thing-in-itself.' As a result, Kant achieves, not a universal science of philosophy, not a rationalization of all objectivity, but only a formal critique of knowledge that sets the limits of reason and in no way extends its domain."[46] Thus, the *Cartesian Meditations* were Husserl's philosophical reflection on the radical nature of the Cartesian and Kantian revolutions in philosophy. In addition, however, as an introduction to transcendental phenomenology, they are also intended to show the fundamental limitations in the thinking of both Descartes and Kant. In this way, phenomenology is seen as both a continuation and the completion of a revolution begun years earlier but still yet to be realized. What is interesting to note, therefore, in regard to the question of Husserl's stance toward history is that in the *Meditations*, Husserl has come to a different assessment on the value and course of history for philosophy, compared with his earlier 1911 essay, "Philosophy as Rigorous Science." Ricoeur makes this point when he states that the *Meditations* manifest a shift in Husserl's thinking, a shift that now locates phenomenology squarely *within* the history of philosophy.

This shift, however, is not without its own problems. As Ricoeur writes in reference to Husserl: "The fact that there is a history after Descartes, who claimed to put an end to the wanderings of thought and to begin philosophy anew, occurs because Descartes was not sufficiently radical or sufficiently true to his own radicalism. Philosophy could triumph over its own history and could realize its 'eternal sense' if it would follow its task through to the end."[47] This notion of the philosophical triumph over history, then, displays a residue of ambivalence on the part of Husserl toward history. On the one hand, the philosopher can look back to history and note the historical watersheds. Furthermore, by delving into the history of these decisive moments within the history of philosophy, the philosopher might better understand the reasons for the failure of philosophy throughout history to realize its essence. On the other hand, once this essence has been realized, which means that once a proper philosophical foundation has been established, history has done its work and has thereby rendered itself obsolete. Again, Ricoeur makes this point well: "The *Cartesian Meditations* suggests the notion that the history of philosophy has a sense insofar as it proceeds toward the suppression of its own history by progress in the direction of the true beginning."[48]

Husserl's stance toward history from this middle period can thus be described as the philosophical appreciation of a history that culminates in the end of history and the true and radical beginning of transcendental phenomenology. Therefore, history begins not at the point of its origination, but only when its end is in sight. In this sense of the term, history will always and only be retrospective. It is history that gives meaning to the past, but this remains a past that is left behind once history is overcome. History is thus the story of endings, and when history comes to its completion, there is likewise an end to history and a beginning to thought.[49]

THE PHENOMENOLOGICAL REDUCTION

That history effects its historical overcoming does not yet answer the second question regarding Husserl's appreciation of historicity. In fact, it is concerning this matter that the *Meditations* displays Husserl's most radical shift in understanding from his earlier period. Recall from "Philosophy as Rigorous Science," that Husserl distinguishes phenomenology from Dilthey's *Weltanschauung* philosophy chiefly on the matter of the order of priority given to either philosophy or history. At this early stage, Husserl still configured this order of relation in terms of temporality. That is to say, Husserl depicts history as a product of philosophy, as though one was the cause, the other the effect. By the time of the *Meditations*, however, Husserl had come to a greater appreciation of the problem that the "pre-givenness" of the world poses for phenomenology; namely, that the world functions as a coconstituent together with the ego. Phenomenology has always sought a balance between its rallying cry "to the things themselves" and the constitutive performance of the ego.[50] For instance, in the classic introduction to phenomenology from his *Phenomenology of Perception*, Maurice Merleau-Ponty writes: "It is a transcendental philosophy which places in abeyance the assertions arising out of the natural attitude, the better to understand them; but is also a philosophy for which the world is always 'already there' before reflection begins—as an inalienable presence; and all its efforts are concentrated upon re-achieving a direct and primitive contact with the world, and endowing that contact with a philosophical status."[51] Descartes gives voice to the same problem in Meditation V: "But before examining whether any such objects as I conceive exist outside of me, I must consider the ideas of them in so far as they are in my thought, and see which of them are distinct and which confused."[52] It has already been demonstrated how this Cartesian question of the existence of the thing has been put in brackets. For this reason alone, the Cartesian spatialization of the subject and object as the inside and outside, respectively, is no longer a working hypothesis: "If transcendental subjectivity is the universe of possible sense," Husserl writes, "then an outside is precisely—nonsense."[53]

Nevertheless, the problem of the relation between the subject and the object remains a problem unresolved. Husserl's proposal from the *Meditations* is as follows: "If (as is in fact the case) there are transcendentally constituted in me, the transcendental ego, not only other egos but also (*as* constituted in turn by the transcendental intersubjectivity accruing to me thanks to the constitution in me of others) an Objective world common to us all, then everything said up to now is true, not alone in the case of my de facto ego and in the case of this de facto intersubjectivity and world, which receive sense and existence-status in my subjectivity."[54] Phenomenology, therefore, is defined as "a self-explication of the ego," by which the objective status of both the transcendental ego and the transcending world are mutually, and primordially, constituted. The one does not come before the other, nor, as Husserl writes, does thinking proceed "from a supposed immanency to a supposed trancendency." This phenomenological process of self-elaboration is a move away from the solipsism of the monadic ego to a universal transcendental philosophy by way of intersubjectivity; it uncovers the "implicit intentionality" that stands as the very intentional structure of consciousness itself; namely, that consciousness is always conscious of something, that the immanent self stands in constant relation to the transcending other. The ego "experiences within himself a world."[55] It is therefore both *constitutive*, as the ground of possibility, and is *constituted* by its experience of that which is not itself[56]—"the validity of world-apperception has already been presupposed." Again, this does not mean that one somehow gets "outside" one's own "island of consciousness,"[57] but that the conscious self is both active and passive, both free and determined, and that there is a fundamental correlation, even agreement, between consciousness and the world.[58]

Regarding the question concerning historicity, this means that the self is always already being made, and thus, that it is impossible for transcendental phenomenology proceeding by the means of the phenomenological reduction, which is nothing other than the elaboration of the self, or *an all-embracing self-investigation,*[59] to achieve eternal validity. Merleau-Ponty would make this point explicit when he writes: "The most important lesson which the reduction teaches us is the impossibility of the complete reduction." And further: "The unfinished nature of phenomenology and the inchoate atmosphere which has surrounded it are not to be taken as a sign of failure, they were inevitable because phenomenology's task was to reveal the mystery of the world and of reason."[60] As Merleau-Ponty understands it, this "unfinished nature of phenomenology" was the very contribution that phenomenology makes to modern thought.

Like Heidegger's *Being and Time,* Husserl's *Cartesian Meditations* gives time to transcendental phenomenology in such a way that the future is left open. "Universal," "all-embracing," and "apodictic" it might be, but "timeless" it is not. Thus, Husserl writes, *the transcendental ego who comes into view is, to be sure, grasped apodictically*—but as having *a quite undetermined horizon,* a horizon restricted only by the general requirement that the world and all I know about it shall become a mere 'phenomenon.'" This is a "mere phenomenon," however, that saves the appearance of the historicity of the self, and of other like philosophical concepts, for phenomenology. As such, it also allows phenomenology to more fully realize its historical purpose, which, as Husserl defined it, was "to show the concrete possibility of the Cartesian idea of a philosophy as an all-embracing science grounded on an absolute foundation."[61] Still, in Husserl's mind, achieving this "radical beginning" to philosophy promises to alleviate the confusion of philosophical concepts, the disunity among the sciences, and the fragmentation of culture. In contrast to Merleau-Ponty, Husserl remained convinced that a proper understanding of philosophical grounds might function as a secure base from which the knowledge of essences might be achieved and on which the edifice of philosophy for future generations might be built.

Time of Crisis

While it was originally Husserl who set the scene for phenomenology, by the time of the publication of the *Cartesian Meditations* in 1931 Husserl had already become concerned that this work—which was intended to be the final introduction to phenomenology and to establish the proper phenomenological ground for philosophy—would lead to more confusion than clarity, and that it would be overshadowed by the growing interest in the philosophies of existence. "The cause for this," writes Ronald Bruzina, "was quite simply—Heidegger." The transformation that Heidegger had effected in phenomenology was more like a "subversion" or a "gross misinterpretation" from Husserl's perspective.[62] As a result, Husserl now found himself in a situation where he not only faced the difficulty of having to introduce the phenomenological method, but also—and even more—he now had to defend it as a worthy endeavor, which itself was a kind of victory for the existentialists.

The problem was that the *Cartesian Meditations* never spells out its concrete relation to the world. In fact, Husserl had even taken pains to distinguish phenomenology as an eidetic science from a more concrete or practical philosophy. Husserl's longtime assistant, Eugen Fink (who himself was working on a revision of Husserl's *Meditations* in what would later be published as the *Sixth Cartesian Meditation*), wrote in his own notes in the margins of Husserl's text: "This whole path [the Cartesian grounding in the apodicticity of the ego] now seems to have been the wrong way to go." Husserl's response after the fact: "So it was! A sheer muddle, and wrongheaded as a course of action."[63] Another way of stating the problem was that in the *Meditations*, Husserl presents the phenomenological reduction as though it were a straightforward process of self-elaboration. This leaves the reader with the appearance that the plausibility of Husserl's phenomenology is based on nothing other than, in David Bell's terms, "the individual philosopher's having undergone some esoteric experience."[64] Or according to Bruzina: "[The *Cartesian Meditations*] seems to move *away from* the world to an apparent self-sufficient, self-present ego. Correspondingly, the phenomenological reduction seems to function to safeguard absolute self-sufficiency on the part of the reflecting ego and absolute purity and independence *from* and *against* the world."[65]

The failure of the *Meditations* was that its rhetoric leaves the impression that it is based on some pure experience that guarantees the absolute freedom of the self. In contrast to Heidegger, this was not a

purity of thought purged of the self-willing ego, nor a thinking necessarily independent of faith. Instead, with Husserl purity stands for
the philosopher's attention only to what is *purely given*. This is a
purity determined by the paradigm of the positive sciences, and thus
has more in common with geometry than mysticism. It is a purity
based on the independence of the ego as that which freely bestows
meaning on the world, the purity of the structure of intentionality.
This is the primary criticism that Levinas levies against Husserl;
namely, that Husserl's phenomenology is finally a philosophy of
freedom, and as such, it does not adequately describe the self as a
being constituted by its relation with the other. As Levinas writes:
"Husserl's phenomenology is, in the final analysis, a philosophy of
freedom, a freedom that is accomplished as, and defined by, consciousness. . . . This means that the real—things and thoughts—has
meaning only in consciousness, which is the very mode of existence
of meaning." Levinas continues: "This is not solipsism, but the possibility of solipsism. It marks the way of being in which existence is its
own starting point."[66] The question, therefore, is whether this problem is one of degree or according to the very nature of Husserlian
phenomenology.

"DE-CARTESIANIZING"
TRANSCENDENTAL PHENOMENOLOGY

According to Fink, at least, it is one of degree; thus the problem can
be corrected from within. Fink's early efforts, therefore, are described
as an attempt to "de-Cartesianize" Husserl's *Cartesian Mediations.*
He accomplishes this by centering not on transcendental subjectivity,
but on the world as an all-embracing framework. As he explains his
revisions in the opening of the *Sixth Cartesian Meditations:* "The
phenomenological inquiry developed here presupposes the 'Médita-
tiones Cartésiennes,' and originates on the basis and within the limits
of the problematic inaugurated there. However, it also goes further
inasmuch as it expressly puts into question the methodological
naiveté which consists in uncritically transferring the mode of cognition that relates to something *existent* into the phenomenological
cognition of the *forming* of the existent."[67] The uncritical transfer of
the knowledge of the object to the mode of knowledge characteristic
of Husserl's *Meditations,* Fink calls "*transcendental naiveté.*" Fink
writes: "It consists in our unfolding and explicating transcendental
life only in the *presentness* . . . in which it is given us by the reduction,
without entering by analysis into the 'inner horizon' of this life, into

the performance of constitution." By entering into the "performance of constitution," one thereby begins the task that lies beyond the phenomenological reduction and regressive phenomenology; namely, that of a "constructive phenomenology." The difficulty this poses for phenomenology is the issue that what is spoken of is no longer what is simply present or what is purely given. On the contrary, the object of constructive phenomenology is precisely what is *not* given, what is "beyond the living present of the actual moment." Constructive phenomenology, in other words, "is nothing other than the sum total of all the problems that go beyond the reductive givenness of transcendental life." Therefore, beyond description and self-elaboration, Fink's "de-Cartesianized" transcendental phenomenology makes apparent the fact that "in order to gain any understanding at all, we have to *'construct.'*" Phenomenology, finally, gives way to a paradox: "the givenness of the theme for phenomenologizing is in constructive phenomenology a *non-givenness.*"[68]

By asserting "non-givenness" as the proper theme for a constructive phenomenology, Fink seeks a release from the exclusive self-reference characteristic of phenomenology as egology. In this way, Fink's project resembles Heidegger's analysis of the hermeneutic circle. As Fink explains, "phenomenology breaks open a *cleft* in the field of transcendental subjectivity." It exposes "an antithesis and split in *transcendental life itself,* a setting of itself against itself: *identity in difference, antithesis in self-sameness.*"[69] In other words, phenomenology is no straightforward process of self-elaboration. On the contrary, by attending to things as they appear, one comes to an awareness of a structure of knowing that by nature *cannot* come to appearance—the constitution of the phenomenological given is by that which is precisely *not given* to phenomenology. As Bruzina writes: "Fink's whole argument leads to the conclusion that it is not possible for the transcendental as properly taken to appear properly *as* transcendental, that is, as 'pre-existent'—*as meontic;* for in itself, not being within the realm of being, it 'is' not something that *can* 'appear' at all, much less in evidentness."[70]

The rupture within Husserlian phenomenology continues and is extended. This time the rupture emerges from completely within, as the outgrowth of Fink's stated attempt "to formulate a series of problems that remained latent in Husserl's phenomenology."[71] As has been shown, the chief problem that Fink has in mind was Husserl's continuing "transcendental naiveté," which can be understood as a misguided confidence in the range of philosophy as a radical and objective science, and more specifically, as a false grounding in a transcendental subject that by nature cannot be given to experience. At least through the *Cartesian Meditations*, Husserl was optimistic regarding the power of reason to overcome philosophical skepticism and cultural relativism. What he failed to recognize, however, was the growing philosophical and cultural resonance with what Ricoeur would later term the "school of suspicion," which is the collective achievement of Karl Marx, Friedrich Nietzsche, and Sigmund Freud. Ricoeur explains:

> If we go back to the intention they had in common, we find in it the decision to look upon the whole of consciousness primarily as "false" consciousness. They thereby take up again, each in a different manner, the problem of the Cartesian doubt, to carry it to the very heart of the Cartesian stronghold. The philosopher trained in the school of Descartes knows that things are doubtful, that they are not such as they appear; but he does not doubt that consciousness is such as it appears to itself; in consciousness, meaning and consciousness of meaning coincide. Since Marx, Nietzsche, and Freud, this too has become doubtful. After the doubt of things, we have started to doubt consciousness.[72]

What remains to be shown, therefore, is whether—and if so, how—Husserl himself liberates his philosophy from this characteristically Cartesian reliance on the self-certain ego. Phenomenology has clearly entered into a crisis, both from within, as its logic reaches its breaking point, and from without, as it now finds itself in need of a defense. Husserl's last great work, *The Crisis of European Sciences and Transcendental Phenomenology*, would be his final attempt to once again make a case for the proper phenomenological understanding of philosophy, as well as the historical ends such a philosophy serves.

THE "LIFE-WORLD"

The question of the relation between phenomenology and history remains central. In fact, it is in this last stage of Husserl's development that the imprint of history is most clearly seen. The irony is that while the imprint of history becomes more visible, this creates a space for that which stands outside history, which is the other of the "life-world," that which cannot be accounted for in the terms of a historical analysis, or the more phenomenological terms of presence or absence, being or nonbeing, and appearance or nonappearance. In other words, the life-world is Husserl's attempt to give voice to that which is not given to phenomenology. This is a profound shift in Husserl's thinking, the importance of which should not be overlooked. In one respect, the life-world can be understood in terms of Kuhn's definition of the paradigm, as that "fundamental unit . . . that cannot be fully reduced to logically atomic components which might function in its stead";[73] or, according to Ricoeur's analysis, the life-world is "a theme which phenomenology came up against in spite of itself." Ricoeur explains: "Phenomenology is thus caught in an infinite movement of 'backwards questioning' in which its product of radical self-grounding fades away. Even the last works devoted to the *life-world* designate by this term an horizon of immediateness that is forever out of reach. The *Lebenswelt* is never actually given but always presupposed. It is phenomenology's paradise lost. It is in this sense that phenomenology has undermined its own guiding idea in the very attempt to realize it. It is this that gives Husserl's work its tragic grandeur."[74] Of course, Husserl's attention to that which is not given to phenomenology is shared, and was preceded, by both Heidegger and Fink. But it is with Husserl more than any other that the inevitability of this discovery for phenomenology is seen in its greatest force, for it was Husserl's paramount interest that phenomenology should lead philosophy to a more solid, scientific grounding. The fact that this endeavor ended in the undoing of itself marks the endpoint of the notion of phenomenology as an autonomous discipline.

THE CRISIS OF HISTORY AND HISTORICAL PHENOMENOLOGY

It is Merleau-Ponty's claim that Husserl's shift in attention toward the life-world can be seen as a turning away from transcendental idealism.[75] He writes: "It was in his last period that Husserl himself became fully conscious of what the return to the phenomenon meant and tacitly broke with the philosophy of essence."[76] Other commentators have suggested that this shift in Husserl's attention is a clear example of Heidegger's direct influence on Husserl, specifically with respect to Heidegger's holistic notion of *Dasein* as a "being-in-the-world" compared with Husserl's developing concern with the life-world. Husserl himself explicitly denies such a Heideggerian influence to his thinking during this period.[77] What seems more probable is that as Husserl seeks to correct certain oversights to his previous introductions to transcendental phenomenology, he is increasingly drawn into the philosophical currents of his time. Heidegger's work is certainly an important element to these currents, but so too are the political and cultural factors that cannot be ignored. From this perspective it can be seen how Husserl's crisis writings from 1934–37 resemble Heidegger's from roughly the same period. This does not mean that one directly influenced the other, but that they both were immersed in a history beyond their making.

Take Heidegger's essay "The Age of the World Picture" (1938), for instance. Here Heidegger identifies the five "essential phenomena of the modern age": (1) Science, by which Heidegger means the modern understanding of knowledge as a product of a procedure of research; (2) Machine technology, which is the outgrowth of the essence of modern metaphysics; (3) Art as aesthetics, which is the understanding that art is merely subjective; (4) Culture, by which the individual becomes lost in the national politics of culture; and (5) Loss of the gods, by which the modern worldview is Christianized and Christian doctrine transforms itself into a worldview. Together these phenomena make up the modern "world-picture," which, as Heidegger writes, "does not mean a picture of the world but the world conceived and grasped as picture." The modern world-picture stands in contrast to both the ancient Greeks and the Middle Ages, for with the Greeks "being" meant being "beheld by what is," and during the Middle Ages "being" meant "belonging" to creation. The openness and vulnerability that Heidegger sees in these more ancient orientations to being contrasts with the modern understanding of being as that which is represented. Heidegger writes: "Here to represent [*vor-stellen*] means to bring what is present at hand [*das Vorhandene*] before oneself as something standing over against, to relate it to oneself, to the one representing it, and to force it back into this relationship to oneself as the normative realm. Wherever this happens, man 'gets into the picture' in precedence over whatever is." The problem with the modern world-picture is that it thinks pictorially (i.e., representationally) at all. As Heidegger writes: "The fundamental event of the modern age is the conquest of the world as picture."[78]

Like Heidegger, Husserl also analyzes the modern philosophical paradigm through the lens of history. The reason for this is that history, both of philosophy and of the sciences, has entered into a crisis. This crisis, Husserl writes, "concerns not the scientific character of the sciences but rather what they, or what science in general, had meant and could mean for human existence." As with Heidegger's argument concerning the representational character of modern thought, Husserl here insists that it is the great "success" of science that is also its greatest shortcoming; namely, that as the sciences become more technologically proficient, so too do they become "indifferent" to "the questions which are decisive for genuine humanity." Put simply,

"Merely fact-minded sciences make merely fact-minded people."
The crisis is one of meaning itself, and the sciences—even a scientific philosophy—apparently have nothing to contribute. Further, by
attending to history the philosopher is aware of at least the following:
First, Husserl saw the history of his own culture's age as "unhappy
times." Second, he saw that things could be otherwise. As Husserl
writes: "It was not always the case that science understood its demand
for rigorously grounded truth in the sense of that *sort* of objectivity
which dominates our positive sciences in respect to method and
which, having its effect far beyond the sciences themselves, is the
basis for the support and widespread acceptance of a philosophical
and ideological positivism. The specifically human questions were
not always banned from the realm of science."[79]

When compared with his earlier works, Husserl's stance toward
history has undergone a complete reversal. In contrast to "Philosophy
as Rigorous Science," here in *The Crisis of the European Sciences*
Husserl is clearly making a claim for the positive value of history for
the renewal of both philosophy and the sciences. And in distinction
from the *Cartesian Meditations*, the value attributed to history is
not the sort that will be forgotten once the crisis of history is overcome. Instead, as Husserl explains, "The work that I am beginning
with the present essay . . . makes the attempt, by way of a teleological-
historical reflection upon the origins of our critical scientific and
philosophical situation, to establish the unavoidable necessity of a
transcendental-phenomenological reorientation to philosophy." This
reorientation to philosophy, furthermore, realizes the complications
of the contemporary philosophical situation; namely, that *"Every
philosopher 'takes something from the history' of past philosophers,*
from past philosophical writings—just as he has at his disposal, from
the present philosophical environment, the works that have been most
recently added and put in circulation."[80] Husserl has come to realize
that even the ideal of science, from which he has built so much of his
understanding of the task of phenomenology, is historically determined and constituted. The modern "world-picture," borrowing
Heidegger's terminology, has had a decisive impact on Husserlian
phenomenology as the life-world that has been presupposed. Accordingly, one of the primary tasks of phenomenology, as defined in the
Crisis, is for the philosopher to step back from the natural attitude in
order to set the life-world in clearer relief. In this way the concrete
value of a phenomenological philosophy is made more apparent, for
one becomes more cognizant of the history by which one is made,
and less removed from the practical consequences of one's thought.

In distinction from Heidegger's historical analysis, Husserl's begins with modernity and with its "primal founder" in Descartes. The significance of this is that while Heidegger seeks out the essence of historical paradigms, Husserl, by the end of his career, attends to the movement within an historical paradigm itself. Husserl, like Heidegger, still is seeking "what is essential to history," or the "a priori of history"[81] as he phrases it, but it seems Husserl has come to realize that even the essence of history has a historical genesis. According to David Carr, this final shift in Husserl's thinking "represents Husserl's attempt to come to terms with . . . the historicism he had attacked in 'Philosophy as Rigorous Science.' Dilthey is the key figure here rather than Heidegger."[82]

One can see that Husserl has come full circle in his reconsideration of the relation of phenomenology to history. History is no longer seen as the "product" of philosophy, as though the two were related causally or temporally. The best philosophy can do now is to set its present history in relief through the exercise of the phenomenological reduction. That would be the final answer Husserl would offer to the question of the historical purpose that philosophy serves. The philosopher cannot escape, overcome, or get behind his or her history and thereby attain an objective knowledge of essences. Rather, as Carr writes, history is now "elevated" to the eidetic level.[83] In other words, Husserl's attention to the life-world demonstrates that even the sciences have a historical origin: "As history teaches us," he writes, "there was not always in the world a civilization that lived habitually with long-established scientific interests. The life-world was always there for mankind before science, then, just as it continues its manner of being in the epoch of science."[84]

What this "elevation" of history means for phenomenology is the realization of the intrinsic limitation of the *epoché.* Again, one cannot get behind the life-world; indeed, one cannot even effectively put it in brackets. That is because the *epoché* itself is historically determined. Pure givenness is only an illusion made possible by the modern world-picture, which is the determining theoretical vantage point of the modern life-world. One cannot get behind the life-world, because the life-world is always already there; it is what is pregiven or presupposed by even the most advanced of theories. It is a problem for Husserlian phenomenology, because by the life-world the structure of knowing is shown to be always in advance of itself. Husserl voices this realization with the following: "Is not the life-world as such what we know best, what is always taken for granted in all human life, always familiar to us in its typology through experience? Are not all its horizons of the unknown simply horizons of what is just incompletely known, i.e., known in advance in respect of its most general typology?"[85] Husserl's attention to the life-world in this final phase of his thinking inches phenomenology ever closer to theology. For like Heidegger's *Faktum* of the vocabulary of being, the meaning of the life-world is determined by a preunderstanding or a foreknowing. And such a structure of foreknowing, as Derrida has demonstrated, is virtually indistinguishable from what is commonly meant by the term "religion."[86]

Conclusion

A final word is necessary before concluding. Both Derrida and Jean-Luc Marion have been involved in the effort of extending or radicalizing Husserl. According to John D. Caputo and Michael J. Scanlon, from their introduction to the collection of essays in *God, the Gift, and Postmodernism,* the key to understanding the difference between Derrida and Marion is to go back to the basic distinction Husserl made between "intention" and "fulfillment."[87] Intention has to do with meaning and signification; fulfillment has to do with givenness. Derrida's attempt at radicalizing Husserl is brought about by showing the structural emptiness to language, which means there might be intention *without* fulfillment. Examples given include non-Euclidean geometry, the poetry of Mallarme or James Joyce, even religion itself by virtue of its structure of faith. In this way thought is freed from the scientific constraints Husserl meant to impose upon phenomenology, but only because such constraints finally could not account for themselves. Phenomenology, in other words, unravels itself; its undoing was the direct consequence of its own undertaking.[88]

With Marion, the undoing is reversed. It is not that one's intention is unfulfilled or that desire remains unsatisfied, but that there is an overflow of givenness, thus intention cannot contain fulfillment. It is not that thought is now liberated to think the impossible, but that the impossible breaks open the bounds of thought. If Caputo and Scanlon are correct, then the question of the extension of Husserl's thought into the world of religion and/or theology would be the following: "Is the impossibility lodged in a givenness that can never be intended or in an intention that can never be given? Depending on the answer, the transgression of the old Enlightenment, the movement beyond the constraints imposed by modernity's conditions of possibility, the apology for the impossible, will take either of two very different forms which bear the proper names Marion and Derrida."[89]

The question then is raised: Is the phenomenological discovery of the life-world also an opening of philosophy toward faith? By "faith" what is meant here is not the data of belief that is then available to be scientifically explicated by theology. Rather, this faith is more akin to the mitigated skepticism of Hume, which plainly states that in order to make one's way in the world practically, by necessity one must take up certain stances that are not founded on certainty or assurances.[90] Or compare this faith with Jamesian pragmatism, which speaks of truth as a "virtual" reality—a truth that is made true only in action, or a truth still awaiting verification.[91] This is the faith of a fideism that argues nondogmatically not for the exclusivity or priority of a particular faith or dogmatic tradition, but more critically, for a kind of faith that is the very condition of knowledge.[92]

Put in other terms, Merleau-Ponty makes the ironic claim that Husserlian phenomenology begins with the *rejection of science.*[93] As was already stated, by the period of the *Crisis* writings, Husserl would agree when he writes that the dream of philosophy as a science is over. But if this is the "beginning" of phenomenology, it was a beginning that has a whole history behind it, and it is a beginning that transforms its future. No longer restricted only to that which is purely given, it now realizes that the *given itself is a historical construct.* Husserl, wittingly or unwittingly, has followed the same path as laid out by Fink—from description to construction. The reason is that by this time Husserl has been convinced of the illusions inherent to the self-justifying circle of modern philosophy. And as a self-justifying science, the end of phenomenology—which as an ideal, was, and remains, a faithfulness and attentiveness to things only as they appear—is realized to be already predetermined. Again, as Husserl writes: "Here arises the ineradicable illusion of a pure thinking which, unconcerned in its purity about intuition, already has its self-evident truth, even truth about the world—the illusion which makes the sense and the possibility, the 'scope,' of objective science questionable."[94]

Finally, to conclude, return to Ricoeur's intriguing suggestion regarding the mixed origins of phenomenological philosophy; namely, the cogito and God. Husserl's understanding and description of phenomenology has followed a path that ends in crisis. Accordingly, the ideal of a purity of discourse is over. By virtue of the phenomenological discovery of history, the self gives way to the Other and philosophy becomes intermingled with faith.

INTERLUDE 2

ON TRANSLATIONS

Testimony is the disjunction between two impossibilities of bearing witness; it means that language, in order to bear witness, must give way to a non-language in order to show the impossibility of bearing witness. The language of testimony is a language that no longer signifies and that, in not signifying, advances into what is without language, to the point of taking on a different insignificance—that of the complete witness, that of he who by definition cannot bear witness.

—Giorgio Agamben, *Remnants of Auschwitz*

Victim and executioner are equally ignoble; the lesson of the [Nazi death] camps is brotherhood in abjection.

—Rousset, as quoted by Giorgio Agamben, *Remnants of Auschwitz*

FROM BORDERS of politic and currency to language and the question of translation, or better, translatability—of meanings lost and renewed, of certain answers giving way to questions, to a way of questioning, or a method of interrogation that may very well be hostile to its native land. From German to French—a transition that cannot forget the principal events of Western Europe in the heart of the twentieth century. It is a history that tells of a people divided, or a desire for conquest and the need for self-preservation. From a war-deprived land that kills even its own to a place that learned the futility of resistance, meaning that resistance never overcomes once and for all.

From a philosophy and theology that take themselves to their own limits whereby the virtues of a purity of discourse might be proclaimed, to a phenomenology turned existentialism—a methodology with its attention turned toward the quality of life, toward a thinking as a way of life, toward thoughtfulness as a kind of revolt.

From philosophy and theology to ethics as first philosophy. From the desire for purity to the realization of intersubjectivity, and even more, of the stranger within or the self thought of only as a trace constituted by the other, by whom oneself is always and already put in question. The self held hostage. The self proclaimed guilty before ever doing any harm. From Heidegger, who was complicit in the Nazi regime, to Barth, who early and directly spoke against Nazism,[1] but who nevertheless remained protected within the boundaries of a neutral land, to Bonhoeffer, who endeavored beyond the self-imposed strictures of Heidegger and Barth only to suffer from the counterforce of such indiscretion.

From conquest, sacrifice, and devastation, to an occupied territory and a politic restrained. No more illusions of a final solution. No more hope of a stable and secure ground. Instead, thinking has become more like a negotiation, both literally and figuratively. A deal struck with the authorities. A pragmatics with oneself. A realization that even the good has a price and that the ethical exchange between oneself and another is never complete so long as justice is still lacking.

Finally, then, from the abstract to the concrete, even more concrete than Heidegger's facticity and Barth's Christological stratagems. More because the freedom and responsibility that will be spoken of begins in the mundane, even banal, choices that one makes; indeed, that one cannot help but make as the consequence of the burden of freedom. Such a freedom is far from the abstract ideals that serve the sound-bite rhetoric of the politician endeared by the populace. As Sartre's rhetoric pronounces, it is a freedom that condemns, because one has no one to blame but oneself when responsibility centers in on existence here and now. This does not mean that sympathy and understanding are lost to justice, only that they are extended to the common good, to the need for a more sympathetic understanding of the irrationality that stands at the root of even the greatest rationality and most systematic of all regimes.

Think of Elie Wiesel's horrifying account of his boyhood in the concentration camp in which he tells his own account of the death of God:

> Never shall I forget that night, the first night in camp, which has turned my life into one long night, seven times cursed and seven times sealed. Never shall I forget that smoke. Never shall I forget the little faces of children, whose bodies I saw turned into wreaths of smoke beneath a silent blue sky.
>
> Never shall I forget those flames which consumed my faith forever.
>
> Never shall I forget that nocturnal silence which deprived me, for all eternity, of the desire to live. Never shall I forget those moments which murdered my God and my soul and turned my dreams to dust. Never shall I forget these things, even if I am condemned to live as long as God himself. Never.[2]

Nevertheless, Wiesel also tells of the life-giving power of religion, of the celebration of Rosh Hashanah, of the praise given to God for a new year. Of the survival of prayer in spite of God: "'What are You, my God,' I thought angrily, "'compared with this afflicted crowd, proclaiming to You their faith, their anger, their revolt? What does Your greatness mean, Lord of the universe, in the face of this weakness, this decomposition, and this decay? Why do You still trouble their sick minds, their crippled bodies?'"[3] Of the indictment of God by the religious:

> Why, but why should I bless Him? In every fiber I rebelled. Because He had had thousands of children burned in his pits? Because He kept six crematories working night and day, on Sundays and feast days? Because in His great might He had created Auschwitz, Birkenau, Buna, and so many factories of death? How could I say to Him: "Blessed are Thou, Eternal, Master of the Universe, Who chose us from among the races to be tortured day and night, to see our fathers, our mothers, our brothers, end in the crematory? Praised be Thy Holy Name, Thou Who hast chosen us to be butchered on Thine altar?"[4]

And finally, of prayer to God in spite of oneself. Wiesel writes, "And, in spite of myself, a prayer rose in my heart, to that God in whom I no longer believed."[5] The seeming utter absurdity of a religion without God, of a theistic faith in which God has already been put on trial, condemned and executed by the hands of those willing executioners who sought the extermination of the Jews.

Or from the other side of the Nazi horror there is Hannah Arendt's damning indictment of Adolf Eichmann, a man too thoughtless to know and exercise his own freedom. An utterly irresponsible cog in a wheel, who nevertheless was shown to be completely responsible and justly worthy of execution. As Arendt writes in the closing lines of her report on the Eichmann trial:

> Let us assume, for the sake of argument, that it was nothing more than misfortune that made you a willing instrument in the organization of mass murder; there still remains the fact that you have carried out, and therefore actively supported, a policy of mass murder. For politics is not like the nursery; in politics, obedience and support are the same. And just as you supported and carried out a policy of not wanting to share the earth with the Jewish people and the people of a number of other nations—as though you and your superiors had any right to determine who should and should not inhabit the world—we find that no one, that is, no member of the human race, can be expected to want to share the earth with you. This is the reason, and the only reason, you must hang.[6]

And last, from the language of the victim and the language of the accuser, to the language of literature, specifically as interpreted through the words of Kristeva. To Kristeva at least, the question of literature delivers itself over to something even more originary, namely, why speak at all? In other words, what is the use of language in the face of the overbearing powers of horror? Certainly not to instruct or edify, for that is merely the surface effect of certain discourses that exact a cost of understanding and perhaps even a violence against oneself. Neither to resolve or overcome, for such a desire in fact manifests precisely the cycle of sadomasochism from which one is seeking a relief. The question of literature, then, settles in the ongoing endeavor to give voice, to speak a language for which one cannot be blamed, but by which one might finally be held accountable. Such is the power of language; it alone allows the possibility of the truth to come to light—a possibility that only remains as such a possibility, a hope, an expectation, a desire, and even more, a commitment.

4

PHENOMENOLOGY TURNED THEOLOGY

A philosophical hermeneutics consists in an ontological investigation that involves no ontotheological amalgamations.

—Paul Ricoeur, *Oneself as Another*

We are infinitely free in theology: we find all already given, gained, available. It only remains to understand, to say, and to celebrate. So much freedom frightens us, deservedly.

—Jean-Luc Marion, *God without Being*

FROM THIS point forward, this study shifts from the more descriptive analysis of the earlier chapters to a more constructive and critical engagement with contemporary trends in philosophical and theological thought. For the sake of clarity, therefore, it is important to restate the problematic. The argument has been made that the very articulation of the problem of philosophical theology—at least as understood by Barth and Heidegger, and how it has subsequently played itself out in the representative figures of Bonhoeffer and Husserl—is itself problematic. That is to say, the notion that both theology and philosophy accomplish their respective tasks best when left uncontaminated by the other leaves the one cut off from the other and the possibility of dialogue denied. It is in this respect that when left to their own devices, Bonhoeffer and Husserl represent the fragmented and incomplete nature of both theology and philosophy.

For instance, we have seen Bonhoeffer's theological endeavor to incorporate the concerns and concepts of the more strictly philosophical tradition through his advance of a theological ontology. The aims of this theological ontology were to offer a comprehensive critique of both the theological and philosophical tendency toward idealism. Yet, when he sets for himself the task of articulating an ethic that is responsive to a "world come of age," he resorts to a dogmatic faith that is guilty of the same self-certain assurances of which he was rightly critical in his earlier writings. We have also seen how Husserl's early efforts at purifying philosophy according to the scientific ideals of phenomenology as a descriptive science eventually gave way to the "crisis" of history, which in turn, according to Ricoeur's analysis, exposed phenomenology to its mixed origins in the cogito and God. In other words, theology and phenomenology are so complexly inter-mixed that the one cannot fulfill even its self-appointed tasks apart from the other.

Bonhoeffer's resort to dogmatism ran counter to his intention, which was the theological affirmation of the world. And Husserl's discovery of history undermined the very notion of phenomenology as an autonomous, scientific enterprise. This demonstrates not only the shortsightedness of the respective articulations of the problem from Barth and Heidegger, but also the self-contradiction.

This allows for the further question concerning what really is at stake in this study. First, I have suggested that both sides of the philosophical-theological divide are driven by the desire for purity, and correlatively, the fear of contamination. This drive might be seen as a response to the problem of ontotheology in the sense that it exposes an uneasiness with the ontotheological condition of being and thought. Also, it has been suggested that this dynamic in con-temporary thought mirrors the biblical injunction of Holiness. Of course, this injunction is no longer understood literally, nor for that matter does it even manifest itself in a self-conscious manner. Never-theless, the notion that one best preserves truth through directing one's attention inward is not only a residue of the Cartesian turn to-ward the subject characteristic of modern philosophy, but even that Cartesian revolution itself can be read as participating in this broader, more fundamental religious dynamic.[1]

Second, I have already confessed my own commitment to the pos-itive value of dialogue. This commitment is certainly not based on some naïve belief that through dialogue differences are necessarily resolved and unity achieved. On the contrary, dialogue just as often exposes irreconcilable differences. Even so—and perhaps for this very reason—a genuine encounter with legitimate differences allows the opportunity for greater reflection, not only of one's own beliefs and commitments, but also on the values of the other and the greater perspective such an encounter with otherness affords. Therefore, by questioning this understanding of the problem of philosophical theology, and by attempting to show not only its limitations but also its contradiction, there is at least the implicit suggestion that the relation of theology to philosophy must be reenvisioned. It is to this task of reenvisioning the relation of theology and philosophy that this text now turns.

What follows will be an analysis of the work of Paul Ricoeur and Jean-Luc Marion. Both Ricoeur and Marion have distinguished themselves by their work in phenomenology as well as by their interest and explicit engagement with the Western theological tradition. However—and this will be the major theme of the present chapter—while they share common texts and a common tradition, the respective models of philosophical theology they provide are as different as the characteristic theological restraint and freedom that determine their diverging paths. For while Ricoeur proclaims his philosophical hermeneutics innocent of the ontotheological problem, Marion accepts the bounds established by the ontotheological condition. Thus, what will be demonstrated is that while Ricoeur reiterates the philosophical divide, Marion finds pleasure in its transgression.

Ricoeur: Theological Restraint and Philosophical Appropriation

In his early study of the philosophy of Paul Ricoeur, Don Ihde concludes with his own summary of the guiding methodological principle and the chief insight of Ricoeur's hermeneutic phenomenology: *"Whether or not with God, at least with man, in the beginning is the word."*[2] Notice the *epoché* at work concerning the question of God, but also the explicitly religious language being appropriated. Making sense of this apparent tension between Ricoeur's theological restraint together with his philosophical appropriation of religion will be the chief point of interest in the ensuing discussion of Ricoeur.

First, a reminder and an observation that will serve as an introduction to Ricoeur: As the reader no doubt recalls, it was Ricoeur's insight into the complications of Husserl's phenomenological development that more than anything else provided the "hermeneutical key" in interpreting the significance of Husserl's discovery of history. This discovery of history, it was argued, opened philosophy to theology in such a way that the presumed autonomy of phenomenology as a scientific enterprise was shown to rest on a prior origin, an origin

that was precisely *not* given to thought. In Ricoeur's terms, phenomenology eventually leads to the realization of its mixed origins in the
cogito and God. This would seem to suggest Ricoeur's own sympa-
thies with the values inherent to both a philosophical and a theological discourse.

The observation is less straightforward and, at first glance, might
appear unrelated. It is that Ricoeur insisted on his own preference for
the earlier, more transcendentally oriented Husserl as opposed to the
later, more concrete interest of Husserl's in the life-world. In his
study of Husserl, for instance, Ricoeur writes: "The fruitfulness of
the noetico-noematic analysis of the period of the *Ideas* [*Ideas I:
General Introduction to Pure Phenomenology* (1913)]] has probably
been underestimated by the generation of phenomenologists which
went immediately to the writings of the period of the *Crisis*. That
school of phenomenologists has sought inspiration in a theory of
the *Lebenswelt* for a description which is too quickly synthetic for
my liking. . . . In the early stages at least, phenomenology must be
structural."[3] According to Ihde, this preference of Ricoeur's is, most
importantly, symptomatic of his *"dialectic* of methods," which
translates into "a need to elaborate concepts *indirectly* and *dialecti-
cally* rather than directly and univocally;" also, that "this indirect
route via symbol and through interpretation constitutes the opening
to a hermeneutic phenomenology."[4] From this perspective it could
be said that the problem with Husserl's attention to the life-world in
the *Crisis* was that it was a premature concession to the philosophies of existence. This is not to say that the life-world was necessarily an improper theme for phenomenology, only that the route
one takes in deciphering its significance must be consistent with the
subject matter. In other words, that Husserlian phenomenology
finally entered into a crisis is not strictly the result of its discovery of
history and of its concrete concern with the life-world, but that its
mode of interpretation of phenomena had not learned from the bur-
geoning field of hermeneutics. Like the phenomenological discovery
that it must be more than simply an egology if it is to overcome the
self-justifying circle of science, the field of hermeneutics was coming
to the like realization that interpretation involves more than the
explication of authorial intent. As Ricoeur writes in his essay "On
Interpretation," "[T]here is no self-understanding which is not *mediated* by signs, symbols, and texts; in the last resort understanding
coincides with the interpretation given to these mediating terms. In
passing from one to the other, hermeneutics gradually frees itself
from the idealism with which Husserl had tried to identify phenom-

enology."[5] This calls the interpreter back into the world of culture, symbols, and myth, each of which would be taken up in turn by Ricoeur's three-volume "philosophy of will," together with the extension of these explorations in the symbolics of the unconscious: *The Voluntary and the Involuntary* (1950), *Fallible Man* (1960), *The Symbolism of Evil* (1960), and *Freud and Philosophy: An Essay on Interpretation* (1965). Interestingly, however, while often appropriating specifically religious themes in his hermeneutic phenomenology, Ricoeur still insists that his philosophy should be distinguished from theology.

To reiterate, on the one hand there is Ricoeur's interpretation of Husserlian phenomenology that opens philosophy toward theology, together with Ricoeur's own explicit appropriation of specifically religious themes and resources. On the other there is Ricoeur's own hesitancy when it comes to the possibility of a genuine philosophical theology, what I am calling his theological restraint. What is at stake in Ricoeur's refusal of theology? And how does his own approach to these issues inform the understanding of the problem of philosophical theology along with providing resources for the reenvisioning for which the understanding of this problem calls?

"THE SYMBOL GIVES RISE TO THOUGHT"

In the conclusion to *The Symbolism of Evil*, Ricoeur makes the famous claim that "the symbol gives rise to thought."[6] This claim provides the basis for Ricoeur's entire hermeneutical strategy of interpretation. Interestingly, however, this claim is also a consequence of Ricoeur's particular study of the symbolism of evil. As both the basis and the consequence of interpretation, Ricoeur gives articulation to his own version of the hermeneutical circle, namely, "We must understand in order to believe, but we must believe in order to understand." Another important aspect of this claim is that Ricoeur does not give priority to experience, but to symbolic language that gives a particular experience of thought. In other words, experience is not self-evident. Thus, the task of interpretation must traverse the indirect route through language, which is shown to be "symbolic through and through." The experience that is more evident, in fact, is that of pure reflection, which Ricoeur defines as "a direct exercise of rationality."[7] The question, then, that Ricoeur asks is how the latter might be enriched by the former.

This question is not easily resolved. Ricoeur states that it is not resolved by the "juxtaposition" of reflection and confession, as in the case of Plato's notion of the interruption of philosophy by myth; for example, "here discourse ends, there myth begins." The problem with this position is that it fails to understand the true task of philosophy, which, according to Ricoeur's perspective, is that it "must comprehend everything, even religion." Juxtaposition, in other words, implies an inherent limitation to the appropriative task of philosophy, a limitation that Ricoeur is unwilling to accept. Yet, neither is the question resolved through the means of a philosophical translation of a mythological language, as if the meaning were already there, latent from the beginning. Thus, between the two options of interruption and translation, Ricoeur claims, "we are going to seek a third way—a creative interpretation of the meaning, faithful to the impulsion, to the gift of meaning from the symbol, and faithful also to the philosopher's oath to seek understanding."[8]

This third way, according to Ricoeur's analysis, exposes the necessary relation between symbolism and criticism, or later, as his thinking develops, between textuality and hermeneutics. As he writes: "There exists nowhere a symbolic language without hermeneutics; wherever a man dreams or raves, another man arises to give an interpretation; what was already discourse, even if incoherent, is brought into coherent discourse by hermeneutics. In this respect, the hermeneutics of modern men is continuous with the spontaneous interpretations that have never been lacking to symbols."[9] It is in this respect that the symbol gives rise to thought; namely, in that the symbol requires interpretation. Much like in phenomenology, it is through the structure of intentionality that meaning is bestowed upon phenomena. It is precisely this insight that would be extended by Ricoeur in his study of Freud and in his later interest in the narrative structure of meaning; namely, that it is interpretation that gives meaning, or even more forcefully, that without interpretation there would be no meaning.

As Ricoeur himself tells it, there is a clear evolution to the development of his thinking on this matter, which progresses through three interpretative strategies: (1) interpretation mediated by signs, (2) interpretation mediated by symbols, and (3) interpretation mediated by texts. The first grounds Ricoeur in the basic awareness of language as "the primary condition of all human experience."[10] The second extends this awareness by the understanding that symbols carry at least a double meaning; for example, "language itself is from the outset and for the most part distorted: it means something other than what it says, it has a double meaning, it is equivocal."[11] The necessary consequence of this symbolic equivocation is the conflict of interpretations. As one seeks to resolve or to make sense of this conflict, interpretation moves beyond the meaning derived from symbols alone, to the broader contextual reality of the intrasystematic unity of symbols embedded within texts. Thus, the final evolution in Ricoeur's thought begins with his attentiveness to the importance of an intratextual interpretation. This intratextual interpretation is what Ricoeur calls the reconstruction of the internal sense of a given text. However, interpretation does not end with this act of reconstruction, because the life of a text extends beyond its words on a page. Interpretation, therefore, must not only be intratextual, but also extratextual, in the sense that through the act of interpretation the work of the text is actually restored.[12]

What unites these evolving and expanding interests of Ricoeur's is his consistent understanding of the "appropriative function" of hermeneutics. To return to the concluding chapter of *The Symbolism of Evil*, Ricoeur writes: "What is peculiar to the modern hermeneutics is that it remains in the line of critical thought. But its critical function does not turn it away from its appropriative function; I should say, rather, that it makes it more authentic and more perfect."[13] And from the essay "On Interpretation," the need for this hermeneutical task of appropriation is in response to the ontological condition of language, which is "that there is always a *Being-demanding-to be said* (*un etre-a-dire*) which precedes our actual saying."[14] It is in this sense that the thinking that has arisen from the symbol in turn gives life back to the symbol. The circle of hermeneutics is ongoing.

According to Gerald Bruns, in his work *Hermeneutics: Ancient and Modern*,[15] this endeavor of appropriation is Ricoeur's way of writing himself into the ancient and ongoing quarrel between the philosopher and the poet. In the tradition of Aristotle and Hegel, and in distinction from Heidegger, Ricoeur tries to rein in the chaos of a poetic discourse, or at least to establish the interpretation of such a discourse on proper philosophical grounds. These grounds are not established in terms of the self-transparency of the ego, nor in terms of authorial intent, for this would confuse the difference between first-order and second-order reference. Ricoeur is clear that the meaning of philosophy does not rest in the language of signs, symbols, and texts. If that were the case, then what need would there be for interpretation? On the contrary, not "concealed behind the text," meaning happens in the act of interpretation, which unfolds *"in front of* the text."[16] The meaning is thought of in terms of a *"proposed* world," which then becomes actualized "to the extent that we act on what the text proposes." According to Bruns, this kind of hermeneutical appropriation could be traced back "through Luther and Augustine

to the earliest beginnings of scriptural hermeneutics, where the idea
is to interpret a text by understanding oneself and one's historical
situation in its light."[17] This distinctly theological tradition that
stands in the background of Ricoeur's understanding of hermeneutics adds complications to his claim that his philosophy can be kept
separate from his theological interests and commitments.[18] However,
before turning to that discussion, a fuller account of his hermeneutical appropriation of religion is in order.

EXEGESIS GIVES RISE TO HERMENEUTICS

It has already been shown that Ricoeur's understanding of hermeneutic phenomenology clearly allows for—indeed, it might even be said
that it only arises from—a philosophical appropriation of religion.
From this perspective *The Symbolism of Evil*, which is a critical
engagement with traditionally religious resources and theological
argumentation, is hardly the exception but more likely the rule for
Ricoeur's philosophy, in the sense that it manifests the guiding
methodological framework by which Ricoeur engages in the task of
interpretation. Further evidence for this is from the 1998 work published by Ricoeur jointly with André LaCocque, entitled *Thinking
Biblically*. In this work, the two authors unite their philosophical
and exegetical interests in the form of a dialogue. At the same time,
however, they admit that the possibility of such a dialogue is not
immediately evident and thus is in need of some justification. "At
first glance," they write, "our approaches may appear different to the
point of standing in opposition to each other." And further, "Does
not the one seek to be scholarly, even scientific, and the other to be
philosophic? Is not the one turned toward what lies behind the text,
toward its archaeology, while the other looks toward what comes
afterward, toward its teleology . . . ?"[19] Thus, as they justify and explain
their shared endeavor, they also provide an interesting account of
the relation between hermeneutics and exegesis, and more broadly,
between philosophy and theology.

As for the justification, Ricoeur and LaCocque speak of the "double
movement" characteristic of both of their works. For instance, the
exegete is not solely interested in the recovery of the historical context of a given text, but also must attend to "the role of reading in the
elaboration of the meaning of a text." The exegete's glance is both
backward-looking and forward-looking simultaneously, both recon-
structive and restorative. Similarly with the philosopher, the task is not

complete through the accomplishment of a rational appropriation, for there must also be an attentiveness to the "specificity of the texts found within the biblical corpus," and to the "originality of the Hebrew, then the Christian way of thinking." Together, both the exegete and the philosopher express a respect for "the irreducible plurivocity of the text," by their commitment to a "plurality of readings."[20] No single reading can express the full complexity of a given text. This is in large part due to the fact that with each new reading the text takes on a new life that then engenders further commentary and reflection. A corollary of this is that just as no single reading is complete, neither is any single reader. Thus, the justification for dialogue.

As for the explanation, the work is basically configured in terms of a reading and a response, as each chapter begins with an exegesis of a particular biblical passage and follows with a philosophical reflection on the significance of the reading. Thus, the dialogue is structured in such a way that LaCocque's exegetical reading precedes and serves as the basis from which Ricoeur's philosophical reflections follow; or in terms of Ricoeur's broader interpretative strategy, it might be said that *exegesis gives rise to hermeneutics.*

Concerning our broader interest regarding the relation between philosophy and theology, the two authors make a most intriguing point in their concluding remarks to the preface. They write:

> The philosopher most disposed to a dialogue with an exegete is undoubtedly one who more readily reads works of exegesis than theological treatises. Theology, in fact, is a very complex and highly speculative form of discourse, eminently respectable in its place. But it is a mixed or composite form of discourse where philosophical speculation is already inextricable intermingled with what deserves to be called "biblical thought," even when it does not assume the specific form of Wisdom, but also that of narrative, law, prophecy, or the hymn. Our working hypothesis here is that there are modes of thought other than those based on Greek, Cartesian, Kantian, Hegelian, etc. philosophy.[21]

There are several reasons for the importance of this statement by LaCocque and Ricoeur. Most obviously, it is important because, like the discussion of Barth and Heidegger from chapter 1, it provides a working definition of philosophy and theology or, more precisely, an argument concerning why the two should not be confused or intermingled. Here, at least, theology is characterized as a "highly speculative form of discourse," presumably in contrast to philosophy, which proceeds by and relies on arguments alone. This contrast is spelled out in greater detail in Ricoeur's *Oneself as Another*, where he writes:

> The ten studies that make up this work assume the bracketing, conscious and resolute, of the convictions that bind me to biblical faith. . . . I think I have presented to my readers *arguments alone*, which do not assume any commitment from the reader to reject, accept, or suspend anything with regard to biblical faith. It will be observed that this asceticism of the argument, which marks, I believe, all my philosophical work, leads to a type of philosophy from which the actual mention of God is absent and in which the question of God, as a philosophical question, itself remains in a suspension that could be called agnostic . . . A philosophical hermeneutics consists in an ontological investigation that involves no ontotheological amalgamations. [italics mine][22]

The implied argument concerning why theology must not be confused with either philosophy or "biblical thought" reveals what appears to be an agreement by Ricoeur with the original analysis of the problem of philosophical theology as provided by Heidegger. In fact, the preceding quotes could be read as restatements of the claim made by Heidegger that began this study, namely, "We understand each other best when each speaks in his own language."[23] To theology belongs an "eminently respectable" place. Where that is and what it might look like, LaCocque and Ricoeur do not say. What they do suggest, however, is that this place must not be confused with the place of philosophy, nor even with the place of "biblical thought." To each belong their own distinct realms.

Interestingly, however—and this is where Ricoeur seems at least to be attempting to move beyond Heidegger—is that it is not only philosophy that deserves the designation of genuine thought, but also the biblical tradition, which gives rise to its own specific "mode of thought." In this respect, the task of thought is neither to strip philosophy from the Bible, nor the Bible from philosophy,[24] but to show how "the event of this encounter, once it took place, has become the constitutive destiny of our culture. If it is neither to be deplored nor deconstructed, this destiny indicates a task against which our reflections must measure themselves with total honesty and total responsibility."[25]

In this way, the coming together of Greek philosophy with the biblical tradition constitutes the mixed origins of Western culture, and these mixed origins are thought to be "neither a misfortune that ought to be deplored nor a perversion that ought to be eradicated."[26] This stands in marked contrast with Heidegger, who, as John Caputo has argued in his work *Demythologizing Heidegger,* is guilty of engaging in the myth of pure origin and "monogenesis." Heidegger essentializes the myth of being and by so doing thinks he has purified philosophy from faith, when in fact he has merely put one myth in the place of another. "The issue, then," Caputo writes: "is not divided between mythologizing and demythologizing—as if these always meant the same thing—but between dangerous myths and salutary myths; between privileging, elitist, and hierarchizing myths and myths that promote justice and multiplicity; between exclusionary and oppressive myths and liberating, empowering myths."[27]

With Caputo's critique of Heidegger in mind, it could be said of Ricoeur that he and LaCocque's notion of "biblical thinking" is a corrective to Heidegger's privileging of the myth of being. By highlighting the living tradition of thought that belongs specifically to the biblical tradition, they demonstrate the open-ended nature of biblical thought. The resources might differ between biblical thought and that of the Western philosophical tradition, but the nature of this difference is not, as Heidegger supposed, that the one is open-ended while the other is self-enclosed, and thus, that the one is genuinely thoughtful while the other is merely scientific. On the contrary, according to Ricoeur's analysis, any interpretation—whether philosophical, theological, or biblical—is necessarily open-ended by virtue of its prospective quality.

To repeat Bruns's analysis, Ricoeur's hermeneutical theory makes sense only in light of a concrete, embodied interpretation. No text is complete apart from the dual task of interpretation, which is both the *reconstruction* of the text's meaning and the *restoration* of the text's work. The text's work does not end with the words on a page; this is only its beginning, in the sense that they give rise to the ongoing act of interpretation. In other words, reading gives life to a text as each new interpretation expands the body of a text. The biblical texts therefore give rise to a peculiar kind of thinking that is no less thoughtful, though still different from that of Western philosophy.

RELIGION GIVES RISE TO ORTHODOXY

Nevertheless, this advance of Ricoeur's beyond Heidegger also exposes a fundamental contradiction in his thought, for if the legacy of Western culture is the inextricable intermingling of philosophy with the biblical tradition, what does this say of the prospect of Ricoeur's notion of "philosophical agnosticism," or the theological restraint that characterizes his work as a whole? To go back even further in the analysis, recall Husserl's rather late realization of the inherent limitation of the *epoché.* The bracketing off of the natural attitude can only extend so far. In other words, the philosopher cannot achieve the thoroughgoing asceticism to which Ricoeur purportedly aspires. In this way philosophy, biblical thought, or an amalgamation of the two are no less a "mixed and composite form of discourse" than that of theology. Therefore, what is it that truly separates the one from the other, except that theology might be more explicit about its point of origin and more honest about its speculative nature? Even more, when considering Bruns's suggestion that the structure of Ricoeur's hermeneutical appropriation has its basis in a theological tradition, it would seem that what is at stake is not a choice between philosophy and theology, but the kind of philosophical theology that will be employed. By virtue of the "constitutive destiny of our culture," in other words, philosophy is necessarily intermingled with faith, and this intermingling of philosophy and faith becomes the very condition of thought itself—a condition that is simultaneously both affirmed and resisted in Ricoeur's own work.

A final word then is offered on Ricoeur. Instead of accepting the claim that his thinking stands in contradistinction from theology, I suggest a reading of Ricoeur as one model for a kind of philosophical theology. This raises the question regarding what kind of model this might be. Consider the model of orthodoxy, in which orthodoxy is not defined strictly in terms of "right belief," but more complexly, according to the praxis upon which such belief is grounded. In this way, the development of orthodoxy—at least in the Christian tradition, which has been our primary orientation up to this point—is clearly marked by a historical and political context and clearly serves a political purpose. This understanding of orthodoxy parallels Ricoeur's interest in narrative theory, wherein texts are read according to the concrete models of praxis they both reflect and propose. Furthermore, it is the will "to comprehend everything—even religion," that stands as the most prominent feature that identifies Ricoeur's work with that of orthodoxy. Also, as has been demonstrated, comprehension is not the end, but serves the ongoing cycle of interpretation as biblical faith finally gives way to knowledge. Therefore, to further extend Ricoeur's interpretative strategy, the *religious life gives rise to orthodoxy,* just as orthodoxy in turn creates a space that one might meaningfully inhabit. Ricoeur's thinking serves the life of religion. This service to religion, however, begins in the religious life already begun by the signs, symbols, and texts that stand as the very inspiration and chief resource for Ricoeur's thought.

A point of comparison might prove illustrative. Recall the discussion of Bonhoeffer's ethics, in which it was argued that Bonhoeffer's intention of articulating a Christian ethic responsive to a "world come of age" fell short by its recourse to a theological dogmatism. Likewise with Ricoeur, his conscious bracketing of faith fails to achieve the thoroughgoing philosophical agnosticism it requires of itself. This failure is not to be attributed to a lack of resolution on the part of Ricoeur. On the contrary, it is this very resolution that is here being argued against. For when it comes to the attempt at moving beyond the problem of philosophical theology, Ricoeur's chief value is that he shows the integrity of different traditions of thought, an integrity that is not based in the misdirected desire for purity, but is the consequence of a hermeneutical understanding. That is to say, by appreciating the necessity of interpretation, all thought is realized to be open-ended and any interpretation gives new resources to be thought. Furthermore, it is Ricoeur who demonstrates that any given text—indeed, any tradition to speak of—is an indebted, duplicitous, and equivocal one, with a history at least as complex and varied as that of the mixed origins of Western civilization itself.

What is needed for the reenvisioning of the problem of philosophical theology is not only Ricoeur's understanding of the linguistic structure of experience, but also a genuine appreciation and understanding of the determining factor of experience in setting the bounds of possibility for a meaningful interpretation. Insofar as Ricoeur is correct that the symbol gives rise to thought, the philosopher is no more autonomous than the theologian, because both speak out of a particular tradition, from a particular perspective, and to a particular point of reference. And if such is the case, truth is better served by the acknowledgment of one's convictions, as opposed to the pretense of *"arguments alone,"* which if anything is to be learned from hermeneutics, it is precisely that arguments never stand alone, but are always already encircled.

It is with this in mind that the study now turns to the discussion of Marion and then to the concluding chapter on Levinas, in which the aim is not that of overcoming, for overcoming inevitably comes at the cost of an-other, but with thinking, speaking, and acting otherwise—in short, with a philosophical theology that turns on the question of the Other.

Marion: Freedom and Apophaticism

There is a paradox that stands at the center of the ensuing discussion of the French phenomenologist and sometimes theologian Jean-Luc Marion, especially when set in relation to Ricoeur; namely, Marion discovers the freedom of theology, not as the exercise of autonomy, but by its opposite, which in Marion's case as a Roman Catholic theologian is through the submission to authority. This freedom through submission can be discerned in both Marion's phenomeno-logical and theological works. As Thomas Carlson, a frequent trans-lator and commentator on Marion, points out, the difference is that the former deals with pure possibility, while the latter deals in con-crete actualities.[28] Thus, while there are clear structural similarities to both Marion's phenomenology and theology, as Marion insists, the two must not be confused: "[T]he border passes between revelation as possibility and revelation as historicity. There could be no danger of confusion between these domains."[29] So given, it is in the princi-pally theological works that the paradox is set in its clearest relief. That is because by delimiting theology by the actual, in distinction from the possible, Marion has liberated theology from the paradoxi-cal restrictures of pure possibility.

In this way, Marion can be read as a radicalization of Husserl much in the same way that Husserl sought to radicalize Descartes. That is to say, Marion picks up where Husserl left off, and by so doing, phenomenology effects its own transformation as it passes beyond itself through its articulation of a distinctly theological voice. That phenomenology passes beyond itself through the exercise of theolog-ical freedom, however, is not the same as making the argument that phenomenology in fact is a kind of cryptotheology.

As a point of illustration, consider the differences between Husserl and Ricoeur. With Husserl the ideal of phenomenology as a rigorous science was finally undone, which resulted both in a crisis in the understanding of the proper philosophical grounds for phenomenol-ogy and in *crisis* becoming the proper theme for a phenomenological philosophy. The argument was made in chapter 3 that in the final phase of Husserl's thought, he had come to recognize the fundamental limitations of the *epoché,* and that this philosophical recognition of limits in turn parallels the theological claim that knowledge follows the order of faith. In this way philosophy and theology are no longer thought of in terms of mutual exclusivity, as though the one must purify itself from the other, but in terms of mutual dependency, in which truth turns on the question of the Other. Philosophy is opened up to the otherness of a theological discourse.

With Ricoeur, on the other hand, the appropriative task of philosophy remains unrestricted. Therefore, while he proclaims sympathy for the internal integrity and proper place of theology—much in the spirit of Heidegger's delegation of proper philosophical and theological tasks—and while he also goes beyond Heidegger by insisting on the open-ended nature of any and all interpretative endeavors, the fact that his understanding of hermeneutics does not adequately acknowledge its theological point of origin raises questions concerning the value and even trustworthiness of his purported philosophical agnosticism. The difference, then, is that while Husserl stops short of theology by the honesty and reserve with which he approaches the life-world as a theme for phenomenology, Ricoeur's philosophy is shown to be theologically predetermined, as it sets as the philosophical norm a particularly theological reading of interpretation.

To return to Marion, his theology parallels his phenomenology, which is made possible by Husserl's late realization of the incapacity of phenomenology to realize its dream of philosophy as a rigorous science. Thus, to say that the one passes beyond itself by passing into the other is still not to confuse the two. It is instead the admission of need by the one for the other, but only and precisely as an other.

OVERCOMING ONTOTHEOLOGY

David Tracy was the first to reflect on the central paradox in Marion's theology in his foreword to the English translation of Marion's *God without Being*.[30] Tracy views Marion's theology in terms of basic strategies that have played themselves out in response to the crisis of modernity. The two most basic of these theological strategies have been those that urge correlation between reason and faith (e.g., Tillich, Bultmann) and those that reject correlation in lieu of the primacy and necessary foundation of revelation (e.g., Barth, Bonhoeffer). The reader should recognize the terms of the debate as established by Barth early in the twentieth century. Recall that it was Barth who presented his revelation-centered theology as an alternative to the theology-turned-anthropology of Schleiermacher and his successors in liberal Protestant thought. It is for this reason that Tracy calls Barth Marion's "natural ally in Protestant theology." Like Barth, Marion's theology begins as a critique of the overconfidence of human reason. While capable of thinking being, reason is fundamentally incapable of disclosing God. Such disclosure is only a consequence of the gift of God. Thus, according to Tracy, "Marion has clearly forged a new and brilliant postmodern version of the great alternative for theology: a revelation-centered, noncorrelational, postmetaphysical theology. . . . Marion has developed a rigorous and coherent theological strategy focused on the reality of God's revelation as pure gift, indeed as excess."[31]

While agreeing with Tracy's basic assessment that Marion's theology is best understood from the perspective of a theology of revelation,[32] it should also be noted how Marion's theology provides a corrective to the shortcomings of Barth—most notably, Barth's overvaunted trust in the theological subject. Remember that Barth's attempt at a theological overcoming of modernity rested primarily in his reversal of priority. Thus, in contrast to Schleiermacher, Barth begins not from the standpoint of human experience and human knowledge, but from that of revelation. The shortcoming of this position was that it merely replaces one confidence with another, with the effect of theological dogmatism replacing that of philosophical arrogance. Reversal is only one step in the ongoing process of overcoming. Marion's position is similar to that of Barth insofar as he too begins from the place of revelation. In distinction from Barth, however, Marion's critical theology does not then serve as a foundation from which to build the edifice of a Church dogmatics; on the contrary, Marion's theology realizes itself only in the pragmatics of the religious life. Thus, the circle of knowledge is undone by its giving way to an order of desire that may be either confirmed or disconfirmed only by the lived faith of its practitioners. This theology, therefore, is not a matter of speaking correctly of God, but begins from the experience of God, which can never be spoken of properly. It is not, finally, a matter of knowledge, whether initiated by God or humanity, but proceeds wholly without knowledge and thus is infinitely free.

As a theology of revelation, Marion's *God without Being* is also a response to Heidegger's philosophical delimitation of theology. Recall Heidegger's statement that if he were to write a Christian theology, the word "being" would not appear. What Marion demonstrates, however, as he seemingly follows Heidegger's prescription for theology, is that theology's refusal of "being" does not represent its restriction as merely a self-certain discourse, but that theology cancels out or evacuates being by abandoning it to itself, and thus moves beyond philosophy by virtue of the gift of God's self-disclosure. That is to say, theology delimits the horizon of being, stripping being of its absolute and singular status by putting it in relation to the thinking of God, which stands beyond and before ontology. In relation to such talk of God, ontology is exposed as an idol, or a false attachment that places restrictions on the absolute and unlimited nature of God. As Carlson articulates it: "If onto-theology constitutes an idolatry insofar as it subjects the appearance of God to the limits of conceptual thinking, the Heideggerian critique of onto-theology would itself, for Marion, harbor its own idolatry, insofar as it subjects the appearance of God, beyond onto-theology, to its own conditions: the unquestioned priority of Being and, correlatively, the primacy of that being for whom alone Being is an issue—*Dasein*."[33]

As one thinks the God beyond idolatry, there comes the realization that one has already been called into thought by that which stands beyond ontology, beyond ontotheology, even beyond ontological difference itself, which is the God who is absolutely unthinkable.[34] In other words, the thought of God radically undermines and disrupts thinking altogether, which itself is a product of ontology, such that even the theological thinking that had this effect is disestablished and rendered insufficient to the infinite overflow of the givenness of God. Theologically speaking, Heidegger's prioritization of being is seen by Marion as a form of idolatry, and it fails to overcome the elevation of the subject and its attendant dualism, which has been characteristic of modern philosophy from Descartes to the present. Even from a phenomenological perspective, Heidegger fails to accomplish what he set out for himself. As Marion writes in *Reduction and Givenness:* "It remains that Heidegger no doubt did not accomplish what he nevertheless attempted, more than anyone else, to attain through and for phenomenology. This is so, first, because, whatever the case may be, *Dasein* still remains haunted by the I; next it is so because the 'phenomenon of Being,' even in the already attenuated form of the ontological difference, never shows itself; and finally it is so because the 'phenomenology of the unapparent' henceforth called for never gets beyond either its programmatic status or its contradictory formulation."[35] In response, Marion proposes a theology that is more critical and more radically iconoclastic, and a phenomenology that is more purely passive by handing itself over to the givenness of phenomena. As such, theology and phenomenology share both a common starting point (e.g., the critique of the limitations of metaphysics) and a common aim (e.g., the realization of freedom). Again, in Carlson's words: "Just as Marion's theology would pass beyond metaphysics by freeing God's self-revelation in distance from every limiting concept that would seek to render that God present under the idolatrous conditions of thought, so his phenomenology would pass beyond metaphysics by freeing the phenomenon's self-showing from any a priori conditions, whether those of the thinking subject or those of a metaphysical God."[36]

As was previously stated, at the heart of Marion's theology lies the paradox of freedom. One way Marion speaks of this paradox is through his acknowledgment of the fundamental hypocrisy of theology. To say that theology is fundamentally hypocritical is not a criticism, but simply an appraisal of the double bind in which the theologian finds him/herself. In the introduction to *God without Being,* Marion writes:

> Theology renders its author hypocritical in at least two ways. Hypo-critical, in the common sense: in pretending to speak of holy things . . . he cannot but find himself, to the point of vertigo, unworthy, impure—in a word, vile. This experience, however, is so necessary that its benefi-ciary knows better than anyone both his own unworthiness and the meaning of that weakness . . . ; he deceives himself less than anyone; in fact, here there is no hypocrisy at all: the author knows more than the accuser. He remains hypocritical in another, more paradoxical sense: if authenticity . . . consists in speaking of oneself, and in saying only that for which one can answer, no one, in a theological discourse, can, or should, pretend to it. For theology consists precisely in saying that for which only another can answer, the Other above all, the Christ who himself does not speak in his own name, but in the name of his Father.[37]

First, then, for Marion is a hypocrisy that is in fact the most authentic laying bare of oneself. The theologian thinks and speaks as if he knew the Word of God, yet by precisely what he does know, he knows more than others the inadequacy of such knowledge. According to what has been said concerning Barth, it is this latter point that seems forgotten in his later work, and it is why a dogmatic theology, perhaps by its very nature, is shortsighted or misleading, if not altogether contradictory. This explains Marion's primary—by which I mean his first—theological task; namely, the identification of various forms of idolatry, which includes even the deconstruction of the death of God theologies, undoubtedly the most iconoclastic of all the most recent theological movements.[38]

Another way Marion expresses this paradox is through his claim that pleasure is the only justification for the writing of theology.[39] As he writes in the opening to *God without Being,* "One must admit that theology, of all writing, certainly causes the greatest pleasure." And he continues, "to try one's hand at theology requires no other justification than the extreme pleasure of writing."[40] This is an important point, because without it the reader might confuse the desideratum of theology with that of silencing thought. One might be led to this conclusion because Marion's theology is so thoroughly self-conscious of the double bind of hypocrisy that its words might double back on themselves with the effect of the devaluation of language altogether. It is true that language fails to capture God, and to the extent that a theological language is intended for this purpose, it must finally fall silent by its very own incapacity. According to Marion, however, this is neither the intent nor the final consequence of theology. On the contrary, if Marion is correct then whatever silence might momentarily be effected through the exercise of theological iconoclasm only feeds into the proper language of theology, which is one of extreme pleasure and infinite freedom. The theologian writes for the sake of writing and speaks for the sake of speaking. If this sounds overly indulgent, remember where this theology begins; that is, from the point of revelation, which in the Christian context, is Christ, the Word incarnate. Just as it was God who spoke creation into being, so too might humans speak of the "God without being," for it is not the being of God that gives words to speak, but the Word of God that brings creation into being. It is God's Word that is given priority, and this moves theology beyond the modern preoccupation with onto-theology toward a genuine theology of language. The theologian now, perhaps for the first time since faith was confused with knowledge, is free to speak, and by so doing, to participate in the life-giving power of language.

BEYOND "NEGATIVE THEOLOGY"

Not only a postmodern theology of revelation, Marion's theology also reaches back to premodern texts, most especially those from the apophatic tradition. It is here that the theologian is given to a certain kind of speech, which is the naming of God. However, this is an iconic naming, as opposed to an idolatrous one. With the icon the name is not fixed according to the order of knowledge, rather the icon itself provokes a desire for the infinite in the sense that it traces itself beyond itself, from the visible to the visible unto infinity. As Marion writes: "The icon does not result from a vision but provokes one. . . . The icon summons the gaze to surpass itself by never freezing on a visible, since the visible only presents itself here in view of the invisible. The gaze can never rest or settle if it looks at an icon; it always must rebound upon the visible, in order to go back in it up the infinite stream of the invisible. In this sense, the icon makes visible only by giving rise to the infinite gaze."[41] This iconic naming of God, therefore, is in fact no naming at all, nor even its opposite, which would be a de-naming. Rather it is an act of *de-nominating*, as one name for God gives way to another. This is a critical "negative theology" that is constantly alert to the human tendency toward idolatry. But to be alert is the best one can do, humanly speaking, for divine disclosure rests strictly with God. This latter point is key to understanding Marion's strong critique of Derrida's treatment of "negative theology."

First, one must examine Derrida's presentation of "negative theology" from his 1980 essay, "How to Avoid Speaking: Denials." In this essay, Derrida distinguishes between "negative theology" and his own ongoing project of deconstruction. The reason for this distinction, Derrida tells the reader, is because the two have so often been compared that some have wondered whether there is indeed any real difference between the one and the other. To this question Derrida responds rather bluntly, "No, what I write is not 'negative theology.'"[42] The most important distinction, it seems, is Derrida's charge that "negative theology" is actually driven by a hyperessentialism. In Derrida's words, "'negative theology' seems to reserve, beyond all positive predication, beyond all negation, even beyond Being, some hyperessentiality, a being beyond Being." This hyperessentialism does not come in the form of any positive knowledge; on the contrary, "negative theology" "knows unknowing itself in its truth." As such, it relies upon a "pure intuition" that "remains inaccessible to speech"[43]—not only inaccessible, but also unaccountable. Negative theologies begin and end with the name of God, all the while confessing ignorance. Structured like a prayer, it also contains the hidden promise of God's presence. By contrast, deconstruction is structured according to the *khora*, which is a strange kind of structure, because the *khora* is that "place" where referentiality of any sort is held suspect. As Derrida writes of it: "Radically nonhuman and atheological, one cannot even say that it gives place or that there is the *khora*. . . . *Khora* is not even that, the *es* or *id* of giving, before all subjectivity. . . . The impossibility of speaking of it and of giving it a proper name, far from reducing it to silence, yet dictates an obligation, by its very impossibility: *it is necessary* to speak of it and there is a rule for that."[44] Therefore, Derrida opposes the *khoric* structure of an impossible necessity with the apophatic structure of an unknown presence. The former admits an ignorance it would wish to, but that cannot be, overcome. The latter hides its true intention of saving the name of God. With respect to the "place" of the *khora*, in other words, "negative theology" comes too late to the scene. As Derrida writes: "At the moment when the question 'how to avoid speaking?' is raised and articulates itself in all its modalities—whether in rhetorical or logical forms of saying, or in the simple act of speaking—it is already, so to speak, *too late*. There is no longer any question of not speaking. Even if one speaks and says nothing, even if an apophatic discourse deprives itself of meaning or of an object, it takes place. That which committed or rendered it possible *has taken place*."[45] Speaking of the *khora*, Derrida tells of a "language before language, a past that was never present and yet remains unforgettable."[46]

As Mark C. Taylor poses this Derridian alternative, the difference between deconstruction and (negative) theology is that deconstruction harbors an end that is without end: "The endless approach of the end of theology harbors an end that is not merely an end of *theology* but is another end . . . a different end that is not the end of difference. This alternative end, which eludes the closed economy of ontotheology, implies the irreducible opening of the a/theological imagination. The task of thinking at the end of theology is to think beyond the end of theology by thinking the 'beyond' of an end that is not theological."[47] Accepting this alternative end without end as the task of thought requires a kind of thinking that thinks otherwise than by the totalizing, comprehensive gaze of ontotheology. That is because, as Taylor writes: "ontotheology leaves nothing unthought," while "the task of thinking at the end of theology is to think nothing otherwise than by not thinking. The nothing remains after (the) all has been thought marks the end of theology by inscribing an end that does not belong to theology. This end implies the closure of theology, which at the same time is the opening of a previously unimaginable a/theology."[48]

Marion responds to this treatment of "negative theology" in an essay entitled, "In the Name: How to Avoid Speaking of 'Negative Theology,'" which was first delivered at Villanova University at the "Religion and Postmodernism Conference," at which both Marion and Derrida were present. Marion's response comes in several different guises. Speaking as both logician and as historical exegete, Marion reminds the audience, and presumably Derrida as well, that the terms "negative theology" and "metaphysics of presence" should be read more as problems to be overcome than as descriptive concepts to be trusted. He explains:

> For neither the Alexandrian nor Cappadocian Fathers, nor Irenaeus nor Augustine, nor Bernard, Bonaventure, nor Thomas Aquinas—all of whom resort to negations when naming God and build a theory of this apophasis—none of them use the formula "negative theology." As a result, it can reasonably be supposed that this formula is nothing but modern. Consequently, we will from now on no longer consider the phrases "metaphysics of presence" and "negative theology," if by chance we have had to use them, as anything but conceptual imprecisions to be overcome or as questions awaiting answers—never as secure bases.[49]

Next, Marion takes on the role of the psychoanalyst, asking why, if nowhere present in the primary texts themselves, would Derrida take up "negative theology" as a theme to distinguish from deconstruction. Marion's answer is that it is because "negative theology" presents deconstruction with its first and foremost rival. Thus, "for deconstruction, what is at issue in 'negative theology' is not first of all 'negative theology,' but deconstruction itself, its originality and its final pre-eminence."[50] This, according to Marion, explains the need of deconstruction to deconstruct the claims of "negative theology," even to the point of employing a misnomer that purportedly distinguishes the ancient rival from what is new to the scene. This deconstruction of "negative theology," in other words, is in fact a form of self-defense, which in archetypal fashion replays the Oedipal complex with its own tragic consequences.

It is in the explication of these consequences that Marion takes on his third and most urgent role, that of the Christian theologian. The issue at hand is whether what Derrida improperly refers to as "negative theology" remains a viable option. Having already questioned both the accuracy and justification of Derrida's account, Marion next approaches his theme from a less defensive position, which gives him the needed space to develop a more proper understanding of Christian theology on its own terms rather than those prescribed by the critic. "In short," Marion asks, "can Christian theology as a theology evoked by Revelation remove itself in principle, if not in actual accomplishment, from the 'metaphysics of presence'—or is it, in the final analysis, reducible to this metaphysics? Which amounts to asking: Is Christian theology subject to deconstruction, or not?"[51]

Key to Marion's answer to this all-important question is that apophasis is a part of a larger strategy "that includes not two but three elements. . . . The game is therefore not played out between two terms, affirmation and negation, but between three, different from and irreducible to each other." It is for this reason that the term "negative theology" is a problem to be overcome, for "negative theology" is not strictly negative, but neither is it fundamentally affirmative. Such predicative terms simply do not apply. It is not a matter of saying or un-saying, or naming or un-naming. In Marion's words, "It is solely a matter of de-nominating." Such de-nomination does not fix the divine essence, because it "does not name him properly or essentially, but . . . marks his absence, anonymity, and withdrawal. . . . In this sense, praise in mystical theology would in the case of divine proper names only reproduce an aporia that is already unavoidable in the proper names of the finite world." Furthermore, by virtue of the "purely pragmatic" nature of theological discourse, "it is no longer a matter of naming or attributing something to something, but of aiming in the direction of . . . , of relating to . . . , of comporting oneself towards . . . , of reckoning with . . . —in short, of dealing with . . ."[52]

Notice here that Marion's description of Christian theology is working on two fronts simultaneously. Not only is he offering a corrective to what he considers to be Derrida's misreading, but he is also offering a challenge to those who would wish for theology a self-confidence of which it is not capable. Consider, for instance, John Milbank's critique of Marion, in which he finally accuses Marion of a radical indeterminacy that tempers the distinctiveness, clarity, and full weight of the Christian message; or, as Marion himself voices this critique: "goodness remains undetermined and, in any case, without essential impact."[53] For Marion, however, this is how it should be when one considers Christian theology as purely pragmatic discourse. That is because "it is no longer a matter of saying something about something, but of a pragmatics of speech, more subtle, risky, and complex. . . . It is no doubt no longer a matter of saying but of hearing, since according to the conventional etymology that Dionysius takes from Plato, bountiful beauty bids."[54]

Therefore, what Marion offers is a wariness of both a heightened skepticism and a theological arrogance. Neither gives proper articulation to what Marion considers to be a whole tradition of a *theology of absence.*[55] In this way, Derrida's critique of "negative theology"—that it is an effort to *save the name* of God—is misplaced, because if Marion is correct, "the theologian's job is to silence the Name and in this way let it give us one."[56] The name of God is not at issue, except to the extent that the idolatrous namings of God by those who confuse theology with metaphysics bars one from the encounter with the God who is *without* being, and without even a proper name we could call his own. So too is Milbank's critique off the mark, because

God is not in need of a translator. In fact, Marion suggests the relationship is precisely reversed, which is to say that humans stand as the recipients of that which cannot be named, but instead only de-nominated. Furthermore, such de-nomination leads to the purely pragmatic speeches of prayer and praise, which is the third way beyond either affirmation or negation, and by which humans stand as the recipients of a diving naming.

ON FREEDOM

To conclude, let us return to the theological paradox of freedom. In one sense, this means that freedom is realized not through the exercise of autonomy, but through the submission to authority. On this matter, Marion writes unapologetically as a Roman Catholic theologian, *"only the bishop merits, in the full sense, the title of theologian.* This proposition may appear paradoxical, but at the risk of simplifying, we must insist on it."[57]

In another sense, as the previous analysis has demonstrated, this means that Marion accepts the articulations of the problem of philosophical theology by both Heidegger and Barth. While paradoxical, in the sense that both Heidegger and Barth present their understandings of the problematic as though philosophy and theology were each mutually exclusive, this need not be a contradiction. That is because Marion does not remain bound to either one; instead, he operates on both fronts simultaneously by following the prescription for theology as set by Heidegger, and by so doing, he realizes more fully Barth's ideal of a radically self-critical orthodoxy. Marion's philosophical theology, therefore, is a *theology in consequence of philosophy.* Beyond cooperation (e.g., Barth) differentiation (e.g., Heidegger), or appropriation (e.g., Ricoeur), Marion models the structural parallels between philosophy and theology. And while Marion insists on distinguishing the two, by his own work he demonstrates the need of the one for the other, as each effects the other's completion.[58]

In yet another sense, it has been suggested that silence might be the unintended consequence of such a thoroughgoing iconoclastic theology. Such is not the case, however, in spite of appearances to the contrary. For though it is the case that the theologian speaks for the sake of exposing the idolatry inherent in language, and though this purpose is achieved when such idolatrous language is silenced, what this means is not a complete silence of language altogether, but the silence of idolatry and the birth of theology. As strange as it may seem, this silence cannot be achieved except through a theological language. That is the point that must be understood in reference to Marion, and it is also why he insists on the distinction between phenomenology and theology in spite of the fact that between the two there are such great and obvious structural parallels. *Language invites theology,* even while the chief task of the theologian is that of silencing a certain kind of language. Theology needs no other justification than that of language to begin with, for it is by language's natural propensity toward idolatry that theology receives its iconoclastic mandate. And when compared with phenomenology, though structurally similar, the differences between phenomenology and theology are the differences between pure possibility and pure historicity— phenomenology attends to the possible, theology to the historic. In other words, what Marion is asserting is that theology requires a commitment of faith. For as pure possibility suspends all presuppositions, historicity gives words to speak, words with concrete and pragmatic meanings, words that are historically determined and theologically bound. Words, even, that might bring a certain pleasure. But nevertheless, words that remain the words of an-other.

Conclusion

In summary, recall the critique of Ricoeur offered earlier in the chapter; namely, that Ricoeur's thought demonstrates a profound and ever-widening appreciation of the linguistic structure of experience and the consequent necessity of interpretation. However—and this is the problem—this appreciation only moves in one direction. It does not in turn reflect back on the determining factor of experience in shaping a given interpretation, and even more fundamentally, in shaping a hermeneutical theory. The result is not, as Ricoeur himself would claim, that he effectively suspends theological judgment and religious conviction, but on the contrary, that these form the very basis for his model of interpretation—*a basis that remains unacknowledged and uncritical.* In the final analysis, therefore, Ricoeur is best understood according to the model of religious orthodoxy in which faith and practice translate into knowledge, albeit indirectly, through interpretation. As such, he does not escape the problem of ontotheology but only furthers it by running it underground.

In contrast, Marion embraces his dual role as both philosopher and theologian. Like Ricoeur, Marion admits the linguistic structure of experience, along with the need for interpretation—in Marion's case, whether a phenomenological or theological interpretation. But by his exercise of a theological freedom, he provides what Ricoeur leaves lacking; namely, an admittedly invested and equally critical interpretation that lives by faith in response to the historical actuality of revelation. Paradoxically, far from having the effect of thus limiting what may or may not be said, such a commitment to the concrete particularities of language actually translates into an infinite freedom that transgresses the bounds of philosophy and theology. Why, then, concern ourselves with the problem of philosophical theology? As Marion would answer: for the pleasure of transgressing bounds.

INTERLUDE 3

ON BIBLIOLATRY

As enclave of the other within the other, otherness becomes crystallized as pure ostracism: the foreigner excludes before being excluded, even more than he is being excluded. Fundamentalists are more fundamental when they have lost all material ties, inventing for themselves a "we" that is purely symbolic; lacking a soil it becomes rooted in ritual until it reaches its essence, which is sacrifice.

—Julia Kristeva, *Strangers to Ourselves*

The scandal of the evangelical mind is that there is not much of an evangelical mind.

—Mark A. Noll, *The Scandal of the Evangelical Mind*

THERE ARE more borders than meet the eye. As Kristeva tells us, we are strangers even unto ourselves.

One such case that demonstrates this truth is that of the Southern Baptist Convention (SBC), the largest of all Protestant denominations in the United States and perhaps, by a certain standard of measure, still the most successful.[1] Southern Baptists have grown from a small subculture on the frontiers of what was then the American Southwest to the dominant religion not only of America's "Bible Belt," but also of American Evangelical Christianity at large. What began in the eighteenth century as a countercultural movement that was known for its opposition to class privilege, certain forms of racism and sexism, and all forms of institutional religion, has become the bulwark of "traditional values," cultural assimilation, and religiously motivated political activism.[2] Yet, for all its apparent success, its future as a denomination is uncertain. As a headline from the *New York Times* reads, "Rift among Baptists Leaves Two Denominations in One."[3]

The focal point of this internal division among Southern Baptists is difficult to discern. Some insist that it is simply a matter of power politics, and that the growing resistance among the more moderate Baptists to the SBC has more to do with their feeling of being disenfranchised than it does with actual doctrinal differences.[4] To this one might add the brute facts of the continued growth of the SBC in spite of the internal conflict. It is with this fact in mind that SBC leaders confidently state that even if the moderate Baptists formed a wholly new denomination, their loss would quickly be replaced by the almost fifteen hundred new congregations formed each year under the auspices of the SBC.[5]

Others view the Baptists' predicament as a reflection of a larger cultural phenomenon in which denominational loyalties are losing their hold. Still others claim that the political disputes are evidence of deeper issues that will not be easily resolved. Such issues involve the SBC's increasingly staunch stance on issues such as abortion, homosexuality, the ordination of women, and most significantly, at least with regard to the internal debates, biblical inerrancy.

It is this final issue that has proven to be the spark that has ignited the engine of controversy, most especially because by the SBC's attempt to preserve its traditional teachings on the authority of the Bible, its more ancient tradition of being an anti-creedal, anti-institutional religious movement, seems to have been compromised. The issue is whether Southern Baptists have made the Bible into an idol, or, according to the particular rhetoric of the controversy, whether they are correctly or incorrectly charged as "bibliolaters."

This charge has been levied against the SBC because of the recent revision it adopted in its official confession of faith, entitled the *Baptist Faith and Message.* Baptists have traditionally distinguished confessions from creeds because, as stated in the *Baptist Faith and Message* itself, confessions "are only guides in interpretation, having no authority over the conscience." As such, they are meant merely to express "a consensus of opinion . . . for the general instruction and guidance of our own people and others concerning those articles of the Christian faith which are most surely held among us."

The significance of this relates to what is most prized in the hearts of Baptists; namely, the notion of soul competency, which is the radical extension of the Protestant reformation's insistence on the priesthood of believers. The notion of soul competency means that each individual—no matter his/her education, socio-economic status, vocation, nationality, or gender—has both the ability and the full competence to interpret scripture according to the guidance of the Holy Spirit. This means that in matters of faith, Baptists have traditionally stood for absolute freedom of thought and liberty in conscience. This explains the Baptist justification of the separation between church and state, which has been one of its most noteworthy cultural legacies. Theologically speaking, this means there are no mediators between God and the individual except that of Jesus Christ. The rejection of creeds, therefore, can be considered a distinctively Baptist form of iconoclasm through which the notion of soul competency is preserved. And thus, the suggestion by some that the *Baptist Faith and Message* has become more "creedal" and less "confessional" strikes at the very heart of the Baptist identity.

Concerning the recent revision in the *Baptist Faith and Message* itself, the issue is regarding the proper standard of biblical interpretation. The present controversy formally began in 1963, when the following statement was inserted into the confession: "The criterion by which the Bible is to be interpreted is Jesus Christ." This addition to the creed was meant to provide a guide for biblical interpretation that might maintain the integrity and authority of Christian conviction and still resolve whatever discrepancies and/or inconsistencies the reader of the Bible might observe. Most certainly, this standard of interpretation was influenced by the currents of the historical-critical method of biblical interpretation that had been developing for roughly the past two hundred years. However, when set in the context of Bultmann's method of demythologization, Bonhoeffer's call for a "religion-less" interpretation of scripture, the onset of the death of God movement, and the beginnings of feminists' critiques of the andro-centrism and patriarchy existent throughout the pages of the Bible, one cannot help but wonder at the source and disproportion of recent claims being made by prominent SBC leaders; namely, that this 1963 revision to the *Baptist Faith and Message* "has become a gaping hole in the wall of sound Bible interpretation through which a rapid succession of erroneous teachings, especially in the institutions of higher learning, invaded our community of faith."[6] The fear is that no matter how justified its original intentions, the revision set the SBC on a "slippery slope" of biblical interpre-tation.

Indeed, if the 1963 revision were to blame for the intrusion of higher criticism within the ranks of the Southern Baptist biblical scholars, the obvious response would be to eliminate this addi-tion, which was precisely what occurred in 2000. Leaders of the SBC have called the 2000 revision "a necessary corrective" that protects biblical interpretation from the "aberrant view" that seeks "to use Jesus as a wedge between God and the Scriptures He Himself inspired."[7] Yet while it may protect the Bible from criti-cism, this protection does not come without a price. First, it has functioned symbolically as a line drawn in the sand, providing a quick and easy reference for distinguishing between those who are on the inside from those who are on the outside of the SBC mainstream. Given the already fragile unity of the SBC and the heightened political sensitivities, it should come as no surprise that the immediate response to this change in the SBC's confes-sion of faith by the more moderates within its fold would be one of suspicion, if not outright hostility.[8]

More importantly for our purposes, however, is the question of the Baptist identity and the measures taken in order to insure its continuity. This insurance has taken one of two forms: It has either purged itself of unwanted influences from within, or pro-tected itself from corrupting influences from outside. The protec-tion from external corruption is what receives most attention. Southern Baptists have become increasingly outspoken not only with regard to the perceived moral laxity of the culture of their surroundings (e.g., the SBC boycott of the Disney corporation for its hiring practices with regard to homosexuality), but also with regard to their evangelical fervor as they have reaffirmed in recent years their missionizing efforts toward Jews, Roman Catholics, and Mormons, among others.

However, it is this need for self-purging that is of most interest for our present concerns. For instance, drawing battle lines as symbolic markers of identity, regardless of whether it is done consciously or unconsciously, is still a deliberate act intended to expose its divided community's innermost convictions and loyalties. In this respect the 2000 revision to the *Baptist Faith and Message* functions less as guide and an expression of consensus and more as a test of faith. The distinction between creed and confession has been blurred, and this effects a fundamental transformation in the Baptist character. Its priorities have shifted from giving privilege to the liberty of individual conscience to throwing the full force of its institutional authority behind the effort of preserving the "high view of Scripture," which it perceives to be under assault from within.[9]

The question of "bibliolatry," therefore, is integral to the structure of the Southern Baptist identity: On the one hand, a "high view" of scripture, which is demanded by the SBC, maintains the traditional Southern Baptist understanding of revelation; that is, that the Bible is the inspired word of God. On the other hand, this understanding is no longer the outgrowth of a consensus, but instead functions as a safeguard, prerequisite, and test of faith. In other words, there might be a continuity to biblical interpretation, but the community's comportment to that interpretation has undergone a decided shift. As such, the nature of the community has been transformed.

This is where the theological question of idolatry is central. That is because those who accuse the SBC of "bibliolatry" do not mean that Southern Baptists literally worship the Bible, but that the SBC's comportment to scripture has been elevated as its primary identity marker.[10] As Marion specifies in his description of the human tendency toward idolatry, the icon is distinguished from the idol not as though they belonged to two different classes of beings, but rather, the "icon and the idol determine two manners of being for beings."[11] As such, the same biblical interpretation can be either iconoclastic or idolatrous depending on its mode of apprehension; also, it may pass from one rank to the other without the least bit of change in the givenness of the thing itself. Or as Gabriel Vahanian writes, "Rationally, God cannot be distinguished from the idol;" and further, "that idolatry is but a caricature of faith in God." This caricature of faith is in contrast to the iconoclastic essence of Christianity, by which Vahanian means the "attempt, not to re-create, but to transfigure the world and man's situation in it, including all the everyday aspects of existence."[12] Or finally, consider Huston Smith's account of "the Protestant Principle": "Stated philosophically," Smith writes, "it warns against absolutizing the relative. Stated theologically, it warns against idolatry."[13]

Each of these accounts of idolatry represents a more subtle temptation than the obvious construction and worship of false images of the divine. If true, these signify a more covert form of idolatry, which, ironically, stems from the very effort at preserving the divine. In the case of the SBC, this would mean that the attempt at preserving the authority and integrity of the revealed word of God is contrary to its intentions by its transformation of the iconoclastic essence of the biblical witness into an idol.

To put it in other terms, the problem is not that the authority of the Bible has been undermined; that is merely the consequence of a tradition that gives privilege to the liberty of individual consciences. Rather, the problem is one of an uneasy alliance and the perception that a community needs to be purified in order to secure its identity. The Southern Baptist predicament is primarily a battle waged from within, as the consequence of its historical affirmations now threatens to undermine its tradition. Its self-preservation is also its self-transformation, as its self-protection demands the ostracization of its own.

5

OTHERWISE THAN OVERCOMING

The sheer originality and range of Levinas's thought demand nothing less than a fundamental reorientation of Western spirit—philosophy, logic, rhetoric, praxis, ontology, science, art, politics, religion—in the light of morality and justice.

—Alphonso Lingis, "Foreword," *Otherwise than Being*

WHAT IF the problem with modern thought was not, as supposed, the intermixing of philosophy and theology? What if the ontotheological problem meant something entirely different from the misguided effort at securing knowledge? Would it still need to be overcome?

Or might the desire for overcoming itself be the problem? If Henri Bergson is correct, then once this problem has been properly stated it is also solved, which is still not to say overcome, especially when considering the possibility that overcoming is itself the problem. Therefore, in this closing chapter, let us pose the possibility that the problem is not ontotheology, but the desire for its overcoming. Stated in this way, we may thereby move beyond the well-rehearsed strategies of modern and postmodern philosophical and theological thought, which, at least according to the models explored in the preceding chapters, have been shown to be misguided or shortsighted, if not altogether contradictory and counterproductive.

For review, recall the three contemporary views concerning the relationship between philosophy and theology as stated in the introduction: (1) Theology overcomes ontotheology by escaping the problem;

(2) Philosophy overcomes ontotheology by passing through and beyond the problem; and (3) Ontotheology is not overcome, and this causes both theology and philosophy to be read in light of the Other. The first two of these views have been explored throughout the preceding chapters. What should be obvious is that they represent two sides of the same coin. As such, their various shortcomings suggest the possibility that it is the very articulation of the problematic that is to blame; thus, the overcoming of ontotheology gives way to its acceptance as the very condition of possibility in which the two discourses of theology and philosophy must be set. As stated previously, ontotheology is not a mistake, nor is it the problem. Rather, the problem is the attempt at overcoming what continually establishes itself as the very condition of life and thought.

Key to the proposal of this concluding chapter will be the work of Emmanuel Levinas. For not only is Levinas credited with redirecting contemporary thought in accordance with an ethic of responsibility, but also it is Levinas who articulates an alternative strategy for contemporary philosophical and theological thought. This is a strategy that is *otherwise than overcoming*; thus, it also allows for the redefinition of the problem, which the previous views have left wanting.[1] Furthermore, it was Levinas who was the unacknowledged influence on the thinking of Marion. It is Levinas's influence on Marion that gives him the needed resource by which he could draw on the best of contemporary philosophical and theological thought, while not also falling into the same predetermined path of thought.

It is also Levinas, in combination with both Marion and Derrida, who rounds out the reenvisioning of philosophical theology for which we are striving. That is to say, all three thinkers share an understanding of what I have introduced as the ontotheological condition of thought; however, where Marion speaks of pleasure and Derrida speaks of the desire for the impossible, Levinas insists on a responsibility that is infinite in its scope. Therefore, he stands to Marion and Derrida as the hyperbolic prophet, demanding a responsibility that cannot be satisfied but that nevertheless stands as the very condition of thought's possibilities. Thus, this chapter will revisit the debate between Marion and Derrida on "negative theology" and their differing understandings of the pragmatic function of language. This time, however, the influence of Levinas will be written into the exchange in such a way that the alternatives of Marion and Derrida are not posed as a choice between two contrasting positions, but as a stance of thought that bears with it certain ethical implications.

Levinas: Beyond Barth and Heidegger

First, a few comments must be made on why Levinas represents a genuine alternative to the understanding of the problematic as it has been thus far articulated, since Levinas's thinking has been compared with that of Barth's,[2] and because his indebtedness to the early thought of Heidegger is well known.[3] This being the case, the question must be asked regarding the point of distinction in the thought of Levinas; with this in mind, the possibilities for the renewal of thought might be made more apparent.

"TOUT AUTRE EST TOUT AUTRE"

At the close of his comparative study of Barth and Levinas, entitled *The Argument to the Other*, Steven Smith writes: "Theology reaches toward humanity, as theological anthropology and ethics, while philosophy reaches toward the infinity of God in responding to the enigmatic goodness of just relation with the neighbor, in the form of philosophical theology." Smith continues: "The presumption by which we set up Barth's and Levinas' arguments as irreducibly competitive paradigms of theology and philosophy is really a corollary of the presumption of their shared argument. Only by virtue of their common gesture of arguing to the Other can they think from such purely irreconcilable starting points for theological and philosophical reason, viz. differently identified personal others."[4]

Note here the common thematics of a distinctively Barthian paradigm of understanding. First, Smith agrees with Barth in distinguishing theology from philosophy according to the respective *direction of thought*. Theology, in Smith's terms, begins from the point of the revelation of God and "reaches toward humanity," while philosophy begins in concrete human experience and reaches upward "toward the infinity of God." This sounds remarkably similar to what Barth calls theology's "mighty act of condescension" and philosophy's "mighty elevation."[5] Second, like Barth's notion of the cooperation that exists between philosophy and theology, Smith views philosophy and theology as "irreducibly competitive," but also realizes this competition is predicated on the basis of their "shared argument." Thus, while differing in the starting point and the direction of thought, philosophy and theology nevertheless share a common aim, which is, in Smith's language, "beyond a preoccupation with transcendence, a very distinctive way of describing it, arguing from it, and holding consistently to it."[6]

The problem with Smith's comparison is that Barth is given the exclusive privilege of establishing the point of contact. In other words, Smith has unwittingly reinstantiated the divide between philosophy and theology by allowing Barth's analysis of the defining features of both philosophy and theology to predetermine the reading of Levinas. In effect, Levinas is made to fit within a Barthian paradigm; in this way, Levinas plays the role of the necessary counterpoint in the achievement of this distinctively theological agenda.

Another comparison between Barth and Levinas comes from the "radical orthodox" thinker Graham Ward, in his book *Barth, Derrida and the Language of Theology.*[7] For Ward, the significance of this comparison is not its reinstantiation of the philosophical-theological divide; indeed, from Ward's perspective, both Barth and Levinas are "unavoidably theological" in the sense that "the problem of otherness . . . *is* a theological problem." Elsewhere he makes this point more fully: "Levinas's philosophy of Saying can then be directly compared with Barth's theology of the Word. The comparison reveals why Barth, as a theologian, cannot avoid the metaphysics of language, and, similarly, why Levinas, as a philosopher of language, cannot avoid being theological."[8] The significance is three interrelated themes that emerge from the comparison between Barth and Levinas: (1) Both Barth and Levinas situate ethics beyond ontology, which means that both agree that there is an *asymmetrical* relationship between either human beings and God, or between the self and the Other, and that this relationship is precisely that which is constitutive of being, thought, and action. (2) Both Barth and Levinas seek ways of giving articulation to this asymmetrical relationship—Barth according to the *analogia fidei,* and Levinas according to the "analogy of appresentation." (3) Both Barth and Levinas consider revelation as a point of "rupture" that "fissures the Kantian unity of apperception."[9]

The value of this dismantling of the foundation of modern subjectivity is that it leads beyond totalizing tendencies of thought in accordance with reason alone, toward a greater and more urgent responsibility of thought and action. And while this accomplishment might be shared by both thinkers, Ward also insists that there is "the Christological difference," which represents "a parting of the ways between Barth's thinking and Levinas's."[10] This difference is, namely, Barth's theological centering on the mediating figure of Christ, in contrast to Levinas's notion of substitution, in which the self is defined as "the-one-for-the-other."[11] In other words, with Barth, the subject is theologically justified; whereas with Levinas, the "subject is a hostage," made unique by "the very fact of bearing the fault of another."[12]

The reader might sense a problem in Ward's analysis as well, inso-far as Ward also appropriates Levinas for the cause of theology, albeit to a lesser degree than that of Smith.[13] However, Ward's appropria-tion is different from Smith's in one important respect. Ward reads Barth, Levinas, and eventually Derrida as well, not as stock charac-ters playing out the ancient and ongoing rivalry between philosophy and theology, but for the purpose of reevaluating the nature of philo-sophical theology itself. In this sense, Barth is no more the prototyp-ical theologian than Levinas is the prototypical philosopher; instead, both contribute to a developing "grammar of signification."[14] And the value of Ward's analysis is that through his reading of their respective contributions to a developing theological grammar, the important differences between them are made more apparent. Barth's *analogia fidei* is not just a theological articulation of transcendence, but it is a specifically Christian theological articulation, one that is thoroughly Christocentric and thus unapologetically dogmatic. Levinas's analogy of appresentation, on the other hand, is a more general statement concerning the very conditions of selfhood; it is an exploration of the ethical preconditions of differentiation, namely, the ethical relation, the self as *subjected* by the other. Put otherwise, Barth's theological grounding in the subject of God has been dispersed by Levinas's read-ing of transcendence as the concrete face-to-face encounter between the self and the other. Barth's "wholly other" is read by Levinas as each and every other with whom one is related in an infinitely com-plex web of mutual and total obligation.

Finally, consider Derrida's reflections in *The Gift of Death*, in which Levinas stands in the background of Derrida's thoughts, while the text itself revolves more explicitly around Derrida's reading of Heidegger and Kierkegaard on the topics of death, responsibility, and religion. These reflections, in contrast to Derrida's earlier writing on Levinas in "Violence and Metaphysics,"[15] are fundamentally in sympathy with Levinas's concerns, especially in the final chapter, which is play-fully and revealingly entitled *"Tout autre est tout autre."*[16] For it is there that the question of the other—which of course, is the spectre of Levinas in Derrida[17]—is most pronounced. Indeed, it is there that the statement regarding the other is revealed as a question, leaving in its trace the seeming incompatibilities between transcendence and immanence or, according to the terms of the present discussion, between Barth and Levinas. In Derrida's words: "One of them [Barth] keeps in reserve the possibility of reserving the quality of the wholly other, in other words the *infinite other*, for God alone, or in any case for a single other. The other [Levinas] attributes to or recognizes in this infinite alterity of the wholly other, every other, in other words, each one, for example each man and woman."[18]

Both apparent options—whether Barth or Levinas, as both Smith and Ward tell us—are equally concrete, so the difference between them is not measured by levels of abstraction. The difference, instead—and this is the point missed by both Smith and Ward—is that by rendering the *infinite other as each and every other*, Levinas has thoroughly decentered philosophical and theological discourse. In contrast to Barth and the contemporary theological tradition that he shaped, Levinas speaks of the concrete in descriptive rather than prescriptive terms. In this sense, when Levinas speaks of the ethical relation, he is speaking of ethics as the very precondition of being and thought, as opposed to qualifying being and thought by a particular ethic. This is why when Levinas was asked whether he thought it necessary for ethics to establish rules, he answered by saying, "My task does not consist in constructing ethics; I only try to find its meaning."[19] It could be said, therefore, that the philosophical critique of theology is countered by Levinas's opening toward the ethical relation. For with Levinas, thinking is at once both concrete and open-ended, conditioned by the face-to-face, while remaining open to the in-breaking of infinity.

Thus Levinas is able to provide an opening to what Barth only promises, namely, the centering in of language upon the point of absolute difference. As Levinas writes in *Totality and Infinity*: "The Other remains infinitely transcendent, infinitely foreign; his face in which his epiphany is produced and which appeals to me breaks with the world that can be common to us, whose virtualities are inscribed in our *nature* and by our existence. Speech proceeds from absolute difference."[20] By contrast, Barth's theology, which is said to decenter, in fact insists on the absolute center of the transcendental signified, which, while it certainly might be the unbound source of mystery, is nevertheless historically conditioned by a tradition of faith. Levinas, on the other hand, speaks of the historically unconditioned other, which is spread out among strangers and friends and stands as the very constitutive base of being itself. This opening represents a profound shift—from dogmatic theology to postmodernism—the latter of which poses the possibility of a theological thinking without or beyond a religious dogmatism. In John Caputo's terms, this way of thinking is a "religion without religion," which means, "*sans* the concrete, historical religions; . . . *sans* the concrete messianisms of the positive religions that wage endless war and spill the blood of the other, and that, anointing themselves God's chosen people, are consummately dangerous to everyone else who is not so chosen."[21]

DELIVERANCE FROM THE "THERE IS"

When speaking of Levinas's intellectual development, the story inevitably leads to the "great event" of Heidegger.[22] As Levinas responded when asked about the importance of Heidegger: "[A] man who undertakes to philosophize in the twentieth century cannot not have gone through Heidegger's philosophy, even to escape it. This thought is a great event of our century."[23]

First, therefore, it should be noted that Levinas never forgets the debt of gratitude he owes to Heidegger, albeit a "regrettable debt."[24] Levinas also affirmed the "absolute novelty" of Heidegger's *Being and Time*,[25] such novelty that it absolutely redirected Levinas's own interest in Husserl, and more broadly, the contribution that Levinas would make to the phenomenological tradition.[26] Levinas admits that it was Heidegger's description of the factical—*being-in-the-world*—that transformed phenomenology from a strict methodology to a living philosophy. Finally, it was Heidegger who pointed the way to a thinking that precedes objectifying knowledge and representation, even if Heidegger himself failed to follow through on this fundamental insight.

With this recognition in mind, the differences between Levinas and Heidegger—at least as Levinas views the matter—are profound and work on at least two different levels:

(1) Heidegger's redirecting of philosophy according to ontology only scratches the surface of a truth that Heidegger himself persistently fails to recognize. As Derrida makes the point in "Violence and Metaphysics":

> In the style by which strong and faithful thought is recognized (this is Heidegger's style too), Levinas respects the zone or layer of traditional truth; and the philosophies whose presuppositions he describes are in general neither refuted nor criticized. Here, for example, it is a question simply of revealing beneath this truth [of Heidegger's ontology], as that which founds it and is dissimulated within it, "a situation which precedes the division of Being into an inside and outside." However it is also a question of inaugurating, in a way that is to be new, quite new, a metaphysics of radical separation and exteriority.[27]

Thus, as Levinas makes the distinction between metaphysics and ontology, he is drawing on a truth that precedes comprehension. Levinas defines this as "a way of approaching the known being such that its alterity with regard to the knowing being vanishes," or that "which reduces the other to the same."[28]

(2) Heidegger maintains the thought of being and thus, de facto, establishes a system of thought that is totalizing by its essential egocentricity. Adriaan Peperzak expresses it well:

> Even if it is true that the fundamental "passivity" of mortality and contingency is stressed and that the initiative of discovery and truth is more and more attributed by Heidegger to Being itself, the subject of truth, acceptance, and "letting-be" is still the center of a panoramic universe, an open space well protected against the invasions of other humans, other histories, of God. If gods exist, they are there for men. Other humans are mentioned only as companions within anonymous communities, *not* as disturbing forces that rob me of my central place.[29]

For Levinas, Heidegger's "panoramic universe" is simply too simple to account phenomenologically for the case of the self as a *being-with-others*. This is why he places such a high premium on the trace, because the trace testifies to the instability, fluidity, or intermixing of identity, to a responsibility beyond intentionality, a responsibility that extends even beyond the self that is intending. As Levinas describes it: "The comedy begins with the simplest of movements, carrying with them every inevitable awkwardness. In putting out my hand to approach a chair, I have creased the sleeve of my jacket, I have scratched the floor, I have dropped the ash from my cigarette. In doing that which I wanted to do, I have done so many things I did not want to do. The act has not been pure for I have left some traces. In wiping out these traces, I have left others."[30]

The fact that there are no pure actions but only traces, and no pure intending subject but only a subject already involved, already implicated, translates for Levinas into a suspicion of an ontology that is fundamentally complacent, that proclaims its innocence by its taking on the apparently benign posture of simply "letting be." It is what such a posture implicitly presupposes that Levinas explicitly rejects; namely, that there is a pure generosity to being, or that the horizon of being does not play favorites to the forces of rationality that place some within the mainstream, and others outside. For Levinas the more accurate trope for describing the subject's entrance into thought is not that of *letting be*, but that of *being called*. His response to Heidegger, therefore, "is to ask whether the relation with the Other is in fact a matter of *letting be*? Is not the independence of the Other accomplished in the role of being called? Is the person to whom one speaks understood from the first in his or her being? Not at all. The Other is not an object of comprehension first and an interlocutor second. The two relations are intertwined. In other words, the comprehension of the Other is inseparable from his or her invocation."[31]

Thought, therefore, begins with interruption or through the disruption of the Other. And comprehension, by way of rationality, is the attempt to silence such disruptive presences, to bring a unity to thinking, which in fact belies a violence of origins and a dark indeterminacy to being.[32] Again, this latter difference is between the interpretations of the given-being; for Heidegger given being is expressed through the German phrase *es gibt,* and for Levinas it is the French *il y a.* For Heidegger this translates into an innocent, even mystical, neutrality. Thus the nostalgia for which he is accused is his effort to return, if not to an essence, then at least to *a history worth remembering.* But this is one history in place of another—a poetic, even inspired history that stands for the philosopher in the place of the actual. For Levinas the *es gibt* is no more innocent than the history it romanticizes. As he first articulates in *Existence and Existents*: "The bare fact of presence is oppressive; one is held by being, held to be. . . . This presence which arises behind nothingness is neither *a being,* nor consciousness functioning in a voice, but the universal fact of the *there is,* which encompasses things and consciousness."[33] Levinas compares this oppressiveness to insomnia in the sense that the work of being never lets up, never rests:

> The consciousness of a thinking subject, with its capacity for evanescence, sleep and unconsciousness, is precisely the breakup of the insomnia of anonymous being, the possibility to "suspend," to escape from this corybantic necessity, to take refuge in oneself so as to withdraw from being, to, like Penelope, have a night to oneself to undo the work looked after and supervised during the day. The *there is,* the play of being, is not played out across oblivions, does not encase itself in sleep like a dream. Its very occurrence consists in an impossibility, an opposition to possibilities of sleep, relaxation, drowsiness, absence. . . . The *there is* lacks rhythm, as the points swarming in darkness lack perspective.[34]

For Levinas it is precisely such a neutrality to thought that is to blame for many of the horrors of history and the shortcomings of philosophy. Speaking of Heidegger's neutrality in particular, he writes: "*There is* —impersonally—like *it is raining* or *it is night.* No generosity which the German term 'es gibt' is said to express showed itself between 1933 and 1945. This must be said! Illumination and sense dawn only with the existing beings' rising up and establishing themselves in this horrible neutrality of the *there is.*"[35]

It is my claim that Levinas's recognition of neutrality as a horror establishes the priority of ethics in his thinking. Thus, his claim that ethics is first philosophy is his passionate plea for a kind of philosophy that acknowledges its ethical stance. This is different from a thinking that is willing to take a stand, for the latter thinks there is a choice, while Levinas's claim is that such stands are the very conditions of thinking itself and the very possibility by which "a subject would have to be posited."[36] One considers ethics in strictly prescriptive terms, while the other asks the more fundamental question of the ethics of ethics. One preserves the centrality of the ego, while the other upsets the balance by reversing the constituting order of exchange—not the self willing responsibility, but an infinite responsibility collapsing the careful divisions between self and other. This argument for the priority of ethics is why Levinas's thinking represents not just another layer of philosophical argumentation, but instead engenders a new urgency in thought that extends beyond its own shortcomings. Levinas demands a new standard of measure for thought such that his importance is not that he merely prescribes a new path of thought, but that he forces a reconsideration and a reconfiguring of the very problem that is presumed to be fundamental.

To be fair to Heidegger, he too speaks of the self-in-response, but for Levinas it is the response to *what* that is decisive. When naming the originary source of the self's call to being, Levinas suggests that Heidegger resorts to being as a totality. In contrast, Levinas speaks of the concrete call of the other. With Heidegger relation with the other begins with comprehension; with Levinas it begins with the ethical relation. With Heidegger what is called for is merely acceptance; with Levinas there is a revolt, a violence, a genuine meeting of the wills whereby one's self is held hostage. In this respect, from a Levinasian perspective, ethics is much like the Kant of the first and third critiques in that it is a questioning—a questioning of the conditions and possibilities of thinking itself, a kind of questioning that itself demonstrates the primacy of practical reason.[37] This is a realization that the self has no choice but to be involved, to speak, to be invested. In Levinas's words, "The self is a *sub-jectum*; it is under the weight of the universe, responsible for everything."[38] Hardly a neutral, indifferent, or complacent endeavor, but instead a reversal, a transgression, and a commitment—ethics asking the question of the ethics of ethics. And by so doing, the self—the supposed precondition for responsibility—is given over to the Other, by whom and for whom the self is constituted.

Levinas: Between Marion and Derrida

In a way one might consider Marion and Derrida as the embodiments of paths of thought that were begun by Barth and Heidegger, respectively. However, what saves the debate between Derrida and Marion from being merely a reiteration of the philosophical-theological divide is the influence of Levinas on both thinkers. This influence allows both Derrida and Marion to see in the other both complete agreement and, at the same time, utter incompatibility. To reiterate, the reason for Levinas's importance in the present discussion of the problem of philosophical theology is certainly not that he somehow resolves the problem. Instead, the argument is being made that Levinas engenders a kind of questioning that compels the reader to think *beyond* the problem to its very condition. In short, Levinas demands the asking of the question of consequence. Therefore, while much is at stake in this debate between Derrida and Marion, one misses the point if their differences are considered as strictly matters of truth or falsity. On the contrary, from a Levinasian perspective, each is characterized by his own truth and consequence; and if the focus is too narrowly defined by the former, then the latter concern, which is the beginning of an ethical inquiry, is left obscured. Finally, then, the responsibility of a discourse is determined by its consequence; and this realization does not simply reverse the problem from cause to effect, but utterly transforms thought from that of self-concern to that of the question of the Other.

THE CONSEQUENCE OF THOUGHT

For Levinas the consequence of thought is revealed by its origination in ethics. His well-known argument that ethics is first philosophy, which concludes *Totality and Infinity*, makes this point in the sense that philosophy seeks its justification not by virtue of its attainment of certainty, even if such an attainment was an actual possibility, but by its being put into question, or by the judgment by which it is held accountable. In this sense being itself is put into question by the positing of metaphysics as desire, and the truth of being gives way to the responsibility of ethics.[39] As Levinas writes: "Freedom is not justified by freedom;"[40] nor may thought rest content as a mere exercise in thinking. Instead—and this is the great innovation of Levinas—it must answer for itself in terms of the Other. Further, such terms are never self-justifying; thus, the greater the responsibility, the greater the guilt as well: "Judgment is pronounced upon me in the measure that it summons me to respond . . . The summons exalts the singularity precisely because it is addressed to an infinite responsibility. *The infinity of responsibility denotes not its actual immensity, but a responsibility increasing in the measure it is assumed;* duties become greater in the measure they are accomplished. . . . The more I am just [,] the more guilty I am."[41] In other words, this is an ethical responsibility that extends far beyond the mandates of morality: "An inexhaustible responsibility: for with the other our accounts are never settled."[42]

The source of this infinite responsibility is the ethical relation, which is founded by the epiphany of the face. Outstripping phenomenology, the epiphany of the face has an "a-phenomenological" quality, meaning that it is not given to vision, that it refuses to come to light, and thereby, that it breaks open the horizon of thought by its trace of transcendence. The face is an irreducible exteriority that resists comprehension. In Levinas's words, "The face resists possession, resists my powers." But as Levinas notes, this resistance "does not do violence to me, does not act negatively; it has a positive structure: ethical." He continues: "There is here a relation not with a very great resistance, but with something absolutely *other:* the resistance of what has no resistance—the ethical resistance." And then there is the paradox that would later be developed into Levinas's strategy that is otherwise than overcoming: "The being that expresses itself imposes itself, but does so precisely by appealing to me with its destitution and nudity—its hunger—without my being able to be deaf to that appeal. Thus in expression the being that imposes itself does not limit but promotes my freedom, arouses my goodness."[43] Being held responsible, in other words, gives birth to freedom—certainly not a freedom from care, but an authentic freedom set firmly *within* an ethical plane of existence, not an escape from or overcoming of the problem of ontotheology, but its acceptance as the condition and horizon for thought and the very mandate and urgency for responsibility. As one commentator has written, it is not a matter of choosing freedom over responsibility, or vice versa. Instead, "Ethical transcendence wrests the individual free from the social totality, but is reflected within the totality itself when it is a question of assuring the coexistence of responsibility for the other and the equality of all before the law."[44] The face-to-face encounter sets the existential condition from which one's desire is given expression. The call of the other passes beyond itself unto infinity, unto even the very "idea of infinity", which "consists in thinking more than one thinks" and wherein God and philosophy meet.[45]

This call is detected not only in the thinking that thinks more than one thinks, but also in the saying that says more than what is said. From hunger to desire and from thought to language, Levinas's writings are linked by what Alphonso Lingis calls a "striking continuity." Thus, between his two defining works, *Totality and Infinity* and *Otherwise than Being*, Levinas's thinking is "distinguished by different but complementary emphases."[46] Ethical alterity gives way to ethical subjectivity as the call of the other gives way to putting oneself in the place of another, to being held hostage by and for the other, to substitution through which one bears the responsibility and burdens of the other, even answers for the failures and shortcomings of the other. The difference is one of intensification and emphasis. Desire is an insatiable hunger. Language is thought in flux. Between the saying and the said, however, is both *responsibility* and *betrayal*, requiring, as Levinas states, "as much audacity as skepticism shows, when it does not hesitate to affirm the impossibility of statement while venturing to *realize* this impossibility by the very statement of this impossibility."[47] The saying is said at the price of betrayal, but the saying of the said also bears witness to the responsibility of language as it binds together, establishes relation, and sets conditions for justice. The said permits the saying of the impossible, the inexhaustible, that which cannot and will not be thematized. It is Levinas's attempt to answer his friend Derrida's charge that ethical alterity is in fact a form of violence as it effectively silences the subject, rendering the self incapable of speech by its insistence on absolute difference. Derrida's critique is like Wittgenstein's pronouncement that there is no private language, and Levinas's talk of the saying of the said is his acknowledgement of this fundamental condition of the (im)possibility of language. Yes, Levinas answers, the said is a betrayal, but it is also a responsibility, for though it should not be confused with the saying, without it the saying along with the said is silenced. Like the self must answer not only for itself but also for the other, so too must language not only speak that which is known in the said, but must also that which is unknown in the saying of the said, the very desire of language. We are born into language even before we ever speak, even before we know the meaning of what is said. We are called into speech by something other than speech, otherwise than being, the desire, which is also the saying, the infinite, God.

Ethics, therefore, is the very impossibility and possibility of language. It is both a responsibility and a betrayal. The consequence of the ethical questioning engendered by Levinas is a more urgent, more intense appraisal of the fundamental conditions of being, thought, and language. It is a commitment to dialogue with the simultaneous acknowledgement of dialogue's ultimate failure. With respect to the problem of ontotheology, Levinas admits our fundamental circumscribed condition, that we are being pressed and pulled from all directions, that we are called into responsibility, into an impossible moral obligation, and that this call arouses our freedom, our goodness, indeed, the very discovery of our selves. Between faith and thought, between God and philosophy—that is where and how responsibility is discovered and discerned.

AGREEMENT WITHOUT CONSEQUENCE

This brief description of Levinas's understanding of ethics allows us to move from Levinas's reflections on the face-to-face encounter and the differences between the saying and the said to the actual dialogue that took place between Derrida and Marion. As previously stated, this dialogue reveals both complete agreement and utter incompatibility between the two thinkers. This realization is crucial in appreciating Derrida's response to Marion's critique, which is essentially one of agreement on virtually all points of contention. For instance, like Marion, Derrida agrees that "negative theology" is more a problem to be addressed than a reference to a unified field of discourse. Like Marion, Derrida agrees with the importance of the third way, which evidences the purely pragmatic function of language. Derrida also agrees with Marion's point about de-nomination, by which Derrida means "the question of the name and of the name of God, as the proper name which is never proper."[48] Furthermore, Derrida repeatedly points back to his own texts in which he has shown sympathy with—and dare I say, even understanding of—these various dimensions to both religious discourse and the theological tradition.

With such apparent goodwill, agreement, and regard from Derrida, the reader might be fooled into thinking Derrida had nothing either to add or to take away from Marion's account of apophasis. Such is not the case, however. On the contrary, while there might be general agreement on the meanings of terms and the problems to be considered, even structural agreement on the nature and telos of the strategy of apophasis, on the *purely pragmatic* level—which, recall, both Marion and Derrida have agreed is the true gist of the matter—they are more like ships passing in the night. That is because pragmatics, from Marion's perspective, means a concrete, embodied, and incarnate discourse that emerges from a specific paradigm of ritualized activity, liturgical language, and/or ecclesiastical structure of authority.

Recall Marion's claim from *God without Being*, which states that *"only the bishop merits, in the full sense, the title of theologian."*[49] Marion makes this claim as part of a larger point on the "eucharistic site of theology." And from the present critical essay being considered, Derrida detects repeated references made by Marion to the Christian rite of baptism as the (proper?) paradigm for understanding the structure of what Marion means by de-nomination. According to Derrida's tastes—again, consider the importance of an aesthetic sensibility for a purely pragmatic discourse—Marion's pragmatics lacks the universality or formality that he would desire. Perhaps one way of understanding Derrida's distaste would be that he considers Marion's pragmatics at best only conditional. This *conditional pragmatics*, then, would stand in marked contrast to the *purely pragmatic* discourse that both Marion and Derrida "agree" is the desideratum.

Marion's response confirms this point of difference. He expresses gratitude for Derrida's "general agreement," admits that they are working within a shared problematic, and even detects a point of contact on the general structure of the pragmatic function of a theological discourse. Nevertheless, according to Marion's tastes, which are borne out through his reading of Christian theological texts, the matters of agreement are too formal and they lack the specificity required of a truly pragmatic discourse. In other words, by a Christian theological definition pragmatics must be incarnated, which would mean not only fully conditional, but also, paradoxically, fully universal—a scandal no less than the stumbling block that first divided the Jewish hope from the Christian conviction.

Finally, then, what remains from this conversation on "negative theology" and the pragmatic function of language are at least two denominations of postmodern philosophical theology. The one follows the structure of religion as faith, driven by a hope and expectation of that which is not yet come. By its universality it attests to a common need and desire for a justice still lacking. If rightly called a denomination at all, it is a wandering and diasporic one, which has felt the brunt of violence and rests unsettled in any given homeland of its own. This is the Derrida depicted by Caputo, the Derrida driven by an authentic religious passion. The other follows the structure of religion as fulfillment, culmination, and conviction. By its universality it attests to a surplus of meaning, which cannot be contained by any single denomination, nor properly named by any single term. It is an overflowing denomination, full of great paradoxes and internal flexibility; in the world, but not of it; concrete, and thereby also universal. This is Marion, whose phenomenological reflections on the "saturated phenomenon" parallel his Christian conviction to the point where theology lives as the historical consequence of philosophical possibility.

Thus, while the two might agree on much, the consequence of their discourse is revealed only by their differences. With that in mind, a final word must be said on the consequence of dialogue serving as the model for an authentic philosophical theology.

THE CONSEQUENCE OF DIALOGUE

The dialogue being considered here does not hold out for the promise of reconciliation. Quite the contrary, the chief value of dialogue is its eventual exposure of differences, differences that are often irreconcilable but also rich with unknown possibilities. As the American pragmatist William James states: "There can *be* no difference anywhere that doesn't *make* a difference elsewhere—no difference in abstract truth that doesn't express itself in a difference in concrete fact and in conduct consequent upon that fact, imposed on somebody, somehow, somewhere, and somewhen."[50] Thus, between philosophy and theology there are clearly differences of consequence. For instance, consider the case of Derrida and Marion: One's expectation might be the other's fulfillment. Therefore, the consequence of this difference matters with regard to the renewed condition of thought: Does one proceed from expectation to fulfillment, from fulfillment to expectation, or do the two together somehow coexist as a resource for thinking through, thinking about, and thinking from our differences?

The simple matter of fact is that such differences do indeed exist, and it is to the shame of our history that these differences have been for so long ignored, denied, or even sought to be overcome. This is the very power of horror, which is also the precondition of thought's birth: Differences coming together and the consequence of such an exchange just might be a new kind of thinking that is otherwise than overcoming. A genuine philosophical theology for the sake of the other through whom there is no justification, but only heightened responsibility.

Again, in Levinas's terms this would be a dialogue "beyond dialogue"—a dialogue aware of its limitations, a historically aware dialogue that thinks of history not "as a harmonious process in which all problems are resolved, all conflicts settled, in which, in universality, all contradictions are reconciled"—In other words, it is not an "already accomplished history." Rather, it is a "history in the making," which reveals "besides the many problems awaiting their resolution from reason, technology, or dialogue—. . . the existence of insoluble problems; problems inherently insoluble, and delivered over to violence, not just because of our passions, our impatience, and our laziness, but because of the dormant antinomy within them." In short, it is a "new attitude, a paradigm . . . that lasts even after dialogue has become impossible. Beyond dialogue, a new maturity and earnestness, a new gravity and a new patience, and, if I may express it so, *maturity and patience for insoluble problems.*"[51]

Thus, in praise of ontotheology the problem of philosophical theology is not overcome, but passes over to a new problem, which is one of consequence, as it establishes the conditions from which philosophical theology might be thought otherwise.

POSTLUDE

ON THE FEMININE AND ONTOTHEOLOGY

That is how we came to understand that real worries, though pro-
fane, have something to do with the sacred. We were no longer
"outside," but "inside." That's life—in effect.

—Catherine Clément, in *The Feminine and the Sacred*

IN THE introduction to this work, I spoke not only of the objectives
that would be sought and the strategies that would be examined
and employed, but also of this study's urgency. The claim was made
that the effort to rethink ontotheology was urgent both because it
bears certain consequences and because it raises fundamental
questions about the nature of being and thought. It was with this
urgency in mind that the association between ontotheology and
the abject was made. Like the abject, ontotheology is a dilemma
without resolution; it bespeaks the circumscribed condition of
thought's possibility. Furthermore, the efforts to escape or overcome this circumscribed condition, like the various means of
purifying the abject, cover over and thereby distort its fundamental essence. This association teaches us that the endeavor to overcome ontotheology is at best an act of futility.

But this is not all that the association between ontotheology
and the abject teaches us. After all, the abject, as employed by
Kristeva, illuminates the powers of horror. It provides a window

into the theo-logic and psycho-logic of consecration, with and without sublimation. Through her phenomenology of abjection, Kristeva tells us what we already know, which is that the abject is an ontology, that its being is real, that its consequences are concrete. The same must be said for the ontotheological condition: Its relevance is not reserved to the theoretical reflections of philosophers and theologians alone.

Therefore, beyond theology and philosophy there is yet another division that has been raised, but only below the surface in the margins of the text. This other division, issue, and/or theme, is raised within the interludes, which together represent the urgency of this work as a whole. Urgent, yet still displaced, the interludes occupy a subterranean place, serving as a subtext running parallel throughout the "main" text. In one fashion, these interludes might be read as no more than pauses along the way, giving relief and context to the more strictly theoretical interests of the main body. As such, they would be superfluous distractions, an unnecessary excess that contributes little or nothing to the argument of the work. If the interludes were read in this fashion, however, their point would have been missed and the urgency to the effort of rethinking ontotheology would still be left wanting.

Far from being mere illustrations, the interludes are absolutely essential to understanding this work on its own terms. They are the outgrowths to the argument being made, highlighting the spaces left vacant by theory alone, even modeling a style of thought that is "otherwise than overcoming." Without them the argument would be left incomplete and inconsistent with itself. That is not to say that through them the argument is completed, or somehow cinched or resolved. On the contrary, their point is otherwise—hints and provocations along the way, reminders that the task of thinking otherwise is incessant.

The interludes are integral in yet another fashion as well, for by their placement in between the chapters, they stand as interruptions, as questions, or as suggestions for paths not taken. Thus beyond, before, or in between the philosophical-theological impasse, which has been the dominant framework throughout the pages of this text, stands another voice, another frame of reference, whose power it is not to resolve the problem, but as Kristeva describes in her correspondence with Catherine Clément on the feminine and the sacred, to be on the borderline, to acknowledge one's dual nature. A duality graver than the divisions that exist between men and women, or between philosophy and theology, this is a being on the borderline between biology and meaning, between those "who give life" and those "who give meaning."[1] This has to do with what Bergson calls the very "articulation of the real," in which "it is a question of finding the problem and consequently of positing it, even more than of solving it."[2] This goes down to the very root of the ontotheological problem as it reassesses the divided nature of ontotheology, treating it less as a problem to be overcome and more as the inevitable condition of thought. By shifting the frame of reference, by associating ontotheology with the abject, and/or by writing Kristeva into the exchange between philosophers and theologians, the problem becomes reconstituted, which is not to say reinscribed, but rather, in Kristeva's terms, "otherwise placed, even, I daresay, better placed to stand on that 'roof' [of the sacred]."[3]

The question of the interludes, therefore, is also the question of/from women, and the place of the interludes, in effect, is also the place of the feminine when it comes to the problem of ontotheology. This place, as the preceding pages should suggest, might be better designated as a *non*-place, for inasmuch as ontotheology is a problem, it is one that has been raised, fought, and sporadically "overcome" by men alone. This is the underside, the subtext, to the problem of ontotheology; or more precisely, this is one symptom to the misapprehension of ontotheology as a problem. The desire for a purity of discourse not only reinscribes the philosophical-theological divide, but it also helps to maintain the male privilege and androcentric bias of both a philosophical and a theological language. Therefore, if she is to speak to this problem at all and not simply submit to this exclusion, the woman's place is to articulate a different way of speaking and writing. This would be a mixed discourse giving voice to a fluid identity, a cosmopolitanism that knows the price of crossing boundaries (see Interlude 1), a language made accountable (see Interlude 2), and a fidelity made iconoclastic (see Interlude 3).

Therefore, in the place of the extreme pleasure and unlimited freedom of which Marion speaks stands Kristeva's attention to the abject as the irreducible condition of existence. Indeed, there is a cost to freedom, one cannot help but remain circumscribed within abjection, and in the case of Marion's theology, which paradoxically discovers its freedom through its submission to the authority of the bishop, that cost would seem to support and even require women's exclusion from theology. Set in this context, the pleasure of which Marion speaks becomes an absurdity, if not an outright hostility to the woman who is barred from the rights of power and refused the institutional authority that would sanction the credibility of her theological vision.

And in the place of Derrida's talk of religion—which he rightly points out must admit to at least two sources, both the *doxic* and the *sacred*, and thus is always already plural, always already political, and impossibly duplicitous[4]—stands Kristeva's talk of the sacred, or more precisely, the feminine experience of the sacred, which she insists must be distinguished from both religion and belief. As she writes: "What if the sacred were the unconscious perception the human being has of its untenable eroticism: always on the borderline between nature and culture, the animalistic and the verbal, the sensible and the nameable? What if the sacred were not the religious *need* for protection and omnipotence that institutions exploit but the jouissance of that *cleavage*—of that power/powerlessness—of that exquisite lapse?"[5] The difference is that the sacred—whether hysteria or trance, whether a revolt (Clément: "The sacred among women may express an instantaneous revolt that passes through the body and cries out."), a resistance (Kristeva: "A resistance to the Spectacle in which the religion of the Word culminates."), or authorization (Clément: "Is that to say that sex is sacred? Not a sure thing. But let's reverse the terms: because it authorizes the brutal insurrection of the forbidden humors during ceremonies, the sacred is sexual."), whether it is denied or whether it is the source of embarrassment—is and remains, unlike either historical religions or specific beliefs, impossible to be transcended.[6] When distinguishing the sacred from religion and belief, one no longer speaks of, and gets swept up by the "hysteria" of either its "end" or its "return," for the sacred is always with us. This is the point when it comes to the feminine and the sacred, and likewise with women and ontotheology: Though always with us, it is not always present to us, for it is *present otherwise,* speaking and thinking in "another tongue."[7]

These points of comparison are not meant as condemnations, but as questions, as the culmination to a whole series of questions. These questions exemplify the importance of the dialogical intentions of this book, which, like the correspondence between Clément and Kristeva, is meant to be a "book in two voices," a book that came into being "that collects questions in order to shed light on them."[8]

NOTES

Preface

1. Charles E. Winquist, *Desiring Theology*, 141.
2. John D. Caputo, *Against Ethics*, 4.

Introduction

1. Julia Kristeva, *Powers of Horror*, 2, 1.
2. Elizabeth Gross, "The Body of Signification," 86.
3. Kristeva, *Powers of Horror*, 4.
4. Ibid., 17.
5. For example, see Charlotte Allen, "Is Nothing Sacred?: Casting Out the Gods from Religious Studies;" Walter H. Capps, *Religious Studies: The Making of a Discipline*; Russell T. McCutcheon, *Manufacturing Religion: The Discourse on Sui Generis Religion and the Politics of Nostalgia*; and Donald Wiebe, *The Politics of Religious Studies: The Continuing Conflict with Theology in the Academy*.

For my own analysis of this rift within the academic study of religion, see Jeffrey W. Robbins, "Re-Placing Theology: Theologizing the Academic Study of Religion," *CSSR Bulletin*, Vol. 28, No. 4 (November 1999): 118–25.
6. For example, see Charles Taylor, "Overcoming Epistemology," in *Philosophical Arguments*, 1–19; John Milbank, "Only Theology Overcomes Metaphysics," in *The Word Made Strange: Theology, Language, Culture*, 36–54; Thomas A. Carlson, "The Deaths of God in Hegel: Overcoming Finitude and Religious Representation," in *Indiscretion: Finitude and the Naming of God*, 22–49; and Merold Westphal, "Overcoming Onto-theology," in *God, the Gift, and Postmodernism*, 146–63.
7. Martin Heidegger, *Nietzsche, Volume IV: Nihilism*, 210.
8. See Brian D. Ingraffia, *Postmodern Theory and Biblical Theology*, 101.
9. Ibid., 4.
10. Jean-Luc Marion, *God without Being*, xxi.
11. Westphal, 154.
12. Ibid., 163.
13. For example, see Paul Ricoeur, *The Conflict of Interpretations*, 445, and *Oneself as Another*, 23–25.

14. For instance, see Phillip Blond, who argues that the ontotheological problem can be located within history. As he writes in the introduction to *Post-Secular Philosophy: Between Philosophy and Theology:* "Prior to God entering philosophy under the name of *causa sui*, I would suggest that theology was not necessarily onto-theological in the Heideggerian sense, even if we can already see the preparation of the ground for the *causa sui* from Scotus onwards" (11).

15. See Louis Dupré, *Passage to Modernity*, 39.

16. Ibid., 6–7.

17. Jonathan Glover, *Humanity: A Moral History of the Twentieth Century*, xii.

1. The Problem of Philosophical Theology

1. See Thomas J. J. Altizer and William Hamilton, *Radical Theology and the Death of God*, xii.

2. Some examples: Graham Ward, a representative of the new school of radical orthodox theologians, writes: "What I am arguing here is that theology's primary concern is with its own possibility, its own relationship as a discourse to the original *Deus dixit*" (in *Barth, Derrida, and the Language of Theology*, 10). On the opposite side of the spectrum is the reevaluation of theology begun by Mark C. Taylor's groundbreaking work *Erring*, in which he writes that postmodernism is like a "wound" inflicting theological thinking with "the overwhelming awareness of death—a death that 'begins' with the death of God and 'ends' with the death of our selves" (in *Erring: A Postmodern A/theology*). This wounded theology is an outgrowth of Paul Tillich's theology of culture. As Robert P. Scharlemann writes: "To speak of a theological understanding of the postmodern is to enter the context of what Tillich identified as cultural theology, or theology of culture. The idea that there can be a theology, indeed, that there is a theology, which is not religious or ecclesiastical, but cultural in origin" (in *Theology at the End of the Century*, 7).

What all these various and oftentimes conflicting accounts of theology have in common, I am arguing, is a shared appreciation for the problems inherent in the search for foundations. Where does theology begin such that, in Sallie McFague's words, it is neither "idolatrous" nor "irrelevant"? How might the theologian make a case for the value of theological thinking in an age and culture grown weary and suspicious of dogmatism? What possibilities are there for the theologian to speak truthfully of the "Word of God"?

3. See, for example, Daniel L. Migliore, "Reappraising Barth's Theology," in *Theology Today*, 309–15. Migliore writes: "Any history of twentieth-century theology will be largely the story of the revolutionary work and influence of Karl Barth. Energetic pastor for ten years in a small Swiss village, courageous resistance leader of the church against Nazism, brilliant biblical interpreter, Christo-centric church theologian, lover of Mozart's music—his stature can be measured only by comparison with other theological giants like Augustine, Aquinas, Luther, and Calvin."

4. See, for example, James M. Robinson and John B. Cobb Jr., *The Later Heidegger and Theology*, and Robert S. Gall, *Beyond Theism and Atheism: Heidegger's Significance for Religious Thinking*.

5. Kristeva, *Powers of Horror*, 110, 112.

6. Jacques Derrida makes a similar observation when he writes: "First of all, in the alternative between sacredness without belief (index of this algebra: 'Heidegger') and faith in a holiness without sacredness, in a desacralizing truth, even making of a certain disenchantment the condition of authentic holiness (index: 'Levinas'—notably the author of *From the Sacred to the Holy*)" (in "Faith and Knowledge: the Two Sources of 'Religion' at the Limits of Reason Alone," 64).

7. One interesting historical analogue would be Augustine's debate with, and eventual suppression of, the Donatists; specifically, how this early Church controversy has been described by Peter Brown in his biography of Augustine. According to Brown, the early Augustine shared much in common with the Donatists. This is precisely the reason he was originally drawn to the Manicheans. That is to say, both the Manicheans and the Donatists are concerned with rigidly maintaining purity. Augustine, on the other hand, after his conversion to the Catholic faith, is portrayed by Brown as a recovering perfectionist. Quoting Augustine, Brown writes:

> "Whoever thinks," Augustine will then write, "that in this mortal life a man may so disperse the mists of bodily and carnal imaginings as to possess the unclouded light of changeless truth, and to cleave to it with the unswerving constancy of a spirit wholly estranged from the common ways of life—he understands neither What he seeks, nor who he is who seeks it."
>
> Augustine, indeed, had decided that he would never reach the fulfillment that he first thought was promised to him by a Christian Platonism: he would never impose a victory of mind over body in himself, he would never achieve the wrapt [*sic*] contemplation of the ideal philosopher. It is the most drastic change that a man may have to accept: it involved nothing less than the surrender of the bright future he thought he had gained at Cassiciacum. (147)

The mature Augustine, in other words, realizes that while purity might be a noteworthy desire, in actuality it is a hindrance to the experience of grace and an inadequate foundation for ecclesiology. The difference between himself and the Donatist, therefore, was that the Donatist felt the need to preserve and protect the purity of the gospel, which had first been threatened by persecution and then by compromise. Augustine, on the other hand, is confident in the Church's ability to absorb alien cultures without losing its identity. "This identity," Brown writes, "existed independently of the quality of the human agents of the Church: it rested on 'objective' promises of God, working out magnificently in history, and on the 'objective' efficacy of its sacraments" (214).

8. Barth's terminology, "Word of God," is deliberately extreme as the utmost demand of theological thinking. However, the Word of God remains always as a theological striving. The theologian's words, in other words, should never be confused with God's Word, just as the words of scripture should not be equated with the Word of God. For Barth's clearest analysis of this tension constitutive of theological thinking, see Karl Barth, *The Word of God and the Word of Man*.

9. Karl Barth, *The Epistle to the Romans*, 10–11 (hereafter referred to as *Romans*).

10. Ibid., 1.

11. While reflecting on Barth's understanding of the nature of theological language, Graham Ward speaks of this complexity in interpretation as "a rupture of meaning that places everything in question simply by being other than meaning (though not necessarily meaningless). This rupture is read theologically as the judgment under which God places all human knowledge" (24).

12. Barth, *Romans*, 8.

13. Karl Barth, *Church Dogmatics*, I/1, 113.

14. Barth, *Romans*, 10.

15. See, for instance, Ralf K. Wüstenberg, who writes: "Over against German Idealism . . . , Kant possesses for Barth the advantage of a self-limitation of philosophical thinking . . ." Wüstenberg continues: "Barth concurs when the *thing in itself* becomes for Kant at least unknowable, and for the Neo-Kantians a mere boundary or limiting concept. He argues that in exactly the same way, *God in and for himself* cannot be known unless he first makes himself *known* through revelation" (in *A Theology of Life*, 47–48).

16. As Gabriel Vahanian writes: "A theology of the Word, according to the tradition of the Reformation, is always essentially a *corrective* theology. Like a teacher, it attempts to inform and transform by *confronting* the student, not by indoctrinating him." G. Vahanian, "Introduction," in *The Faith of the Church*, 12.

17. Barth, *Church Dogmatics*, I/2, 868.

18. Barth, *Church Dogmatics*, I/1, 769.

19. Barth, *Wolfgang Amadeus Mozart*, 55.

20. William Stacy Johnson, *The Mystery of God: Karl Barth and the Postmodern Foundations of Theology*. Johnson's reading of Barth, though new in the sense of reading Barth as a precursor to postmodernity, mirrors much of traditional Barthian scholarship in the sense of reading Barth's theology as a critical endeavor. For instance, see Vahanian, Lowe, and Ward above. Also see Eberhard Jüngel, a one-time student of Barth's, who writes: "Barth's theology was, from the beginning, an avowed enemy of systems. It remained so even in the very systematically written *Church Dogmatics*. What is systematic about this theology is that it resolves to make progress precisely by constantly correcting, or else completely changing, its direction" (in *Karl Barth: A Theological Legacy*, 27).

21. Johnson, 35.

22. Ibid., 14.

23. Again, note the similarities between Barth and Kant. Barth's theological analytic of the "wholly other" is similar to Kant's analytic of the sublime, from his *Critique of Judgment*. Borrowing language from Jean-François Lyotard, both cases might be considered as examples of "pure subjective thinking," which serves, ironically, as a critique of both the subjectivity and objectivity of modern thought. For an analysis of the critique that is inherent to reflective judgment, see Lyotard, *Lessons on the Analytic of the Sublime*.

24. Johnson writes: "It [theology] decenters scripture, for scripture is not identical with the 'Word of God' but is a 'sign' that seeks to bear witness to who

God is. It decenters the human self, for our 'real' humanity, made visible in Jesus Christ, exists out in front of us as a task still waiting to be performed. And yes, it decenters our reflections about Jesus Christ too" (185).

25. Ibid.

26. Barth, *Romans*, 35.

27. It is this ethical component that Johnson understands to be at the heart of Barth's theological project. Johnson writes: "Barth views ethical inquiry primarily as a process of continually putting one's own preconceived notions of the moral life into question . . . Barth's ethics offers 'one of the most powerfully anti-modern statements by a Christian theologian since the Enlightenment.' Yet Barth's challenge to modernity is not merely 'anti-modern,' and even less is it naively 'pre-modern,' but it points to a possibility that may be designated genuinely 'post-modern'" (154).

28. See Clifford Green, "Introduction," *Karl Barth: Theologian of Freedom,* 28–29.

29. Barth, *Romans*, 90.

30. Ibid., 57.

31. Ibid., 141.

32. Ibid., 231, 60.

33. Ibid., 238. This strictly negative appraisal of religion will be tamed as Barth's theology shifts from dialectics to dogmatics. See especially his discussion of "True Religion," in *Church Dogmatics*, I/2, 325–61.

34. Karl Barth, "Biblical Questions, Insights and Vistas," in *Karl Barth: A Theological Legacy*, 59–60.

35. Karl Barth, "Philosophy and Theology," in *The Way of Theology in Karl Barth*, 79–81.

36. See Karl Barth, *Anselm: Fides Quaerens Intellectum.*

37. Ibid., 90. See also G. Vahanian, who made this point clear over a generation ago: "It is time to dispel the erroneous conception that Barth has no use for things of this world and that like Tertullian he finds nothing in common between Athens and Jerusalem. Similarly, we must resist the widespread opinion, based on mis-interpreted and extrapolated utterances from his earlier theological writings, that the lapsidary formula 'God is all, man is nothing' gives the real measure of his thinking" (in Vahanian, "Introduction," 12).

38. Barth, "Philosophy and Theology," 86–87.

39. Ibid., 85.

40. Ibid., 84–85.

41. Stephen W. Sykes, "Introduction," in Barth, *The Way of Theology in Karl Barth*, 5.

42. See Karl Barth, "Concluding Unscientific Postscript on Schleiermacher," and "Feuerbach," in *Karl Barth: Theologian of Freedom*, 66–97.

43. On the critical impasse between Barth and Schleiermacher and its continued relevance for contemporary theological thought, see James O. Duke and Robert F. Streetman, eds., *Barth and Schleiermacher: Beyond the Impasse?*

44. Barth, *Romans*, 47, 49.

45. Ibid., 53.

46. This is where my interpretation parts ways with Johnson. For Johnson, Barth's argument for theology as a discrete discipline should be understood as a kind of "emergency measure" necessitated by the other disciplines' failure to live up to their theological calling. If we take Barth's essay "Philosophy and Theology" seriously, however, we discern a deeper cooperation that rests not on a final unity of thought brought about by a theological sublimation, but an ongoing dialectic and dialogue between truly different ways of thinking. And because both philosophy and theology remain human discourses, neither is any closer to the ultimate truth that they share in common.

47. Bernd Jaspert and Geoffrey W. Bromiley, eds., *Karl Barth—Rudolf Bultmann: Letters, 1922–1966*, 38.

48. Charles Marsh, *Reclaiming Dietrich Bonhoeffer: The Promise of His Theology*, 52, 41.

49. Barth, *Church Dogmatics*, I/2, 280.

50. Marsh, 51.

51. The phrase is borrowed from Graham Ward in his discussion of the similarities and differences between Barth and Emmanuel Levinas. See chapter 5.

52. It is no accident and should come as no surprise, therefore, that the next great voice in German Protestant theology after that of Barth would be that of Jürgen Moltmann, whose work *The Crucified God: The Cross of Christ As the Foundation and Criticism of Christian Theology* centered on the theme of the suffering of God. Insofar as Moltmann represents a theological tradition that is continuous with that of Barth, one should read this particular critique of Barth's shortcoming not as a dead end, but more like a road not taken. In other words, it would have been neither inconceivable nor inconsistent for Barth, like Moltmann, to move beyond the theological strategy of reversal, which proved so powerful as a critique of modernity. However—and this is precisely the point of the critique—this would have involved the critical examination of the philosophical concepts and theories employed, which was an effort that Barth refused.

53. As Ward writes of Barth's understanding of the nature of theological language:

A hermeneutic circle is being described which moves within and understands the divine intra-dialogue, and faith is the condition for entry. But Barth insists that there are two radically different forms of hermeneutical activity in operation. On the one hand, there is a human being's continuous attempt "to answer the riddle of his own existence . . . to strike a balance between himself and his world." The question provoking the hermeneutical activity here is an existential one. . . . On the other hand, by faith, human beings participate in a second hermeneutic activity, that of the Trinity, in which God speaks and human beings are brought to understand the meaning of that Word. In this hermeneutic activity, where there is an equation of word with object and the communication is direct, God speaks and interprets God by God (Jesus Christ) through God (Holy Spirit) to God. No synthesis is possible between these two activities, the one anthropological and the other theological; the latter reveals the former to be an idol, or, in terms of linguistics, the endless play of signifiers" (15–16).

54. Martin Heidegger, *Being and Time*, 2–3.

55. Ibid., 17–23.

56. Ibid., 219, 227.

57. Ibid., 219–46.

58. Martin Heidegger, *The Piety of Thinking*, 6.

59. Ibid., 21.

60. This suggestion was made by Heidegger in the course of a conversation he had in 1953 with a group of German Protestant theologians on the significance of his philosophy for theology. In Ibid., 59–71.

61. Gall, ix.

62. Ibid., 26.

63. Heidegger as quoted in Gall, 26.

64. Gall, 27, 26.

65. For instance, see Theodore J. Kisiel and John van Buren, eds., *Reading Heidegger from the Start: Essays in His Earliest Thought*, 213–30; John D. Caputo, *Heidegger and Aquinas*; John Macquarrie, *Heidegger and Christianity*; and George Kovacs, *The Question of God in Heidegger's Phenomenology*.

66. Gall, 25.

67. Ibid., 28.

68. For an analysis of the differences between these two kinds of thinking, see Heidegger's "Memorial Address," in *Discourse on Thinking*, 43–57.

69. For a study of this shift in Heidegger's thought, see James Risser, ed., *Heidegger Toward the Turn*, and Dominique Janicaud and Jean-François Mattéi, *Heidegger from Metaphysics to Thought*.

70. Martin Heidegger, *Identity and Difference*, 55.

71. Barth, *Church Dogmatics*, I/2, 280.

72. Heidegger writes: "[F]or Hegel, the matter of thinking is the idea as the absolute concept. For us, formulated in a preliminary fashion, the matter of thinking is the difference *as* difference" (in *Identity and Difference*, 47).

73. As Joan Stambaugh writes in the introduction to *Identity and Difference*: "Identity is belonging-together. If the element of *together* in belonging-together is emphasized, we have the metaphysical concept of identity which orders the manifold into a unity mediated by synthesis. This unity forms a systematic total-ity of the world with God or Being as the ground, as the first cause and as the highest being. But if the element of *belonging* in belonging together is empha-sized, we have thinking and Being held apart and at the same time held together (not fitted together) in the Same" (ibid., 12–13).

74. Heidegger writes: "Different things, thinking and Being, are here thought of as the Same. What does this say? It says something wholly different from what we know otherwise as the doctrine of metaphysics which states that identity belongs to Being. Parmenides says: Being belongs to an identity. . . . We must acknowledge the fact that in the earliest period of thinking, long before thinking had arrived at a principle of identity, identity itself speaks out in a pronounce-ment which rules as follows: thinking and Being belong together in the Same and by virtue of the Same" (ibid., 27). And later, in his discussion of Hegel, Heidegger writes: "But the same is not the merely identical. In the merely identical, the

difference disappears. In the same the difference appears, and appears all the more pressingly, the more resolutely thinking is concerned with the same matter in the same way" (ibid., 45).

75. Ingraffia, 169.

76. As quoted in Hans-Georg Gadamer, "Being, Spirit, God," in *Heidegger Memorial Lectures*, 56.

77. Martin Heidegger, *On the Way to Language*, 10.

78. Frank Kermode, *The Genesis of Secrecy: The Interpretation of Narrative*, vii.

79. For instance, see Martin Heidegger, "The Anaximander Fragment," in *Early Greek Thinking*, 13–58.

80. Emmanuel Levinas, "Signature," 181.

81. See John D. Caputo, *Demythologizing Heidegger.*

82. See Ingraffia, 110–22.

83. Gall, 33.

84. See Derrida, "Faith and Knowledge."

Interlude: On Political Boundaries and Profit

1. Paul writes to the Corinthians: "For though I am free with respect to all, I have made myself a slave to all so that I might win more of them. To the Jews, I became as a Jew in order to win Jews. To those under the law, I became as one under the law (though I myself am not under the law) so that I might win those under the law. To those outside the law, I became as one outside the law (though I am not free from God's law but am under Christ's law) so that I might win those outside the law. To the weak, I became weak so that I might win the weak. I have become all things to all people, that I might by all means save some" (1 Cor. 9:22).

2. Julia Kristeva, *Nations without Nationalism*, 15–16.

3. Ibid., 2.

4. Eduardo Galeano, *Open Veins of Latin America*, 249, 241.

5. Ibid., 243–44.

2. The Path of Theology

1. It should be noted that others have voiced this critique before. For instance, see Thomas J. J. Altizer, "American and the Future of Theology," in *Radical Theology and the Death of God*. Of Bultmann and Tillich, Altizer writes: "Yet few if any theologians confess that our time demands a radical transformation of faith. Rudolf Bultmann's demythologizing stops short of demythologizing the *kerygma*, and Paul Tillich's method of correlation demands a preservation of the form of the traditional Christian symbols" (10).

2. See Jacques Derrida, "How to Avoid Speaking: Denials," in *Derrida and Negative Theology*, 73–142.

3. For instance, in a letter from June 8, 1944, Bonhoeffer writes:

Efforts are made to prove to a world come of age that it cannot live without the tutelage of "God." Even though there has been a surrender on all secular problems, there remains the so-called "ultimate questions"—death, guilt—to which only "God" can give an answer, and because of which we need God and the church and the pastor. So we live, in some degree, on these so-called ultimate questions of humanity. But what if one day they no longer exist as such, if they too can be answered "without God"? Of course, we now have the secularized offshoots of Christian theology, namely existentialist philosophy and psychotherapists, who demonstrate to secure, contented, and happy mankind that it is really unhappy and desperate and simply unwilling to admit that it is in a predicament about which it knows nothing, and from which only they can rescue it [in *Letters and Papers from Prison*, 326].

4. Robert P. Scharlemann, "Authenticity and Encounter: Bonhoeffer's Appropriation of Ontology," 254.

5. Dietrich Bonhoeffer, *Letters and Papers from Prison*, 280.

6. Ibid., 369.

7. Ibid., 369–70.

8. See Friedrich Nietzsche, who writes: "In this, it seems to me, we should agree that these skeptical anti-realists and knowledge-microscopists of today: their instinct, which repels them from *modern* reality, is unrefuted—what do their retrograde bypaths concern us! The main thing about them is *not* that they wish to go 'back,' but that they wish to get—*away*. A little *more* strength, fight, courage, and artistic power, and they would want to *rise*—not return!" In *Beyond Good and Evil: Prelude to a Philosophy of the Future*, 17.

9. See Bonhoeffer, *Letters and Papers from Prison*.

10. By this I mean to include not only the explicit concerns of *Act and Being* (1929), but also his doctoral dissertation of 1927, *Sanctorum Communio*, which Bonhoeffer wrote when he was only twenty-one years old. While this chapter will not treat this earliest work of Bonhoeffer's in much detail, the argument regarding the defining characteristics of Bonhoeffer's theological ontology will make clear how his social philosophy plays a fundamental role in his theology such that a theological ontology resists ontology's natural tendency toward idealism.

11. This is a phrase used by Clifford Green to describe the unifying programmatic that runs throughout Bonhoeffer's works. It is important to note that a theology of sociality is not to be confused with sociology. Sociality has to do with the conditions that make the science of sociology possible. See Green, *Bonhoeffer: A Theology of Sociality*, 25–26.

12. Ibid., 21.

13. Ibid., 24.

14. Ibid., 32 (italics his).

15. Dietrich Bonhoeffer, *Sanctorum Communio*, 51 (italics his).

16. Green, 27–28 (italics his).

17. Dietrich Bonhoeffer, *Act and Being*, 25.

18. An accusation Bonhoeffer borrows from Hans Michael Müller. See, *Act and Being*, 25 n. 1.

19. Ibid., 27, 30.

20. Ibid., 31.

21. Wayne Whitson Floyd, "Editor's Introduction," *Act and Being*, 11–12.

22. Bonhoeffer, *Act and Being*, 33–35.

23. Ibid., 59, 70, 71.

24. Floyd, 7.

25. Bonhoeffer, *Act and Being*, 38.

26. Ibid., 72. In anticipation of chapter 5, one might say that Bonhoeffer's critique of ontology's tendency toward idealism was in fact the same that the Jewish philosopher Emmanuel Levinas will eventually levy against Heidegger.

27. A few examples from *Act and Being:* "God alone can speak of God" (92); "faith is something essentially different from religion" (93); "There is, therefore, no method for the knowledge of God; human beings cannot place themselves into the existential [existentiell] situation from which they could speak of God, for they are not able to place themselves into the truth. They can try to think in reference to this situation, but as long as they speak 'about' God, their thinking will remain self-enclosed outside the truth" (92); "Therefore, only those who have been placed in the truth can understand themselves in truth" (81).

28. Ibid., 83, 85. This is not to diminish the formative influence Barth had over Bonhoeffer. Indeed, as Charles Marsh has demonstrated, "Bonhoeffer's theology is possible only in view of Barth's revolution in theological method" (ix). Marsh writes that Bonhoeffer "admired Barth until the end as the theologian who showed him the way to Christian freedom, and thus as a kind of mentor or parent, challenging, praising, and provoking him—prodding him along the way of his uncertain pilgrimage" (7).

29. Marsh, 24.

30. Ibid., 24, 25.

31. Bonhoeffer, *Act and Being*, 25.

32. For a description of the stages of Bonhoeffer's developing theological interest in ethics, see the "Editor's Preface," in Dietrich Bonhoeffer, *Ethics*, 15–18.

33. See Søren Kierkegaard, *Fear and Trembling.* This comparison between Bonhoeffer and Kierkegaard should come as no surprise given the previously mentioned formative link between Kierkegaard and Barth, and between Barth and Bonhoeffer. Perhaps what Bonhoeffer most shares in common with Kierkegaard is that both begin their reflections from the standpoint of the radical nature of the Biblical faith. In Kierkegaard's terminology, the leap of faith is an existential embrace of the infinite paradox. For Bonhoeffer, the radical demand of faith is spoken of as a "costly grace." See Dietrich Bonhoeffer, *The Cost of Discipleship.*

34. Bonhoeffer, *Letters and Papers from Prison*, 361.

35. Caputo, *Against Ethics*, 4.

36. Bonhoeffer, *Ethics*, 11.

37. Ibid., 21.

38. Ibid., 66.

39. Ibid., 67.

40. Martin Luther King Jr., "Letter from Birmingham City Jail," in *A Testament of Hope,* 289–302.

41. Bonhoeffer, *Ethics,* 68.

42. Ibid., 68.

43. Hannah Arendt, *Eichmann in Jerusalem,* 247.

44. Bonhoeffer, *Ethics,* 69.

45. Ibid.

46. Ibid.

47. Ibid., 69, 70.

48. Ibid., 70.

49. Ibid., 70–88.

50. Ibid., 88.

51. This confession of guilt ranges from such varying things as the Church's failure to proclaim clearly the message of the gospel, to its failure to protest against the innocent suffering of countless people, and to its desire for "security, peace, and quiet." Ibid., 112–16.

52. Ibid., 119.

53. For example, see Alisdair MacIntyre, *After Virtue,* and Stanley Hauerwas, *The Peaceable Kingdom.*

54. Narrative theology and virtue theory form the theoretical backbone to "postliberal theology." Christian educator Alister E. McGrath describes postliberal theology as follows:

> Building upon the work of philosophers such as Alisdair MacIntyre, postliberalism rejects both the traditional Enlightenment appeal to a "universal rationality" and the liberal assumption of an immediate religious experience common to all humanity. Arguing that all thought and experience is historically and socially mediated, postliberalism bases its theological program upon a return to religious traditions, whose values are inwardly appropriated. Postliberalism is thus *anti-foundational* (in that it rejects the notion of a universal foundation of knowledge), *communitarian* (in that it appeals to the values, experiences, and languages of a community, rather than prioritizing the individual), and *historicist* (in that it insists upon the importance of traditions and their associated historical communities in the shaping of experience and thought).

According to McGrath, "postliberalism" is particularly important for the contemporary understanding of systematic theology and Christian ethics, for it views theology as essentially a "descriptive discipline" that is to be judged not by extrinsic universal criteria, but rather by its "intrasystemic" coherence. Likewise with Christian ethics, its task is the "identification of the moral vision of a historical community (the church), and with bringing that vision to actualization in the lives of its members" (in *Christian Theology: An Introduction,* 109–10.

55. Hauerwas, 24.

56. Ibid., 3.

57. Ibid., 9–10.

58. Bonhoeffer, *Ethics*, 30.
59. Ibid., 17, 25.
60. Ibid., xvii.

3. The Path of Phenomenology

1. Thomas S. Kuhn, *The Structure of Scientific Revolutions*, 1–2.

2. Ibid., 10–11.

3. This argument that phenomenology's discovery of history opens philosophy toward theology is contemporaneous with the variations of the argument of the inherently theological character of history. For instance, see Langdon Gilkey, *Reaping the Whirlwind: A Christian Interpretation of History*, in which he writes: "Once again, history has a religious dimension for those who exist within it: it not only shapes them, sets before them issues of ultimate concern, faces them with deep anxiety, tempts them to sin, and calls forth their courage, creativity and compassion. It also poses for them the deepest of reflective issues concerning human existence in time, the form of history's events, and the shape of the ultimate horizon of temporal being. On the most existential level it calls for a philosophy or a theology of history," (35). Gilkey continues: "Any examination of our historical, and especially our political, experience, reveals a dimension of ultimacy in that experience that must be understood, illumined and dealt with in terms of religious symbols," (37). For Gilkey, in other words, the very fact that human beings are historical beings necessarily gives rise to a sense of religiosity and theological reflection.

Also, see Jaroslav Pelikan, *Historical Theology: Continuity and Change in Christian Doctrine*, who speaks of "the intimate connection between the discipline of history and the study of theology" (ix).

Finally, see Reinhold Niebuhr, *Faith and History*, who argues that the *meaning* of history is only disclosed through faith.

4. Paul Ricoeur, *Husserl*, 84.

5. For an overview of the various strands of phenomenology that developed from Husserl, see Dermot Moran, *Introduction to Phenomenology*.

6. Ricoeur, *Husserl*, 4.

7. See Rüdiger Safranski, *Martin Heidegger: Between Good and Evil*, 71–88.

8. Ibid., 3, 4. Heidegger's transformation of phenomenology would later be described by Moran as phenomenology being "radically historicised" by the "fusing [of] it with principles of interpretation, hermeneutics," (190).

9. Paul Ricoeur, "On Interpretation," in *The Continental Philosophy Reader*, 150.

10. That "crisis" as a particularly *theological* theme is a point that is certainly intended throughout this chapter, though it is one that will remain largely undeveloped. Recall from chapter 1 that "the permanent *krisis* between time and eternity" is the starting point of Barth's dialectical theology. Also recall that this theological crisis had its origins in, or at least was a response to, the historical and cultural crisis in which it emerged; namely, that of World War I and the failure of

modern, liberal theology to speak definitively the Word of God. In this respect, Husserl's turn toward crisis as a theme for phenomenology is intended to suggest an opening of philosophy to theology.

11. Eugen Fink offers an alternative account of the development of Husserl's phenomenology: (1) *Psychologism* (1887–1901), (2) *Descriptive Phenomenology* (1901–13), and (3) *Transcendental Phenomenology* (1913–38). See Moran, 65–66. The benefit of Fink's account is that it includes the earliest of Husserl's work. The drawback is that it fails to account for the importance of the imprint of history in Husserl's latest crisis philosophy. On the importance of this late shift in Husserl's thinking, Moran writes: "[B]eginning in the 1920's but especially in the 1930's, for example in the *Crisis*, Husserl began to recognize that 'static' constitutive phenomenology needed to be supplemented by a phenomenological study of the historical genesis of all meaning, not just cultural meanings but scientific meanings also. Besides 'constitutive phenomenology' Husserl came to recognize the need for a 'genetic phenomenology', a project which came to the fore in the *Crisis* but which existed in subterranean form in his manuscript researches for many years prior to the publication of that work" (Moran, 125).

12. This interpretation of the development of Husserl's thought in the direction of history is indebted to Ricoeur, who was the first to undergo a serious investigation into the question of history in Husserl's thought. For instance see Ricoeur, *Husserl*, 143–74.

13. For an analysis of Dilthey's understanding of the "worldview," see Theodore Plantinga, *Historical Understanding in the Thought of Wilhelm Dilthey*, 134–43; and H. A. Hodges, *Wilhelm Dilthey: An Introduction.*

14. According to Ricoeur, there are three criteria that must be met in order for Husserl to regard a philosophy properly scientific. Ricoeur writes: "Under the name of philosophical science Husserl means three things: first he means *radicality* in the manner of raising the question of the starting point; next he means the *universality* of a method devoted to the explication of strata and levels of sense; and finally he means the *systematic character* of structures thus brought to light" (in *Husserl*, 139).

15. As Hodges writes concerning the comparative task of the historical philosopher, the task is "not to dismiss the various systems as so many illusions, but to disengage the central vision of each and bring them together, since it is not separately, but by complementing and correcting one another, that they tell their real tale. The means by which this is done is a study which Dilthey calls 'philosophy of philosophy'—a comparative and critical *Weltanschauungslehre* which will analyze the metaphysical consciousness and the way in which *Weltanschauungen* arise out of it" (99).

16. Plantinga argues that Husserl's charge of relativism against Dilthey is based on a confusion between 'relativity,' a term Dilthey regularly uses, and 'relativism,' an epistemological problem that Dilthey, like Husserl, hoped to counter. 'Relativity' denotes both the sense of being in relation and the cultural awareness of difference or variety. Put simply, one can affirm 'relativity' without necessarily being a 'relativist.' Furthermore, Dilthey's own response to Husserl was that he

denied the possibility of metaphysics, not the possibility of knowledge. In this sense, Dilthey's project has much in common with phenomenology's employment of the *epoché* as the suspension of the natural attitude. See Plantinga, 134–35.

17. Edmund Husserl, *Phenomenology and the Crisis of Philosophy*, 125, 127.

18. Ibid., 127–28.

19. Quentin Lauer, "Introduction," in *Philosophy and the Crisis of Philosophy*, 8.

20. Jacques Derrida, "'Genesis and Structure' and Phenomenology," in *Writing and Difference*, 160.

21. As Derrida writes: "Pure truth or the pretension to pure truth is missed in its *meaning* as soon as one attempts, as Dilthey does, to account for it from within a determined historical totality, that is, from within a factual totality, a finite totality all of whose manifestations and cultural productions are structurally solidary and coherent, and are all regulated by the same function, by the same finite unity of a total subjectivity" (in "Genesis and Structure," 160).

22. Ibid., 161.

23. See Ricoeur, *Husserl*, 139.

24. Husserl, *Philosophy and the Crisis of Philosophy*, 71, 72, 73.

25. Ibid., 136.

26. Ibid., 146.

27. Ibid., 140, 142.

28. Moran, 133, 135.

29. This anticipates the discussion in chapters 4 and 5 of Marion's *God without Being* and Levinas's *Otherwise than Being*.

30. Husserl, *Philosophy and the Crisis of Philosophy*, 146.

31. Safranski, 72.

32. Moran, 2.

33. See chapter 1.

34. Safranski writes: "It was only the idea of historicity that unveiled for him [Heidegger] the whole questionableness of metaphysics. . . Heidegger learned from Dilthey that truths, too, have their history" (145–46).

35. Heidegger, *Being and Time*, 17–23.

36. Moran, 190.

37. It was not until years later that Husserl recognized the importance of this rupture for the future of phenomenology. Take, for instance, a letter written by Husserl to Gustav Albrecht in December of 1930:

> So this year I've thought and thought, written and written, having always before my eyes these times inimical to me, the younger generation deluded by the collapse, by what I would say I might make them gain the ears that hear and the eyes that see. What is tragic in the situation is that, while I'm absolutely certain that in the last decade I've brought my phenomenological philosophy to a maturity, to clarity and purity, to a breadth of problems and methods encompassed that traces out the genuine meaning and path for philosophy for all future—a new generation has come on the scene that misinterprets my published fragments and incomplete beginnings in their deepest sense, that propagates a presumably improved phenomenology

and reveres me as the old man who is now passed by. So I am once again alone philosophically, the way I was when I began; and yet how fulfilled, how sure the future! [As quoted by Ronald Bruzina, "Introduction," in Fink, *Sixth Cartesian Meditation*, xvi.]

And only one year later in 1931, as Dermot Moran reports, Husserl declares himself "the greatest enemy of the so-called 'phenomenological movement'" (in Moran, 2).

Compare these comments from Husserl with a letter written by Heidegger to Karl Jaspers years earlier, in 1922: "Husserl has gone totally to pieces—if indeed he ever was in one piece—which I have lately been increasingly questioning—he vacillates this way and that and utters trivialities such as would reduce one to tears. He lives by his mission of being 'the founder of phenomenology,' no one has any idea what that is—anyone who has been here for a semester realizes what's happening—he is beginning to suspect that the people are no longer following him" (as quoted by Safranski, 128).

38. Safranski, 96–97.

39. See Moran, 16.

40. See note 37.

41. Safranski, 176.

42. See Heidegger, "What are Poets for?" in *Poetry, Language, Thought*, 89–142.

43. For instance, see Heidegger, *Early Greek Thinking*; "A Dialogue on Language," in *On the Way to Language*, 1–56; and *Poetry, Language, Thought*.

44. Edmund Husserl, *Cartesian Meditations*, 4.

45. Lauer writes: "[T]he Socratic-Platonic revolution, which represented the definitive turn to the 'logos' of being, thus preparing the way for all future 'scientific' developments; the Cartesian revolution, with its emphasis on the subjective thematic in both experience and reason; the 'transcendental' revolution of Kant, in which subjectivity becomes the 'source' of all necessity and, therefore, of all knowledge in the strict sense; and, finally, the 'phenomenological' revolution, that so radically reforms all knowing that not only the form but also the content of every act of knowing has its source in subjectivity" (in Lauer, "Introduction," *Phenomenology and the Crisis of Philosophy*, 31).

46. Ibid., 32.

47. Ricoeur, *Husserl*, 82–83.

48. Ibid., 83.

49. Heidegger makes a similar point when he writes of the historical overcoming of metaphysics: "Experienced in virtue of the dawning of the origin, metaphysics is, however, at the same time past in the sense that it has entered its ending" (in *The End of Philosophy*, 85). Mark Taylor makes an analogous point in *Erring:* "The 'end' of the endgame, however, is at the same time the beginning of an unending game. From the perspective of the end of history, the 'final' plot seems to be 'that there is no plot'" (in *Erring*, 73).

50. Moran writes: "For Husserl it is not that consciousness *creates* the world in any ontological sense—this would be subjective idealism, itself a consequence of a certain *naturalising* tendency whereby consciousness is cause and world is effect—but rather that the world is opened up, made meaningful, or disclosed

through consciousness. . . . Since consciousness is *presupposed* in all science and knowledge, then the proper approach to the study of consciousness itself must be a *transcendental* one—one which, in Kantian terms, focuses on the *condition for the possibility of* knowledge, though, of course, Husserl believes the Kantian way of articulating the consciousness-world relation was itself distorted since it still postulated the thing in itself" (Moran, 144).

51. Maurice Merleau-Ponty, *Phenomenology of Perception*, vii.

52. René Descartes, *Discourse on the Method and Meditations on First Philosophy*, 90.

53. Husserl, *Cartesian Meditations*, 84.

54. Ibid.

55. Ibid., 85, 136.

56. On the concept of 'constitution' in Husserl's work, Fink notes that it is an 'operative,' as opposed to a 'thematic' concept. This means that it is a concept that Husserl frequently employs but never elucidates. See Eugen Fink, "Operative Concepts in Husserl's Phenomenology," in *Apriori and World: European Contributions to Husserlian Phenomenology*, 67–70.

57. Husserl, *Cartesian Meditations*, 83.

58. Moran argues that it is for this reason that Husserl's transcendental phenomenology is to be distinguished from subjective idealism; namely, because even as it is the transcendental consciousness that gives meaning and being to the world, so too is there a correlation between consciousness and the world that is always already pregiven. See Moran, 164–66.

59. Ibid., 156.

60. Merleau-Ponty, xiv, xxi.

61. Husserl, *Cartesian Meditations*, 149, 152.

62. Bruzina, in Fink, *Sixth Cartesian Meditation*, x, xii.

63. As quoted by Bruzina, in Fink, *Sixth Cartesian Meditation*, xxxvii.

64. David Bell, *Husserl*, 162. Moran makes a similar point: "Husserl's critics believe his discoveries are too heavily dependent on others 'seeing' things just in the manner Husserl does, because he lays such a heavy stress on essential intuition rather than on theory formation, hypothesis testing, or even deductive argumentation. If someone disputes Husserl's phenomenological discoveries he can only argue that they have got it wrong; they haven't seen what he has in the phenomenon" (Moran, 188).

65. Bruzina, in *Sixth Cartesian Meditation*, xxxvii.

66. Levinas, *Discovering Existence with Husserl*, 84, 85.

67. Fink, *Sixth Cartesian Meditation*, 2.

68. Ibid., 5, 57, 59, 62, 65.

69. Ibid., 20, 23.

70. Bruzina, in ibid., lviii.

71. Fink, 1.

72. Paul Ricoeur, *Freud and Philosophy*, 33.

73. Thomas S. Kuhn, 11.

74. Ricoeur, "On Interpretation," 150, 149.

75. See Moran, 181.

76. As quoted in David Carr, "Introduction," in Husserl, *The Crisis of European Sciences and Transcendental Phenomenology*, xxx (hereafter referred to as *Crisis*).

77. Moran, 182.

78. Martin Heidegger, *The Question Concerning Technology and Other Essays*, 116–17, 129, 131, 134.

79. Husserl, *Crisis*, 5–7.

80. Ibid., 3, 392.

81. Ibid., 322, 349.

82. Carr, in Husserl, *Crisis*, xxxvi.

83. Ibid., xxxvii.

84. Husserl, *Crisis*, 123.

85. Ibid., 123–24.

86. Derrida writes: *"We act as though we had some common sense of what 'religion' means through the languages that we believe . . . we know how to speak. We believe in the minimum trustworthiness of this word. Like Heidegger, concerning what he calls the* Faktum *of the vocabulary of being . . ., we believe . . . we pre-understand the meaning of this word, if only to be able to question and in order to interrogate ourselves on this subject. Well—we will have to return to this much later—nothing is less pre-assured than such a* Faktum *(in both of these cases, precisely) and the entire question of religion comes down, perhaps, to this lack of assurance"* (in Jacques Derrida, "Faith and Knowledge," 3).

87. John D. Caputo and Michael J. Scanlon, "Introduction," in *God, the Gift, and Postmodernism*, 6–8.

88. Or in terms of Derrida's essay, "Genesis and Structure," this is Husserl's failure to reconcile the structuralist demand with the genetic demand. As Derrida writes: "Husserl, thus, ceaselessly attempts to reconcile the *structuralist* demand (which leads to the comprehensive description of a totality, or a form or a function organized according to an internal legality in which elements have meaning only in the solidarity of their correlation or their opposition), with the *genetic* demand (that is the search for the origin and foundation of the structure). One could show, perhaps, that the phenomenological project itself is born of an initial failure of this attempt" (in "Genesis and Structure," 157).

89. Caputo and Scanlon, "Introduction," 7–8.

90. For example, Hume writes:

For here is the chief and most confounding objection to *excessive* scepticism, that no durable good can ever result from it; while it remains in its full force and vigour. We need only ask such a sceptic, *What his meaning is? And what he proposes by all these curious researches?* He is immediately at a loss, and knows not what to answer. . . . And though a Pyrrhonian may throw himself or others into a momentary amazement and confusion by his profound reasonings; the first and most trivial event in life will put to flight all his doubts and scruples, and leave him the same, in every point of action and speculation, with the philosophers of every other sect, or with those who never concerned themselves in any philosophical researches. When he awakes from his dream, he will be the first to join in the laugh against himself, and to confess, that all his objections are mere amusement, and can have no other tendency than to show the whimsical condition of mankind, who must act and reason and believe; though they are not able, by their most diligent enquiry, to satisfy themselves concerning the foundation of these operations, or to remove the objections, which may be raised against them. [In David Hume, *An Enquiry Concerning Human Understanding*, trans. Antony Flew (Chicago: Open Court, 1996), 190–91.]

For an in-depth study of the question of faith in Hume, see Delbert James Hanson, *Fideism and Hume's Philosophy: Knowledge, Religion, and Metaphysics* (New York: Peter Lang Publishing, 1993).

91. On truth as a "virtual" reality, see William James, "Knower and Known," *William James: Writings 1902–1910*, 881–89. Concerning pragmatism's claim that truth is "made," James writes: "This thesis is what I have to defend. The truth of an idea is not a stagnant property inherent in it. Truth *happens* to an idea. It *becomes* true, is *made* true by events. Its verity *is* in fact an event, a process: the process namely of its verifying itself; its veri-*fication*. Its validity is the process of its valid-*ation*" (*in* "Pragmatism," Ibid., 574).

92. On this point I am indebted to Oz Lorentzen, who makes the argument for this understanding of faith in his unpublished dissertation *Re-Covering Fideism: An A-modern Model of Language and Thought* (Syracuse University, 1998).

93. Merleau-Ponty writes: "It is a matter of describing, not of explaining or analysing. Husserl's first directive to phenomenology, in its early stages, to be a 'descriptive psychology,' or to return to the 'things themselves,' is from the start a rejection of science," viii.

94. Husserl, *Crisis*, 134.

Interlude: On Translations

1. Of the German Evangelical Church under National Socialism, Barth would say, "I cannot see anything in German Christianity but the last, fullest and worst monstrosity of neo-Protestantism," in Eberhard Busch, *Karl Barth: His Life from Letters and Autobiographical Texts*, 230. See also, "The Barmen Declaration," in which Barth drafted the Confessing Church's opposition to German Christians' cooperation with the Nazis. In *Karl Barth: Theologian of Freedom*, 148–51.

2. Elie Wiesel, *Night*, 32.

3. Ibid., 63.

4. Ibid., 64.

5. Ibid., 87.

6. Arendt, *Eichmann in Jerusalem*, 279.

4. Phenomenology Turned Theology

1. For example, see Levinas, "God and Philsophy," in *Emmanuel Levinas: Basic Philosophical Writings*, 129–48.

2. Don Ihde, *Hermeneutic Phenomenology: The Philosophy of Paul Ricoeur*, 181.

3. Ricoeur, *Husserl,* 214–15.

4. Ihde, 6, 7.

5. Ricoeur, "On Interpretation," 151.

6. Paul Ricoeur, *The Symbolism of Evil,* 347–57.

7. Ibid., 351, 347.

8. Ibid., 347, 348.

9. Ibid., 350.

10. Ricoeur, "On Interpretation," 151.

11. Ricoeur, *Freud and Philosophy,* 7.

12. Ricoeur, "On Interpretation," 151–53.

13. Ricoeur, *The Symbolism of Evil,* 350.

14. Ricoeur, "On Interpretation," 154.

15. Bruns, *Hermeneutics: Ancient and Modern.*

16. Ricoeur, as quoted in Bruns, 238.

17. Ibid., 238–39, 240.

18. See, for instance, Paul Ricoeur, *Oneself as Another,* 23–25.

19. André LaCocque and Paul Ricoeur, *Thinking Biblically,* ix, x.

20. Ibid., x, xv.

21. Ibid., xv–xvi.

22. Ricoeur, *Oneself as Another,* 24.

23. Heidegger, *The Piety of Thinking,* 65.

24. Ricoeur's acceptance of the mixed origins of Western thought's constitutive destiny stands in direct contrast with others who share his philosophical interest in the contributions of biblical thought. Besides the examples of Barth and Heidegger as described in chapter 1, perhaps the clearest contrast is from Ingraffia, *Postmodern Theory and Biblical Theology.* Ingraffia's stated intention, for instance, is to undo, or "tease apart," whatever synthesis has been achieved between biblical theology and philosophy. As he writes in the introduction:

> Most work on postmodernism and theology to date seeks a reconciliation between these two discourses, a postmodern theology of some sort (even if this be an "a/theology"). In Western intellectual thought, this unavoidably means some sort of secularized, "demythologized" or "radical" Christianity. I seek to deny the possibility of such a synthesis, to set up an either/or between postmodern thought and biblical theology. Following in the tradition of Paul, Pascal, Luther, Kierkegaard, Barth, Bonhoeffer, and more recently, Jürgen Moltmann, I seek to separate the God of the Bible from the god of the philosophers, for it is the confusion between these two Gods which has caused Christianity to be uncritically equated with ontotheology [14].

25. LaCocque and Ricoeur, xviii.

26. Ibid.

27. Caputo, *Demythologizing Heidegger,* 209, 3.

28. See Thomas A. Carlson, "Translator's Introduction: Converting the Given into the Seen," in Jean-Luc Marion, *The Idol and Distance: Five Studies.*

29. Jean-Luc Marion, "Metaphysics and Phenomenology: A Relief for Theology," 590.

30. David Tracy, "Foreword," *God without Being*, ix–xvi.

31. Ibid., xii.

32. Marion is in agreement with Tracy's assessment, when, at the close of his work entitled *On Descartes' Metaphysical Prism*, he hints at the need for this theological strategy in the effort at overcoming metaphysics. There, after a painstaking investigation of Descartes's reversal of the metaphysical tradition through his exercise of ontotheology, Marion writes of what possibilities remain after Descartes:

> "Overcoming metaphysics"—without sinking to the rank of an appalling buzzword, this formula can signify only: (a) inverting Platonism (Nietzsche), (b) destroying the history of ontology (Heidegger), and (c) deconstructing meaning (Derrida). However diverse these three projects might be, they have two characteristics in common: first, they overcome metaphysics only diachronically, at the terminal point of its unfolding. Accordingly, not a single one of them could have been practiced or could have appeared before the historic or historiological closure of metaphysics. . . . Pascal, in contrast, introduces a new mode of overcoming: (d) destitution. Destitution can be carried out synchronically, contemporaneously with each of the epochs of metaphysics. It succeeds in doing so without destruction, without interdiction, and without putting forth its own claims, because it alone abandons metaphysics to itself. Destitution passes through metaphysics and surpasses its limits (which it thus discerns better than metaphysics does) because it passes to another instance besides metaphysics, which it therefore has no need to combat. Another instance—in Pascal's terms, another order.

In Jean-Luc Marion, *On Descartes Metaphysical Prism: The Constitution and the Limits of Onto-theo-logy in Cartesian Thought*, trans. Jeffrey L. Kosky (Chicago: University of Chicago Press, 1999), 351.

33. Carlson, "Converting the Given into the Seen," xix–xx.

34. Marion, *God without Being*, 44–45.

35. Jean-Luc Marion, *Reduction and Givenness*, 2.

36. Carlson, "Converting the Given into the Seen," xix.

37. Marion, *God without Being*, 1–2.

38. On this point, Marion writes: "[T]he 'death of God' exclusively concerns the failure of the metaphysical concepts of 'God'; in taking its distance from all metaphysics, it therefore allows the emergence of a God who is free from onto-theology; in short, the 'death of God' immediately implies the death of the 'death of God'" (ibid., xxi).

39. In spite of their significant differences, most notably in regard to the legacy of the death of God theologies, on this point of pleasure as the justification for theology, Marion and Mark C. Taylor are very close. For instance, see part 2 of Taylor's *Erring: A Postmodern A/theology*, in which he maps a prospective future for a "deconstructive a/theology." Karl Barth also seems to be in agreement when he writes of Anselm's "theological scheme": "It ought to be noticed first of all that this [the ontological proof] is not the only result of *intelligere* that all the

way through Anselm recognizes and has before him. As *intelligere* is achieved, it issues—in joy. The dominating factor in Anselm's mind is that even the Church Fathers wrote about it in order to give the faithful joy in believing by a demonstration of the *ratio* of their faith" (in *Anselm: Fides Quaerens Intellectum*, 15).

40. Marion, *God without Being*, 1.

41. Ibid., 17, 18.

42. Derrida, "How to Avoid Speaking: Denials," 77.

43. Ibid., 77, 80.

44. Ibid., 106–07.

45. Ibid., 97.

46. Ibid., 99.

47. Mark C. Taylor, "How to Do Nothing with Words," in *Tears*, 203.

48. Ibid., 204, 206.

49. Marion, "In the Name," 21.

50. Ibid., 22.

51. Ibid., 23.

52. Ibid., 24, 28, 29.

53. Ibid., 32. For Milbank's treatment of Marion, see Milbank, "Only Theology Overcomes Metaphysics," in *Theology, Language, Culture: The Word Made Strange*, 36–54.

54. Ibid., 32–33.

55. Marion explains, "By theology of absence . . . we mean not the non-presence of God, but the fact that the name God is given, the name which gives God, which is given as God . . . serves *to shield God from presence* . . . and offers him precisely as an exception to presence." "In the Name," 37.

56. Ibid., 39.

57. Marion, *God without Being*, 153. For my own comments on this rather strange assertion from Marion, see the postlude.

58. Carlson has even gone so far as to suggest an isomorphism between Marion's philosophy and theology: "[T]he structure of Marion's phenomenological vision and the structure of his theological vision are strikingly similar, if not isomorphic: if I see the givenness of the phenomenon, which means if I give myself to it by repeating the act of giving, this is only because that givenness first gave me to myself and moved me to receive givenness in my very being; if I love God, which means if I give myself to him in the love that gives me to others, this is only because God first loved me even when I was not, and moved me to love in my very being" (in "Converting the Given into the Seen," xxxi).

Interlude: On Bibliolatry

1. Noll's observation about the "success" of the evangelical movement in the United States might be applied to the SBC as well. Noll writes: "On any given Sunday in the United States and Canada, a majority of those who attend church hold evangelical beliefs and follow norms of evangelical practice, yet in neither country do these great numbers of practicing evangelicals appear to play significant roles in either nation's intellectual life" (10).

2. For an excellent account of this transformation, not only in the Southern Baptist Convention, but also in American Methodism, see Christine Leigh Heyrman, *Southern Cross: The Beginnings of the Bible Belt.*

3. Gustav Niebuhr, "Rift among Baptists Leaves Two Denominations in One," *The New York Times* (June 6, 2000).

4. In response to this charge, Morris H. Chapman, president and chief executive officer of the Executive Committee of the SBC, writes: "SBC critics such as *Texas Baptists Committed* assert that the controversy in the SBC was about power and politics. This is not so. The root of the controversy in the Southern Baptist Convention was about theology!" Yet, in concluding his plea for a peaceful and reasoned resolution to the conflict between moderate and conservative Baptists, Chapman himself resorts to the most blatant of political rhetoric: "In recent years," Chapman writes, "America has been honoring the veterans, living and dead, of World War II. No one likes war. But how grateful we are for those who sacrificed in war to preserve those things worth fighting for" (in *The Truth about the SBC and Texas,* 11).

5. As Niebuhr reports: "The president of the Southern Baptist Convention, the Rev. Paige Patterson, acknowledged that moderates had 'formed a denomination within the denomination.' Mr. Patterson said he would not be surprised if 1,500 or more moderate congregations were to leave the convention in the coming years out of the more than 40,000 total congregations that belong. But they would quickly be replaced, he said, adding that the denomination started 1,479 new churches in 1999 and that its increasingly conservative stance had been attracting established congregations as new members, like the Thomas Road Baptist Church in Lynchburg, Va., where the Rev. Jerry Falwell is pastor. 'We're gaining, not losing,' Mr. Patterson said."

6. Bill Merrell, "Bibliolatry—A Fraudulent Accusation," in *The Truth about the SBC and Texas,* 5.

7. Ibid., 5, 3.

8. As Merrell writes: "Reactions to the *Baptist Faith and Message* Committee report to the Southern Baptist Convention in Orlando were of two very distinct kinds. The first was overwhelming affirmation and approval by Southern Baptists. The other was another kind altogether—suspicious, resentful, and hostile" (2).

To confirm Merrell's assessment, in the weeks and months after the revisions were enacted, two important events occurred. First, one of the most prominent and widely respected of all Southern Baptists, former President Jimmy Carter, announced that he would be leaving the SBC. Second, the Baptist General Convention of Texas (BGCT) threatened to discontinue its funding of the SBC, which is significant because there are over 2.7 million Texas Baptists and the annual budget of the BGCT is over $51 million.

9. As Chapman writes: "The attempts by denominational leaders to 'keep the peace' by such actions as recommending the 1963 *Baptist Faith and Message* . . . [was] ineffectual in addressing the real problem: the continued influence of many teachers and leaders who did not hold to a high view of Scripture. When moral suasion, passionate appeals, and public criticism failed to alter the *status quo,* conservatives devised and publicly announced a strategy to utilize the time-

honored, democratic electoral system of the Southern Baptist Convention to elect conservative presidents, officers, and directors of the agencies, who would seek conservative personnel to serve Southern Baptists" (11).

10. This means that Merrell misunderstands the meaning of the charge of "bibliolatry," and thus his response that it is a "fraudulent accusation" is misplaced. Merrell writes: "The accusation of bibliolatry is fraudulent! We submit that anti-SBC leaders cannot tell Southern Baptists of one example of a conservative Baptist worshipping the Bible or placing the Bible over Jesus" (5).

11. Marion, *God without Being*, 8.

12. Gabriel Vahanian, *Wait without Idols*, xi.

13. Huston Smith, *The World's Religions: Our Great Wisdom Traditions*, 359.

5. *Otherwise than Overcoming*

1. This distinctively Levinasian strategy begins with the transcendence of the *other*, which, as Levinas states in *Otherwise than Being*, is not to be mistaken for "being otherwise," but instead is defined as "passing over to being's *other*, otherwise than being. Not *to be otherwise*, but *otherwise than being*." Levinas continues: "To be or not to be is not the question where transcendence is concerned. The statement of being's *other*, of the otherwise than being, claims to state a difference over and beyond that which separates being from nothingness—the very difference of the *beyond*, the difference of transcendence" (3).

2. See Graham Ward, *Barth, Derrida and the Language of Theology*, most especially chapter 7, entitled "Barth's Theology of the Word and Levinas's Philosophy of Saying," 147–70; and Steven G. Smith, *The Argument to the Other*.

3. For instance, Levinas himself speaks of the regrettable debt he owes to Heidegger: "It [Levinas's thinking with regard to death] distinguishes itself from Heidegger's thought, and it does so in spite of the debt that every contemporary thinker owes to Heidegger—a debt that one often regrets" (as quoted in Jacques Derrida, *Adieu: to Emmanuel Levinas*, 13). Also, not without significance, Levinas lists Heidegger's *Being and Time* (together with Plato's *Phaedrus*, Kant's *Critique of Pure Reason*, Hegel's *Phenomenology of Mind*, and Bergson's *Time and Free Will*) as one of the five "finest books in the history of philosophy" (in Levinas, *Ethics and Infinity*, 37–38).

4. S. Smith, 240, 242.

5. See Barth, "Philosophy and Theology," 85–87.

6. S. Smith, 2.

7. Ward gives his own definition of radical orthodoxy in the introduction to this work, and in so doing, he also makes a call for a "new approach to philosophical theology; an approach that would be both philosophically radical and yet theologically orthodox" (xviii).

8. Ibid., 147, 9.

9. Ibid., 156.

10. Ibid., 163–64.

11. See Levinas, "Substitution," in *Otherwise than Being*, 99–129.

12. Ibid., 112.

13. This might be considered a problem, because Levinas himself repeatedly denied the claim that his work should be read as being theological. For instance, when asked whether he was a theologian, he responded by saying: "My point of departure is absolutely non-theological. This is very important to me; it is not theology which I do, but philosophy" (in Adriaan Peperzak, *To the Other: An Introduction to the Philosophy of Emmanuel Levinas*, 210).

14. Ward, 170.

15. In this essay, Derrida argues against Levinas's philosophy of difference and in favor of Husserl's phenomenology of the other as an alter ego. According to Derrida's argument, Husserl, while still recognizing the other as a problem for phenomenology, nevertheless justifies his thought of the other through his notion of the "analogical appresentation." By contrast, as Derrida writes in "Violence and Metaphysics," Levinas "*in fact* speaks of the infinitely other, but by refusing to acknowledge an intentional modification of the ego—which would be a violent and totalitarian act for him—he deprives himself of the very foundation and possibility of his own language" (125). In short, Levinas fails to recognize the "necessity due to the finitude of meaning" (127). Thus, Derrida concludes, "In effect, *either* there is only the same, which can no longer even appear and be said, nor even exercise violence. . .; *or* indeed there is the same *and* the other, and then the other cannot be the other—of the same—except by being the same (as itself: ego), and the same cannot be the same (as itself: ego) except by being the other's other: alter ego" (128).

16. "*Tout autre est tout autre*" translates to "every other is wholly other."

17. Derrida himself testifies to this claim that the idea of the Other is credited to Levinas's thought, when, while delivering Levinas's eulogy, he draws on the following assessment of Levinas made by Maurice Blanchot: "But we must not despair of philosophy. In Emmanuel Levinas's book [*Totality and Infinity*]— where, it seems to me, philosophy in our time has never spoken in a more sober manner, putting back into question, as we must, our ways of thinking and even our facile reverence for ontology—we are called upon to become responsible for what philosophy essentially is, by welcoming, in all the radiance and infinite exigency proper to it, the idea of the Other, that is to say, the relation with *autrui*. It is as though there were here a new departure in philosophy and a leap that it, and we ourselves, were urged to accomplish" (as quoted in Derrida, *Adieu*, 8–9). See also, Robert Bernasconi, "The Trace of Levinas in Derrida," in *Derrida and Difference*, 17–44; and Simon Critchley, *The Ethics of Deconstruction*.

18. Jacques Derrida, *The Gift of Death*, 83.

19. Levinas, *Ethics and Totality*, 90. This reading of Levinas is in contrast with Moran, who writes of Levinas: "The ethical dimension is a dimension where the descriptive and prescriptive meet, or where they are originally inseparable. It is this deliberate ambiguity which makes Levinas's ethics difficult to classify" (321).

20. Levinas, *Totality and Infinity*, 194.

21. Caputo, *The Prayers and Tears of Jacques Derrida*, xxi. Others have seen the consequence of this shift as ushering in a "secular theology." For example, see Winquist, *Desiring Theology*, and Crockett, *Secular Theology*.

22. See Robert Bernasconi, "Fundamental Ontology, Metontology, and the Ethics of Ethics," 76–93; and Luk Bouckaert, "Ontology and Ethics: Reflections on Levinas' Critique of Heidegger," 402–19.

23. Levinas, *Ethics and Infinity*, 42.

24. Derrida, *Adieu*, 13.

25. Levinas, *Ethics and Infinity*, 39.

26. See Derrida, "Violence and Metaphysics." For instance, referring to Levinas's own eventual critique of Husserl, Derrida writes: "In 1930 Levinas turns toward Heidegger against Husserl. *Sein und Zeit* is published, and Heidegger's teaching begins to spread. Everything which overflows the commentary and 'letter' of Husserl's text moves toward 'ontology,' 'in the very special sense Heidegger gives to the term.'" In his critique of Husserl, Levinas retains two Heideggerean themes: (1) "despite 'the idea, so profound, that in the ontological order the world of science is posterior to the concrete and vague world of perception, and depends upon it,' Husserl perhaps was wrong to see in this concrete world, a world of perceived objects above all'. . . (2) if Husserl was right in his opposition to historicism and naturalistic history, he neglected 'the historical situation of man . . . understood in another sense.' There exist a historicity and a temporality of man that are not only predicates but 'the very substantiality of his substance.' It is 'this structure . . . which occupies such an important place in Heidegger's thought'" (87).

Or as Adriaan Peperzak writes: "Husserl started the revolution in philosophy called 'phenomenology'; Heidegger exploited hidden possibilities of phenomenology and transformed it into a new ontology; Levinas developed and tried to overcome phenomenological ontology by a radical renewal of 'metaphysics,' rehabilitating the existent . . . by a thought 'beyond being'" (in *Beyond: The Philosophy of Emmanuel Levinas*, 38).

27. Derrida, "Violence and Metaphysics," 88.

28. Levinas, *Totality and Infinity*, 42.

29. Peperzak, *To the Other: An Introduction to the Philosophy of Emmanuel Levinas*, 17.

30. Levinas, "Is Ontology Fundamental?" in *Philosophy Today* 33, 2 (1989): 122.

31. Ibid., 124–25.

32. As Peperzak writes: "'Letting be,' the permission given to all beings to present themselves in the splendor of their being, has in fact been practiced as an exercise of power and domination. The reduction of particulars to universality is the first theoretical form of violence" (in *Beyond*, 51–52).

33. Levinas, *Existence and Existents*, 65.

34. Ibid., 65–66.

35. Levinas, "Signature", 181.

36. Levinas, *Existence and Existents*, 66.

37. As Levinas writes: "If one had the right to retain one trait from a philosophical system and neglect all the details of its architecture . . . , we would think here of Kantianism, which finds a meaning to the human without measuring it by ontology and outside of the question 'What is there here . . . ?' that one

would like to take to be preliminary, outside of the immortality and death which ontologies run up against. The fact that immortality and theology could not determine the categorical imperative signifies the novelty of the Copernican revolution: a sense that is not measured by being or not being; but being on the contrary is determined on the basis of sense" (in *Otherwise than Being*, 129).

For an examination of the similarities between Kant and Levinas, see Peter Atterton, "The Proximity between Levinas and Kant: The Primacy of Pure Practical Reason," 244–60.

38. Levinas, *Otherwise than Being*, 116.

39. See Levinas, *Totality and Infinity*, 302–07.

40. Ibid., 303.

41. Ibid., 244.

42. Levinas, "The Rights of Man and the Rights of the Other," in *Outside the Subject*, 125.

43. Levinas, *Totality and Infinity*, 197–200.

44. Pierre Hayat, "Preface," in *Alterity and Transcendence* (New York: Columbia University Press, 1999), xviii–xix.

45. See Levinas, "God and Philosophy."

46. Alphonso Lingis, "Foreword," *Otherwise than Being*, xi.

47. Levinas, *Otherwise than Being*, 7.

48. Caputo and Scanlon, *God, the Gift, and Postmodernism*, 45.

49. Marion, *God without Being*, 139–60, 153.

50. William James, *Pragmatism and Other Writings*, 27.

51. Levinas, "Beyond Dialogue," in *Alterity and Transcendence*, 85, 87.

Postlude

1. Kristeva borrows this distinction from Hannah Arendt. In Catherine Clément and Julia Kristeva, *The Feminine and the Sacred*, 13–15.

2. Henri Bergson, *The Creative Mind*, 50–51.

3. Clément and Kristeva, *The Feminine and the Sacred*, 27.

4. See Derrida, "Faith and Knowledge."

5. Clément and Kristeva, *The Feminine and the Sacred*, 26–27.

6. Ibid., 10, 27, 20.

7. See Noëlle Vahanian, *Language, Desire, and Theology: A Genealogy of the Will to Speak*.

8. Clément and Kristeva, *The Feminine and the Sacred*, 3.

BIBLIOGRAPHY

Agamben, Giorgio. *Remnants of Auschwitz: The Witness and the Archive.* Translated by Daniel Heller-Roazen. New York: Zone Books, 1999.

Allen, Charlotte. "Is Nothing Sacred?: Casting Out the Gods from Religious Studies." In *Lingua Franca* (November 1996), pp.30–40.

Altizer, Thomas J. J., and William Hamilton. *Radical Theology and the Death of God.* Indianapolis: Bobbs-Merrill, 1966.

Arendt, Hannah. *Eichmann in Jerusalem: A Report on the Banality of Evil.* New York: Penguin Books, 1994.

———. *The Origins of Totalitarianism.* New York: Harcourt, 1973.

Aristotle. *Metaphysics.* Translated by Richard Hope. Ann Arbor: University of Michigan Press, 1994.

Atterton, Peter. "The Proximity between Levinas and Kant: The Primacy of Pure Practical Reason." In *Eighteenth Century: Theory and Interpretation,* vol. 40, no. 3 (fall 1999).

Barth, Karl. *Anselm: Fides Quaerens Intellectum.* Translated by Ian Robertson. London: SCM Press, 1960.

———. *Church Dogmatics.* Translated by G. T. Thomas and Harold Knight. Edited by G. W. Bromiley and T. F. Torrance. Edinburgh: T & T Clark, 1956.

———. *The Epistle to the Romans.* Translated from the sixth edition by Edwyn C. Hoskyns. Oxford: Oxford University Press, 1968.

———. *The Faith of the Church: A Commentary on the Apostle's Creed According to Calvin's Catechism.* Translated and with an introduction by Gabriel Vahanian. New York: Living Age Books, 1958.

———. *Karl Barth: Theologian of Freedom.* Edited by Clifford Green. Minneapolis: Fortress Press, 1991.

———. *The Way of Theology in Karl Barth: Essays and Comments.* Edited by H. Martin Rumscheidt; with an introduction by Stephen W. Sykes. Allison Park, Penn.: Pickwick Publications, 1986.

———. *Wolfgang Amadeus Mozart.* Translated by Clarence K. Pott. Grand Rapids, Mich.: W. B. Eerdmans, 1986.

———. *The Word of God and the Word of Man.* Translated by Douglas Horton. Gloucester: Peter Smith, 1978.

Bell, David. *Husserl.* London: Routledge, 1991.

Bergson, Henri. *The Creative Mind: An Introduction to Metaphysics.* Translated by Mabelle L. Andison. New York: Citadel Press, 1992.

Bernasconi, Robert. "Fundamental Ontology, Metontology, and the Ethics of Ethics." In *Irish Philosophical Journal*, vol. 4 (1987).

———. "The Trace of Levinas in Derrida." In *Derrida and Différance*. Edited by David Wood and Robert Bernasconi. Coventry, Eng.: Parousia Press, 1985.

Blond, Phillip, ed. *Post-Secular Philosophy: Between Philosophy and Theology*. London: Routledge, 1998.

Bouckaert, Luk. "Ontology and Ethics: Reflections on Levinas' Critique of Heidegger." In *International Philosophical Quarterly* (September 1970).

Bonhoeffer, Dietrich. *Act and Being: Transcendental Philosophy and Ontology in Systematic Theology*. Translated by H. Martin Rumscheidt, with an introduction by Wayne Whitson Floyd. Minneapolis: Fortress Press, 1996.

———. *The Cost of Discipleship*. New York: Collier Books, 1963.

———. *Ethics*. Translated by Neville Horton Smith. Edited by Eberhard Bethge. New York: Simon and Schuster, 1995.

———. *Letters and Papers from Prison*. Edited by Eberhard Bethge. New York: Macmillan, 1979.

———. *Sanctorum Communio: A Theological Study of the Sociology of the Church*. Translated by Reinhard Krauss and Nancy Lukens. Minneapolis: Fortress Press, 1998.

Brown, Peter R. L. *Augustine of Hippo: A Biography*. Berkeley and Los Angeles: University of California Press, 1969.

Bruns, Gerald L. *Hermeneutics, Ancient and Modern*. New Haven, Conn.: Yale University Press, 1992.

Busch, Eberhard. *Karl Barth: His Life from Letters and Autobiographical Texts*. Translated by John Bowden. Grand Rapids, Mich.: W. B. Eerdmans, 1994.

Capps, Walter H. *Religious Studies: The Making of a Discipline*. Minneapolis: Fortress Press, 1995.

Caputo, John D. *Against Ethics: Contributions to a Poetics of Obligation with Constant Reference to Deconstruction*. Bloomington: Indiana University Press, 1993.

———. *Demythologizing Heidegger*. Bloomington: Indiana University Press, 1993.

———. *Heidegger and Aquinas: An Essay on Overcoming Metaphysics*. New York: Fordham University Press, 1982.

———. *Prayers and Tears of Jacques Derrida: Religion without Religion*. Bloomington: Indiana University Press, 1997.

Caputo, John D., and Michael J. Scanlon, eds. *God, the Gift, and Postmodernism*. Bloomington: Indiana University Press, 1999.

Carlson, Thomas A. *Indiscretion: Finitude and the Naming of God*. Chicago: University of Chicago Press, 1999.

Clément, Catherine, and Julia Kristeva. *The Feminine and the Sacred*. Translated by Jane Marie Todd. New York: Columbia University Press, 2001.

Critchley, Simon. *The Ethics of Deconstruction: Derrida and Levinas*. Oxford: Blackwell, 1992.

Crockett, Clayton, ed. *Secular Theology: American Radical Theological Thought*. London: Routledge, 2001.

Deleuze, Gilles. *The Logic of Sense.* Translated by Mark Lester, with Charles Stivale. New York: Columbia University Press, 1990.

————, and Félix Guattari. *What is Philosophy?* Translated by Hugh Tomlinson and Graham Burchell. New York: Columbia University Press, 1994.

Derrida, Jacques. *Adieu: to Emmanuel Levinas.* Translated by Pascale-Anne Brault and Michael Naas. Stanford, Calif.: Stanford University Press, 1999.

————. *The Gift of Death.* Translated by David Willis. Chicago: University of Chicago Press, 1995.

————. "How to Avoid Speaking: Denials." Translated by Ken Frieden. In *Derrida and Negative Theology.* Edited by Harold Coward and Toby Fashay. Albany: SUNY Press, 1992.

————. *Of Grammatology.* Corrected Edition. Translated by Gayatri Chakravorty Spivak. Baltimore: Johns Hopkins University Press, 1998.

————. *The Truth in Painting.* Translated by Geoff Bennington and Ian MacLeod. Chicago: University of Chicago Press, 1987.

————. *Writing and Difference.* Translated by Alan Bass. Chicago: University of Chicago Press, 1978.

————, and Gianni Vattimo, eds. *Religion.* Stanford, Calif.: Stanford University Press, 1998.

Descartes, René. *Discourse on the Method and Meditations on First Philosophy.* Edited by David Weissman. New Haven, Conn.: Yale University Press, 1996.

Duke, James O., and Robert F. Streetman, eds. *Barth and Schleiermacher: Beyond the Impasse?* Philadelphia: Fortress Press, 1988.

Dupré, Louis. *Passage to Modernity: an Essay in the Hermeneutics of Nature and Culture.* New Haven, Conn.: Yale University Press, 1993.

Fink, Eugen. "Operative Concepts in Husserl's Phenomenology." In *Apriori and World: European Contributions to Husserlian Phenomenology.* The Hague: M. Nijhoff, 1981.

————. *Sixth Cartesian Meditation: The Idea of a Transcendental Theory of Method.* Translated and with an introduction by Ronald Bruzina. Bloomington: Indiana University Press, 1995.

Freud, Sigmund. *Civilization and Its Discontents.* Translated by James Strachey. New York: W. W. Norton, 1961.

Gadamer, Hans-Georg. "Being, Spirit, God." Translated by Steven W. Davis. In *Heidegger Memorial Lectures.* Edited by H. Gadamer. Pittsburgh: Duquesne University Press, 1982.

Galeano, Eduardo. *Open Veins of Latin America: Five Centuries of the Pillage of a Continent.* Translated by Cedric Belfrage. New York: Monthly Review Press, 1973.

Gall, Robert S. *Beyond Theism and Atheism: Heidegger's Significance for Religious Thinking.* Boston: M. Nijhoff, 1987.

Gilkey, Langdon. *Reaping the Whirlwind: A Christian Interpretation of History.* New York: Seabury Press, 1976.

Glover, Jonathan. *Humanity: A Moral History of the Twentieth Century.* New Haven, Conn.: Yale University Press, 1999.

González, Justo L. *Mañana: Christian Theology from a Hispanic Perspective.* Nashville: Abingdon Press, 1990.

Green, Clifford J. *Bonhoeffer: A Theology of Sociality.* Grand Rapids, Mich.: W. B. Eerdmans, 1999.

Gross, Elizabeth. "The Body of Signification." In *Abjection, Melancholia, and Love: The Work of Julia Kristeva.* Edited by John Fletcher and Andrew Benjamin. London: Routledge, 1990.

Hanson, Delbert James. *Fideism and Hume's Philosophy: Knowledge, Religion, and Metaphysics.* New York: P. Lang, 1993.

Harnack, Adolf von. *What is Christianity? Sixteen Lectures Delivered in the University of Berlin during the Winter Term 1899–1900.* Translated by Thomas Bailey Saunders. New York: G. P. Putnam's Sons, 1904.

Hauerwas, Stanley. *The Peaceable Kingdom: A Primer in Christian Ethics.* Notre Dame, Ind.: University of Notre Dame Press, 1983.

Heidegger, Martin. *Being and Time: A Translation of Sein und Zeit.* Translated by Joan Stambaugh. Albany: SUNY Press, 1996.

———. *Discourse on Thinking: A Translation of Gelassenheit.* Translated by John M. Anderson and E. Hans Freund. New York: Harper & Row, 1966.

———. *Early Greek Thinking.* Translated by David Farrell Krell and Frank A. Capuzzi. San Francisco: Harper & Row, 1975.

———. *The End of Philosophy.* Translated by Joan Stambaugh. New York: Harper & Row, 1973.

———. *Identity and Difference.* Translated and with an introduction by Joan Stambaugh. New York: Harper & Row, 1969.

———. *Nietzsche, vols. 1–2.* Translated by David Farrell Krell. San Francisco: HarperSanFrancisco, 1991.

———. *Nietzsche, vol. 4: Nihilism.* Translated by Frank A. Capuzzi. New York: Harper & Row, 1982.

———. *On the Way to Language.* Translated by Peter D. Hertz. New York: Harper & Row, 1971.

———. *The Piety of Thinking: Essays.* Translated by James G. Hart and John C. Maraldo. Bloomington: Indiana University Press, 1976.

———. *Poetry, Language, Thought.* Translated by Albert Hofstadter. New York: Harper & Row, 1971.

———. *The Question Concerning Technology, and Other Essays.* Translated and with an introduction by William Lovitt. New York: Harper & Row, 1977.

Heyrman, Christine Leigh. *Southern Cross: The Beginnings of the Bible Belt.* New York: Alfred A. Knopf, 1997.

Hodges, H. A. *Wilhelm Dilthey: An Introduction.* New York: H. Fertig, 1969.

Hume, David. *An Enquiry Concerning Human Understanding.* Chicago: Open Court, 1996.

Husserl, Edmund. *Cartesian Meditations: An Introduction to Phenomenology.* Translated by Dorion Cairns. Dordrecht, Netherlands: Kluwer Academic Publishers, 1991.

———. *The Crisis of European Sciences and Transcendental Phenomenology: An Introduction to Phenomenological Philosophy.* Translated by David Carr. Evanston, Ill.: Northwestern University Press, 1970.

———. *Phenomenology and the Crisis of Philosophy: Philosophy as a Rigorous Science, and Philosophy and the Crisis of European Man.* Translated and with an introduction by Quentin Lauer. New York: Harper & Row, 1965.

Ihde, Don. *Hermeneutic Phenomenology: The Philosophy of Paul Ricoeur.* Evanston, Ill.: Northwestern University Press, 1971.

Ingraffia, Brian D. *Postmodern Theory and Biblical Theology: Vanquishing God's Shadow.* Cambridge: Cambridge University Press, 1995.

James, William. *Pragmatism and Other Writings.* Edited by Giles Gunn. New York: Penguin Books, 2000.

———. *William James: Writings 1902–1910.* New York: Penguin Books, 1987.

Janicaud, Dominique, and Jean-François Mattéi. *Heidegger from Metaphysics to Thought.* Translated by Michael Gendre. Albany: SUNY Press, 1995.

Jaspert, Bernd, and Geoffrey W. Bromiley, eds. *Karl Barth-Rudolf Bultmann Letters, 1922–1966.* Translated by G. W. Bromiley. Edinburgh: T & T Clark, 1982.

Johnson, William Stacy. *The Mystery of God: Karl Barth and the Postmodern Foundations of Theology.* Louisville, Ky.: Westminster John Knox Press, 1997.

Jüngel, Eberhard. *Karl Barth: A Theological Legacy.* Translated by Garrett E. Paul. Philadelphia: Westminster Press, 1986.

Kant, Immanuel. *Prolegomena to Any Future Metaphysics That Will Be Able to Come Forward as a Science: The Paul Carus Translation.* Extensively revised by James W. Ellington. Indianapolis: Hackett Publishing, 1977.

Kermode, Frank. *The Genesis of Secrecy: On the Interpretation of Narrative.* Cambridge: Harvard University Press, 1979.

Kierkegaard, Søren. *Fear and Trembling: Repetition.* Edited and translated by Howard V. Hong and Edna H. Hong. Princeton: Princeton University Press, 1983.

King, Martin Luther, Jr. *A Testament of Hope: The Essential Writings and Speeches of Martin Luther King, Jr.* Edited by James M. Washington. San Francisco: HarperSanFrancisco, 1991.

Kisiel, Theodore J., and John van Buren, eds. *Reading Heidegger from the Start: Essays in His Earliest Thought.* Albany: SUNY Press, 1994.

Kovacs, George. *The Question of God in Heidegger's Phenomenology.* Evanston, Ill.: Northwestern University Press, 1990.

Kristeva, Julia. *In the Beginning Was Love: Psychoanalysis and Faith.* Translated by Arthur Goldhammer. New York: Columbia University Press, 1987.

———. *Nations without Nationalism.* Translated by Leon S. Roudiez. New York: Columbia University Press, 1993.

———. *Powers of Horror: An Essay on Abjection.* Translated by Leon S. Roudiez. New York: Columbia University Press, 1982.

———. *Revolution in Poetic Language.* Translated by Margaret Waller. New York: Columbia University Press, 1984.

———. *Strangers to Ourselves.* Translated by Leon S. Roudiez. New York: Columbia University Press, 1991.

Kuhn, Thomas S. *The Structure of Scientific Revolutions.* Chicago: University of Chicago Press, 1962.

LaCocque, André, and Paul Ricoeur. *Thinking Biblically: Exegetical and Herme-neutical Studies.* Translated by David Pellauer. Chicago: University of Chicago Press, 1998.

Levinas, Emmanuel. *Alterity and Transcendence.* Translated by Michael B. Smith. New York: Columbia University Press, 1999.

———. *Discovering Existence with Husserl.* Translated by Richard A. Cohen and Michael B. Smith. Evanston, Ill.: Northwestern University Press, 1998.

———. *Emmanuel Levinas: Basic Philosophical Writings.* Edited by Adriaan T. Peperzak, Simon Critchley, and Robert Bernasconi. Bloomington: Indiana University Press, 1996.

———. *Ethics and Infinity.* Translated by Richard Cohen. Pittsburgh: Duquesne University Press, 1985.

———. *Existence and Existents.* Translated by Alphonso Lingis. The Hague: M. Nijhoff, 1978.

———. *Nine Talmudic Readings.* Translated and with an introduction by Annette Aronowicz. Bloomington: Indiana University Press, 1990.

———. *Otherwise than Being, or, Beyond Essence.* Translated by Alphonso Lingis. Pittsburgh: Duquesne University Press, 1998.

———. *Outside the Subject.* Translated by Michael B. Smith. Stanford, Calif.: Stanford University Press, 1994.

———. *Totality and Infinity: An Essay on Exteriority.* Translated by Alphonso Lingis. Pittsburgh: Duquesne University Press, 1969.

———. "Signature." In *Research in Phenomenology,* vol. 8 (1978).

Lowe, Walter. *Theology and Difference: The Wound of Reason.* Bloomington: Indiana University Press, 1993.

Lyotard, Jean-François. *Lessons on the Analytic of the Sublime: Kant's Critique of Judgment.* Translated by Elizabeth Rottenberg. Stanford, Calif.: Stanford University Press, 1994.

MacIntyre, Alisdair. *After Virtue: A Study in Moral Theory.* Notre Dame: University of Notre Dame Press, 1981.

Macquarrie, John. *Heidegger and Christianity: The Hensley Henson Lectures, 1993–1994.* New York: Continuum, 1999.

Marion, Jean-Luc. *God without Being: Hors-texte.* Translated by Thomas A. Carlson; with a foreword by David Tracy. Chicago: University of Chicago Press, 1991.

———. *The Idol and Distance: Five Studies.* Translated and with an introduction by Thomas A. Carlson. New York: Fordham University Press, 2001.

———. "Metaphysics and Phenomenology: A Relief for Theology." Translated by Thomas A. Carlson. In *Critical Inquiry,* vol. 20, no. 4 (summer 1994).

———. *On Descartes' Metaphysical Prism: The Constitution and the Limits of Onto-theo-logy in Cartesian Thought.* Translated by Jeffrey L. Kosky. Chicago: University of Chicago Press, 1999.

———. *Reduction and Givenness: Investigations of Husserl, Heidegger, and Phenomenology.* Translated by Thomas A. Carlson. Evanston, Ill.: Northwestern University Press, 1998.

Marsh, Charles. *Reclaiming Dietrich Bonhoeffer: The Promise of His Theology.* New York: Oxford University Press, 1994.

McCutcheon, Russell T. *Manufacturing Religion: The Discourse on Sui Generis Religion and the Politics of Nostalgia.* New York: Oxford University Press, 1997.

McFague, Sallie. *Metaphorical Theology: Models of God in Religious Language.* Philadelphia: Fortress Press, 1982.

McGrath, Alister E. *Christian Theology: An Introduction.* Oxford: Blackwell, 1994.

Merleau-Ponty, Maurice. *Phenomenology of Perception.* Translated by Colin Smith. New York: Routledge, 1962.

Migliore, Daniel L. "Reappraising Barth's Theology." In *Theology Today,* vol. 43, no. 3 (October 1986).

Milbank, John. *The Word Made Strange: Theology, Language, Culture.* Oxford: Blackwell Publishers, 1997.

Moltmann, Jürgen. *The Crucified God: The Cross of Christ as the Foundation and Criticism of Christian Theology.* Translated by R. A. Wilson and John Bowden. Minneapolis: Fortress Press, 1993.

Moran, Dermot. *Introduction to Phenomenology.* New York: Routledge, 2000.

Niebuhr, Reinhold. *Faith and History: A Comparison of Christian and Modern Views of History.* New York: Charles Scribner's Sons, 1949.

Nietzsche, Friedrich. *Beyond Good and Evil: Prelude to a Philosophy of the Future.* Translated by Walter Kaufmann. New York: Vintage Books, 1989.

Noll, Mark A. *The Scandal of the Evangelical Mind.* Grand Rapids, Mich.: W. B. Eerdmans, 1994.

Pelikan, Jaroslav. *Historical Theology: Continuity and Change in Christian Doctrine.* New York: Corpus, 1971.

Peperzak, Adriaan. *Beyond: The Philosophy of Emmanuel Levinas.* Evanston, Ill.: Northwestern University Press, 1997.

———. *To the Other: An Introduction to the Philosophy of Emmanuel Levinas.* West Lafayette, Ind.: Purdue University Press, 1993.

Plantinga, Theodore. *Historical Understanding in the Thought of Wilhelm Dilthey.* Toronto: University of Toronto Press, 1980.

Rasmussen, Larry. "Patriotism Lived: Lessons from Bonhoeffer." In *Christianity and Crisis,* vol. 45 (June 1985).

Ricoeur, Paul. *The Conflict of Interpretations.* Translated by Charles Freilich. Evanston, Ill.: Northwestern University Press, 1974.

———. *Freud and Philosophy: An Essay on Interpretation.* Translated by Denis Savage. New Haven, Conn.: Yale University Press, 1970.

———. *Husserl: An Analysis of His Phenomenology.* Translated by Edward G. Ballard and Lester E. Embree. Evanston, Ill.: Northwestern University Press, 1967.

———. *Oneself as Another.* Translated by Kathleen Blamey. Chicago: University of Chicago Press, 1992.

———. "On Interpretation." In *The Continental Philosophy Reader.* Edited by Richard Kearney and Mara Rainwater. London: Routledge, 1996.

———. *The Symbolism of Evil.* Translated by Emerson Buchanan. Boston: Beacon Press, 1969.

Risser, James, ed. *Heidegger Toward the Turn: Essays on the Work of the 1930's.* Albany: SUNY Press, 1999.

Robinson, John A. T. *Honest to God.* Philadelphia: Westminster Press, 1963.

Robinson, James M., and John B. Cobb Jr., eds. *The Later Heidegger and Theology.* New York: Harper & Row, 1963.

Rubenstein, Richard L. *After Auschwitz: History, Theology, and Contemporary Judaism,* Second Edition. Baltimore: Johns Hopkins University Press, 1992.

Rubenstein, Richard E. *When Jesus Became God: The Struggle to Define Christianity During the Last Days of Rome.* New York: Harcourt, 1999.

Safranski, Rüdiger. *Martin Heidegger: Between Good and Evil.* Translated by Ewald Osers. Cambridge: Harvard University Press, 1998.

Sartre, Jean-Paul. *Essays in Existentialism.* Edited by Wade Baskin. Secaucus: Citadel Press, 1997.

Scharlemann, Robert P. "Authenticity and Encounter: Bonhoeffer's Appropriation of Ontology." In *Union Seminary Quarterly Review,* vol. 46, nos. 1–4 (1992).

———, ed. *Theology at the End of the Century: A Dialogue on the Postmodern with Thomas J. J. Altizer, Mark C. Taylor, Charles E. Winquist, and Robert P. Scharlemann.* Charlottesville: University of Virginia Press, 1990.

Schweitzer, Albert. *The Quest of the Historical Jesus: A Critical Study of its Progress from Reimarus to Wrede.* New York: Macmillan, 1968.

Smith, Huston. *The World's Religions: Our Great Wisdom Traditions.* San Francisco: HarperSanFrancisco, 1991.

Smith, Steven G. *The Argument to the Other: Reason beyond Reason in the Thought of Karl Barth and Emmanuel Levinas.* Chico, Calif.: Scholars Press, 1983.

Taylor, Charles. *Philosophical Arguments.* Cambridge: Harvard University Press, 1995.

Taylor, Mark C. *Erring: A Postmodern A/theology.* Chicago: University of Chicago Press, 1984.

———. *Tears.* Albany: SUNY Press, 1990.

Tillich, Paul. *Systematic Theology.* Chicago: University of Chicago Press, 1951.

The Truth about the SBC and Texas: A Message of Concern for Southern Baptists in Texas. Nashville: Executive Committee of the Southern Baptist Convention, 2000.

Vahanian, Gabriel. *Wait without Idols.* New York: George Braziller, 1964.

Vahanian, Noëlle. *Theology, Language, Desire: A Genealogy of the Will to Speak.* London: Routledge, 2003.

Wallwork, Ernest. *Psychoanalysis and Ethics.* New Haven, Conn.: Yale University Press, 1991.

Ward, Graham. *Barth, Derrida, and the Language of Theology.* Cambridge: Cambridge University Press, 1995.

Westphal, Merold. "Overcoming Onto-theology." In *God, the Gift, and Postmodernism.* Edited by John D. Caputo and Michael J. Scanlon. Bloomington: Indiana University Press, 1999.

Whitehead, Alfred North. *Process and Reality: An Essay in Cosmology.* Corrected Edition. Edited by David Ray Griffin and Donald W. Sherburne. New York: The Free Press, 1978.

Wiebe, Donald. *The Politics of Religious Studies: The Continuing Conflict with Theology in the Academy.* New York: St. Martin's Press, 1998.

Wiesel, Elie. *Night.* Translated by Stella Rodway. New York: Bantam Books, 1982.

Winquist, Charles E. *Desiring Theology.* Chicago: University of Chicago Press, 1995.

———. *Epiphanies of Darkness: Deconstruction in Theology.* Aurora, Colo.: The Davies Group, 1999.

Wüstenberg, Ralf K. *A Theology of Life: Dietrich Bonhoeffer's Religionless Christianity.* Translated by Doug Stott. Grand Rapids, Mich.: W. B. Eerdmans, 1998.

STUDIES IN RELIGION AND CULTURE